CASTLES AND KINGS

Other works by P. E. Cleator include

The Past in Pieces
Lost Languages
Archaeology
Treasure for the Taking
Ancient Rome

Rockets Through Space
Into Space
The Robot Era
An Introduction to Space Travel

P. E. CLEATOR

CASTLES AND KINGS

Diagrams and Maps by the Author

LONDON
ROBERT HALE LIMITED
63 Old Brompton Road, S.W.7

First published in Great Britain 1963

PRINTED IN GREAT BRITAIN
BY EBENEZER BAYLIS AND SON, LIMITED
THE TRINITY PRESS, WORCESTER, AND LONDON

to

M

and to

W. H. Browning

historian, mentor, friend

CONTENTS

ILLUSTRATIONS

Chapter Headings

Numbered Figures in Text

Photographs

ACKNOWLEDGEMENTS

THE literature of English history has attained such vast proportions that even a cursory study of it, restricted though it may be to one particular aspect of the subject, calls for considerable research—in the present instance, the reading and digesting of some ten million words.

From this mammoth undertaking, it goes without saying, I have emerged heavily in debt to a multitude of authorities, many of whose writings are named in the Selected Bibliography at the end of this book. But as its title implies, the list is far from complete, if only because it had to be severely curtailed through sheer press of numbers, while to it must be added the many standard works of reference which were also consulted, among them *Americana*, *Britannica*, *Chambers's*, *Collier's*, *Compton's*, *Everyman's*, and *Universal*, not to mention all ten volumes of the *Oxford New English Dictionary*.

Valuable assistance of one kind or another has also come from Elizabeth A. Livingstone, of the Clarendon Press, from Jean M. Blad and E. Grainger, of the Photographic Library and the Information Branch of the Ministry of Public Buildings and Works respectively, from my erstwhile co-author (*Architectural Draughtsmanship*) A. Stanley Barnes, F.R.I.B.A., and from the librarians of half a dozen establishments, to all of whom due thanks are tendered.

The photographs are reproduced by arrangement with B. T. Batsford Ltd., Aerofilms and Aero Pictorial Ltd., and (where Crown Copyright is concerned) the Ministry of Public Buildings and Works, while in the preparation of the line illustrations, I have either re-drawn these from contemporary prints and other published sources (maps and plans) or made use of actual photographs (elevations), as elsewhere acknowledged.

And as usual, I am also beholden to my wife and my old friend W. H. Browning for their proof-reading activities, and to Gordon Chesterfield and his colleagues for their painstaking efforts in the realm of production.

P. E. CLEATOR

GENESIS OF THE CASTLE

CELTIC (and pre-Celtic) defensive earthworks, such as the misnamed Maiden Castle near Dorchester, have existed in the British Isles since time immemorial. And when the Romans arrived, they, too, established camps and forts throughout the land, while the enclosed townships (burhs) of their Anglo-Saxon successors were also protected by walls or palisades. But the purpose of all these fortifications was the defence of a community, and the word "castle", a term properly reserved for the private stronghold of an individual, is not applicable to them.

The castle, strictly so-called, was a by-product of the feudalistic society which emerged in Western Europe after the decay of the Carolingian Empire, when territory other than that retained by the King (the royal demesne) was granted out to vassal lords, who proffered oaths of homage and fealty in exchange. The decline of the central authority was thus matched by an increase in the power of the nobility, until eventually the great barons became very much a law unto themselves. This independence inevitably led to rivalries and disputes, which in turn gave rise to acts of encroachment and pillage, so that, of dire necessity, a nobleman's residence began to assume a form which would enable it to be defended against attack.

In France and elsewhere on the Continent, such private strongholds consisted at first of little more than a wooden tower or keep (thus named because the owner kept, or lived, there) which stood on elevated ground and was ringed by a stockade of hewn logs. In flat country, an artificial mound, known as a motte, was raised by making a central heap of earth taken from a surrounding ditch, which cavity was water-filled if there happened to be a stream in the vicinity, but which otherwise remained dry.

The timber keep gradually developed into an elaborate structure of several storeys, replete with halls, storerooms, and even a chapel. It also contained a guardroom. As the top of the mound provided little enough room for housing a garrison, however, a much more extensive base-court came to be added to the foot of the motte. This area, known as the bailey, was also protected by an encircling fence and ditch, an interconnected moat system forming a figure eight about the two components, access from one to the other of which was by way of a sloping wooden bridge. If, during an assault, the lower court were taken, the defenders could then retreat to the tower on the adjacent mound, the steep sides of which could be relied upon to present a formidable obstacle to the attackers.

Although the essential outlines of these motte and bailey castles are described in the writings of contemporary chroniclers, their accounts say little enough about the many variations in detail. But as subsequent investigation has shown, the shape of the bailey was often adapted to suit the requirements of a particular site, nor was it by any means uncommon for there to be more than one bailey. A double motte, on the other hand, was exceptional. It was also unusual for the mound to be located within the bailey, though on occasion it was so placed, standing either centrally or to one side.

Because the early keeps were made of timber, none of them has survived. The remains of their tell-tale mounds, however, abound. They are particularly numerous in Normandy, and also in England, where, until comparatively recently, the existence of hundreds of these grass-grown hillocks was explained by attributing them to the Anglo-Saxons, a complete absence of the stonework traditionally associated with the later castles of the Middle Ages lending support to the theory that the mounds were to be regarded as a form of "burh". It was not until the 1890s that this view was challenged by J. H. Round, who contended, in the face of much learned incredulity and disbelief, that the moated hillocks were a foreign importation introduced by the Normans, prior to the arrival of whom the British Isles contained no castles, properly so-called.

This thesis, which now finds general acceptance, is well supported by archaeological and other evidence. Thus, "motte" is not an English word, while the mounds themselves are to be found in predominantly Celtic regions (for example, Ireland) which the Saxons failed to penetrate. Again, the early Anglo-Saxon records do not contain any mention of castles until about the middle of the eleventh century. And while it is true that the first of these references antedate the coming of the Conqueror, it has to be remembered that they nevertheless relate to a time when the Normanization of the country had already been begun by Edward the Confessor and his friends from overseas.

Among these intimates was a nephew, Ralf of Mantes, who until his death in 1057 held the earldom of Herefordshire, a border territory much troubled by raiders from Wales. The remains of three of the strongpoints which he and his associates caused to be erected in an attempt to stem these Celtic incursions have been identified, with some probability, as Ewias Harold (which available records show to have been in existence prior to 1066); Richard's Castle (named after Osbern Fitz Richard, the son of Scrob, a Norman who settled in the district in 1052); and Hereford Castle itself (a structure which, there is evidence to suggest, was standing in 1055). Significantly, all three sites conform to the conventional motte and bailey pattern.

Only two other castles are known with any certainty to have existed in England in pre-Conquest times, and these are likewise attributable to foreign influence. One is an edifice of which it is recorded that Robert Fitz Wimarc, a Breton according to his name, possessed to the north of London (and now represented, it is thought, by the motte and bailey at Clavering, in Essex), while the other consists of early earthworks on the Dover cliffs, held to be the remnants of the strongpoint Harold Godwinson is known to have constructed there on behalf of Duke William of Normandy.

The castle, then, was a Norman innovation (though not necessarily a Norman invention) which first reached England about the year 1050 in the guise of a timber tower atop a moated hillock. As such, a great advantage was the ease and rapidity with which it could be built, even by unskilled labour—according to Ordericus Vitalis, one of these structures was completed at York in as little as eight days! On the other hand, a serious weakness of the motte and bailey castle was the extensive use made of timber in its construction, for not only was this woodwork liable gradually to deteriorate, but it provided an ever-present fire hazard, a circumstance which assailants were not slow to exploit.

The substitution of a more durable building material was thus merely a question of time, and seems to have been inspired by the military architecture of Fulk the Black, Count of Anjou—the remains of a stone tower at Langeais, in Touraine, work on which was begun in 994, have at all events been attributed to him. Similar keeps, erected as an alternative to the fortified earthen mound, made their appearance in nearby Normandy during the first half of the eleventh century, and in England shortly after the Conquest. Needless to add, their introduction heralded radical alterations in castle construction and design, for, apart from such attendant complications as the need for highly skilled artisans and the greatly increased cost of the work (not to mention the years of effort it often involved), the impracticabilities of erecting a massive stone edifice upon so insecure a foundation as a newly raised mound of earth soon became evident.

ADVENT OF THE KINGS

WHEN the Roman legions withdrew from Britain during the first half of the fifth century A.D., their going was the signal for the arrival of hordes of invading Jutes, Angles, and Saxons, who relentlessly drove the resident Celts into the highlands of the west and north-west of the island. From this Nordic influx, there eventually emerged the seven independent kingdoms of Essex, Wessex, and Sussex (predominantly Saxon); East Anglia, Mercia, and Northumbria (the domain of the Angles); and Kent (Jutes).

In due time these areas of Anglo-Saxon occupation came to acknowledge the suzerainty of Alfred the Great (871–899) and his successors, though not before there had occurred a second Nordic incursion, that of the Danes and Norsemen. The threat offered by these Viking encroachments was successfully contained until the time of Ethelred II the Redeless (Uncounselled), during whose troubled reign Sven I of Denmark (Forkbeard) descended upon England in force and compelled Ethelred to seek refuge in Normandy, the home of his second wife Emma. The newcomer was then accepted by the islanders as their King, in which capacity, despite the efforts of the deposed Ethelred and his supporters, Sven was succeeded by his son Cnut, otherwise known as Canute the Great, at once the ruler of Denmark, England, and (by a later conquest) Norway.

The accession of Canute to the English throne was preceded by the death of Ethelred, the claims of whose surviving offspring the Danish monarch neatly circumvented by marrying their mother, notwithstanding an association he had earlier formed with a certain Elgiva of Northampton, by whom he had two sons, Swein and Harold Harefoot. The not unwilling Emma, leaving her children by Ethelred in the care of her brother, Duke Richard II of Normandy, accordingly resumed her duties as England's Queen, subsequently presenting her new lord and master with another son, by name Harthacnut.

Canute wisely made no attempt to govern his English inheritance by Danes alone, and prominent among the Anglo-Saxons who attained positions of authority under him was Godwin, who became Earl of all Wessex. And it was this son of a former thegn who betrayed Alfred, one of Emma's sons by Ethelred, after the death of Canute in 1035. No doubt with his eye on the succession, though ostensibly on a visit to his mother, Alfred journeyed to England. On arrival, he was met by the scheming Godwin, who diverted the royal visitor to Guildford and into the hands of Harold Harefoot, by whom he was blinded and left miserably to die. By Godwin's treachery and this barbarous act, coupled with the circumstance that Harthacnut, Canute's intended heir, was busy overseas, facing a Norwegian revolt against Danish overlordship, the opportunist Harold attained the English throne, which he continued to occupy until his death in 1040.

He was succeeded by the deprived Harthacnut, one of whose first acts on his arrival from Denmark was to exhume the body of his half-brother and cast it into the Thames. Thereafter, perhaps his greatest service to the country was to drink himself to death within the short space of two years, at the end of which time even the hardened Godwin was persuaded of the desirability of making a change. By now one of the most powerful noblemen in the kingdom, the Earl's choice, which decided that of the Witan (assembly of notables) fell upon Edward, Emma's surviving son by Ethelred, and the Anglo-Saxon lineage was thus restored.

Understandably enough, the new monarch, who was half Norman by blood and wholly Norman by inclination, favoured the company of his lifelong friends and associates from abroad, numbers of whom were promoted to high office, including the archbishopric of Canterbury. This preference for foreigners was much resented by the English nobility, in particular by Earl Godwin, who sought to maintain his influence at Court by arranging a matrimonial alliance. Ignoring the fact that the devout Edward (whose excess of piety was destined to earn for him the sobriquet of The Confessor) was known to have taken a vow of chastity, Godwin somehow prevailed upon the reluctant monarch to share his throne, if not his bed, with his daughter Edith. The marriage took place in 1045, and as time went on, the non-productiveness of the union served increasingly to draw attention to the question of a successor.

This problem was doubtless in Edward's mind when, as early as 1051, he received a visit from his cousin, Duke William II of Normandy, and by all accounts viewed with favour the prospect of his young and forceful kinsman succeeding him. Yet another possibility was opened up when, three years later, the undecided monarch recalled the son of his half-brother Edmund Ironside. But this son, Edward the Exile, whose father had perished in the struggle against Canute, was unavoidably late in answering the royal summons, and it was not until 1057 that he eventually reached England, where he died, in mysterious circumstances, within a few days of his arrival. He was survived by an offspring, Edgar the Atheling, who was, however, a mere boy. Even so, in the eyes of many of his countrymen, this youthful descendant of Alfred the Great was the rightful heir to the throne.

The childless Confessor died in 1066, whereupon Duke William of Normandy, Harold Godwinson of Wessex (who had succeeded to his father's title in 1053) and King Swein of Denmark (a son of Canute's sister Estrith) each announced that he had been promised the vacant throne by the deceased monarch. There was also another claimant, in the person of King Harald III Hardraka of Norway, who demanded the English Crown on the grounds that, years before, his predecessor King Magnus had ended his revolt against Harthacnut on the understanding that if either of them died without an heir, his realms should pass to the survivor.

All these claims ignored the fact that it was not in Edward's power to determine who should succeed him, and that a final decision rested with the Witan—of which body Earl Harold was an influential member. He was thus able to support his own candidacy, and at the same time decry that of the boy Edgar, by arguing that in the face of several threatened invasions from abroad, what the country most urgently needed was the leadership of a mature man, not that of an inexperienced youth. No doubt because of the harsh realities of the situation, this reasoning prevailed. The Atheling, at all events, was passed over in favour of Harold, who at once began making preparations to defend his newly gained kingdom against all comers.

Of the several possible contenders, his most determined opponent was likely to be William of Normandy, if only because, two years earlier, Harold had agreed to relinquish all claim to the throne in favour of the Duke, whose unwilling guest he had been at the time. Presumably he did not afterwards regard as binding a promise which had been extracted under duress, but that he nevertheless considered himself to be under some obligation to his erstwhile host would seem to be indicated by his subsequent fulfilment of an undertaking to assist William's cause by fortifying the cliffs of Dover.

In the event, Swein of Denmark was content to bide his time, and the first to make a move was Harald Hardraka, aided and abetted by King Harold's disgraced and exiled brother Tostig. Accompanied by this renegade, and commanding a fleet of three hundred ships, the Norwegian contender landed in the vicinity of the Humber mouth. At Fulford, near York, he then met and defeated a local force led by the Earls Edwin and Morcar, on receiving news of which disaster Harold of England made a forced march northwards, caught the invaders unawares, and completely routed them at Stamford Bridge. When the fighting was over, both Tostig and Harald Hardraka lay dead upon the field.

It was at this juncture, when King Harold and his battle-weary troops were still at York, that Duke William of Normandy made an unopposed landing on the Sussex coast.

Chapter One

The Norman Nemesis

I

EARLY IN THE tenth century A.D. a band of Scandinavian pirates decided to give up their periodic plundering of the fertile coastal regions of northern Gaul, and settle there instead. The nominal ruler of the land, the French monarch Charles the Simple, acquiesced in the presence of these Normans (Norsemen) by giving his daughter Gisèle in marriage to their leader Rolf, a condition of the match being the bridegroom's adoption of the Christian faith.

The obliging Rolf accordingly submitted himself to the incomprehensibilities of baptismal and other rites, from which he duly emerged as Duke Robert of Normandy and the acknowledged son-in-law of his sovereign lord. The bonds of holy matrimony notwithstanding, however, his subsequent acquisition of an heir was accomplished with the extra-marital assistance of a lady known as Popa, an event which marked the beginning of a family tradition which ordained that mistresses were ever to be preferred to wives. Thus Emma, that daughter of Robert's illegitimate grandson Duke Richard I whose destiny it was to marry two Kings of England (Ethelred the Redeless and Canute the Great) and to become the mother of a third (Edward the Confessor), inevitably found herself born out of wedlock, as did her brother Richard, who in due course inherited the duchy.

As Richard II, he was in turn succeeded by his offspring Richard III, whose brief reign was brought to an end by the administration of poison, it was widely believed at the instigation of his brother Robert the Devil, whom the Norman barons nevertheless accepted as their leader. The new Duke, known also as Robert the Magnificent, had earlier become enamoured of one Arlette, the daughter of a tanner of Falaise, and late in 1027 (or early in 1028) she presented her lover with a son, a boy afterwards referred to with affection by his father as William the Bastard. And it was this child of chance who, as William II of Normandy, invaded England in September 1066, to make good his claim to the throne recently vacated by his cousin Edward.

Duke William—corpulent, choleric, and outstanding as a soldier—was assisted in the enterprise by barons and knights who came not only from his own realm, but also from Brittany, Flanders, Picardy, Boulogne, and elsewhere, a mixed and adventurous following, eager to acquire a share of the promised spoils. The total force, which it may be accepted was considerably smaller than the highly inflated figures contained in contemporary accounts, probably numbered between 8,000 and 10,000 men, perhaps not more than half of whom were cavalry.

The departure from Valery-sur-Somme was delayed for several weeks by unfavourable winds, with the result that the arrival at Pevensey Bay on the Sussex coast could not have been better timed. For the landing, when at last it took place, was accomplished without serious incident on the Thursday of a week, the Monday of which had witnessed the slaughter at Stamford Bridge. But although, as he disembarked, the Duke may have been aware of the possibility that his two most formidable rivals had greatly assisted his cause by their attempt to eliminate one another, he cannot at this time have known which of the two Harolds—Hardraka of Norway, or Godwinson of England—he would soon be called upon to face.

The Normans spent a few days in the landing area, during which they occupied and strengthened an ancient Roman fort. The marshy nature of the district, however, soon persuaded them of its unsuitability as a base, and another position was accordingly taken up at nearby Hastings, where a motte was hastily constructed and one of a cargo of several prefabricated timber keeps erected on its summit. Thus entrenched, and their way of retreat secured, the invaders settled down to await the outcome of their intrusion.

By all accounts, Harold of England was still recuperating at York after his victory over the Norwegians when he received news of the Norman landing. At this, he returned to London in haste and there assembled what followers he could to meet the new threat. His company included contingents of the famous housecarls (picked troops of the royal bodyguard), thegns (members of the lesser nobility), and villeins (peasants), and modern estimations of the size of the army which moved towards Hastings suggest that, in numbers, it about equalled that of the enemy. The equipment and training of the opposing forces, however, differed greatly. The English aristocracy, notwithstanding their possession of horses, preferred to do their fighting on foot, wielding great, two-handed battle-axes, while their Norman adversaries rode into battle bearing lances and swords, supported by archers and cross-bowmen.

It was this dissimilarity of armament which determined both the nature and the outcome of the ensuing struggle for, although it was Harold who marched forth to challenge the invaders, his lack of cavalry forced him to adopt a defensive position on a hilltop when he came to within ten miles of their camp. This vantage point was reached on the night of 13 October, and the initiative then passed to William, who moved forward at once, with the result that by 8 o'clock on the following morning the two armies confronted one another about a mile apart.

The encounter began with a shower of arrows, let loose by the advancing Normans. But neither this nor the sustained infantry assault which followed had any success in dislodging their opponents. A series of cavalry charges likewise failed to penetrate the solid wall of shields presented by the defenders and, as the day wore on, it seemed that the contestants were too evenly matched for a clear-cut decision to be gained by either side. But the resourceful William then launched a double attack, in which his archers, aiming high into the air, covered an advance by his horsemen. Thus simultaneously assailed, and with King Harold himself among the fallen, the English position was finally overrun.

Even with Harold slain and his army completely routed, William can have entertained no illusions as to the limited extent of his success. Thus far, he had won a battle, but hardly a kingdom, and his troops, even with their losses made good by replacements, still had to contend with a hostile population which outnumbered them by at least two hundred to one. Fortunately for the invaders, however, the country was far from united, a circumstance which enabled them to subdue one region without undue interference from another, and thereafter to maintain their hold by leaving a garrison within the precincts of each town or city of importance. Nevertheless, the pacification process required five years to complete.

After his victory at Hastings, it was apparent to William that his next step must be the occupation of London, where a move was already afoot to proclaim Edgar the Atheling King. Accordingly, after receiving the capitulation of Dover, he marched inland by way of Canterbury, and then began a systematic ravaging of the countryside in a bid to bring the encircled Londoners to terms. The plan succeeded, and after tentative representations had been made to the Normans at Wallingford, a further meeting took place at Berkhampstead, where the English notables, the Atheling among them, offered their submission. A formal crowning followed, performed at Westminster Abbey on Christmas Day, in the course of which ceremony Duke William II of Normandy became King William I of England.

Within three months of his coronation, and despite the fact that as yet his forces controlled no more than a small area of the country, the new monarch felt himself sufficiently master of the situation to return home, where matters of some urgency awaited his attention. He left the kingdom in the care of two viceroys, his half-brother Bishop Odo of Bayeux,[1] and William Fitz Osbern, an old and trusted friend upon whom he conferred the earldom of Hereford.

When William returned in the following December, it was to find much of the country in a state of threatened or open rebellion. He was first called upon to march into Devon, there to deal with the inhabitants of Exeter, who were making no secret of their disinclination to acknowledge him. He gained admittance to the town after besieging it for eighteen days, ordered the erection of a castle within its walls and, after making a tour of other parts of the south-west, returned to London.

Here, a number of disturbing defections now occurred. The Atheling, who, with other members of his family, had been

[1] Before Robert the Devil departed this life to join his namesake, Arlette bore him another child, a daughter named Adelaide. On the death of her lover in 1035, she then married Herlwin of Conteville, a Norman nobleman by whom she had two sons—Odo, who became Earl of Kent, and Robert, Count of Mortain, to whom William granted the earldom of Cornwall.

treated with the utmost consideration at William's Court, suddenly repaid this kindness by fleeing with his mother and sisters to Scotland, where King Malcolm III made them welcome. The Northumbrian Earls Edwin and Morcar likewise took their leave, and put themselves at the head of a widespread anti-Norman movement in the north, though prompt and vigorous action on William's part delayed the threatened outbreak. Entering the disaffected area in force, he established castles at such key centres as Warwick, Nottingham, York, and (on his return southwards) Lincoln, Huntingdon, and Cambridge.[1] Through the medium of the Bishop of Durham, he also entered into negotiations with the King of Scots, and put a stop to a proposed invasion of England on the Atheling's behalf.

But in 1069 the impending crisis came to a head. Robert de Comines, sent by William to garrison the north with a company of 500 knights, suffered a surprise attack at Durham in which he and almost his entire following were wiped out. This success inspired an uprising at York, whose citizens declared for the Atheling, though they failed to take the castle, whose defenders, despite the death in action of their commander, managed to hold out until they could be relieved. But, prior to this, it transpired that the insurgents had been in communication with the Danes, with the result that King Swein Estrithson was at last persuaded that the time had come for him to assert his claim to the English throne. To this end, he now despatched a powerful fleet of 240 ships.

Rebels and invaders joined forces on the banks of the Humber. William responded by devastating the surrounding countryside, until eventually the discouraged Danes allowed themselves to be bought off. Much of Yorkshire, meanwhile, together with large areas of neighbouring counties, had been methodically laid waste, neither the people nor their possessions, including their crops, being spared. A hundred thousand or more of the luckless inhabitants who took to the woods in an attempt to escape fire and sword perished miserably of starvation and, in the months which followed, other centres of resistance were similarly treated. Among them was the Isle of Ely, where a Lincolnshire thegn by the name of Hereward made a gallant but unavailing stand.

These ruthless and depopulative measures were no doubt

[1] Of these structures, Warwick Castle was entrusted to Henry, son of Roger of Beaumont, and that at Nottingham to William Peverel. During building operations, scant regard was paid to property already occupying a selected site, and it is on record that at Lincoln, no less than one hundred and sixty-six houses were demolished "for the sake of the castle".

adopted as a last resort, for William looked upon himself as his cousin's rightful successor and desired only that his rule should be regarded as a continuation of the pre-Godwinson administration. But the thegnly ranks of Edwardian days had been sadly depleted by the three great battles of 1066, not the least that which had taken place near Hastings, since when many of the surviving notables had sought refuge abroad, or with Malcolm Canmore (Great Head) in Scotland. And now the uprisings of 1069–70, and the brutal manner of their suppression, had effectively put an end to hopes of Anglo-Norman co-operation, at any rate in so far as the intractable English leaders were concerned.

The rapid decline of the native aristocracy during the first twenty years of Norman rule is clearly revealed by the great Domesday Survey which William ordered towards the end of his reign when, in the words of the author of the Laud (Peterborough) version of the Anglo-Saxon Chronicle, he "sent his men all over England into every shire to ascertain how many hundreds of hides there were in each shire, and how much land and livestock the King himself owned in the country", to such good effect that "not even an ox, nor one cow, nor one pig" escaped notice.

This most exhaustive inquiry was designed to provide information about how the country was divided "on the day when King Edward was alive and dead" (i.e. in 1066) and in the year of the census, and the resulting "Description of all England" (as a royal writ refers to it) shows that by the year 1086, less than a tenth of the land remained in the possession of the old Anglo-Saxon nobility. Of the other nine-tenths or so, rather more than two-fifths were about equally divided between the King and the Church, while the remainder was shared by William's followers, fully half of it by less than a dozen great lords, Odo of Bayeux, Robert of Mortain, and William Fitz Osbern among them.

In accordance with accepted feudalistic practice, these grants of land were made subject to specified services which the recipients acknowledged as owing to the King, including assistance of a military nature. When called upon to do so, each of nearly 200 tenants-in-chief was bound to provide an agreed number (usually a multiple of five or ten) of fighting men, trained and equipped for war, an arrangement whereby the Conqueror, in an emergency, was assured of the availability of as many as 5,000 fully armed knights.[1]

[1] In contrast to the English thegn (a warrior whose service in the field derived from his rank), the Norman knight was ordinarily a person of

It was thanks to the presence of this force, and to the existence of a network of strategically placed castles, that the Norman minority was enabled to impose its will upon the native population. Of the constantly manned strongholds (and doubtless there were others), forty-nine find mention in Domesday, the building of no less than thirty of which is attributed to William himself. Such royal castles were often entrusted to the care of barons with strong local interests, who held them as castellans of the King. Thus it was as custodians, not as lords, that William Peverel and Henry de Beaumont occupied

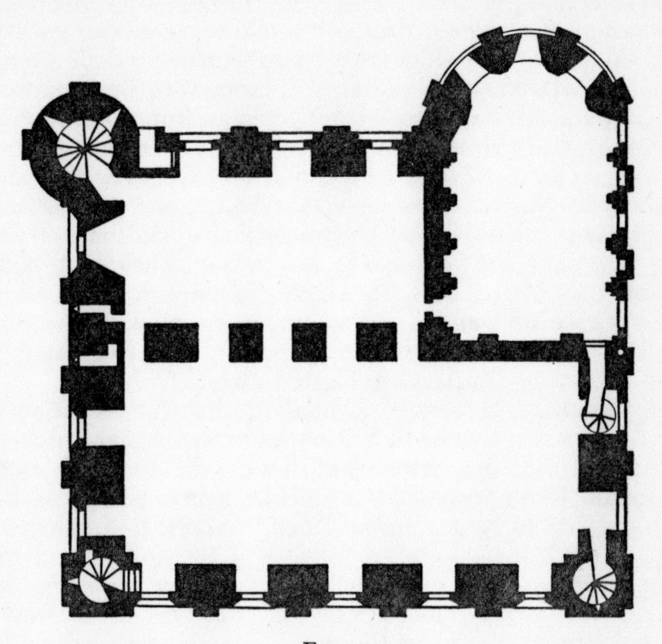

FIGURE 1

The White Tower. First-floor plan of William the Conqueror's Hall Keep, the Tower of London (based on a drawing published by the Royal Commission on Historical Monuments).

Nottingham and Warwick on behalf of William I. Under the Conqueror and his immediate successors, indeed, the building of baronial (as opposed to royal) castles was strictly controlled and made subject to licence, except along actively contested borders (Welsh and Scottish Marches).

insignificant means and of no social standing. His only claim to distinction was the highly specialized military training which made him proficient in mounted warfare.

Almost without exception, these early castles were of the conventional motte and bailey pattern. But for his added protection when resident in London (which already boasted a couple of mound and timber outposts), the King ordered the construction of a more permanent edifice, the lasting qualities of which may be judged from the fact that it is still standing. This was the great rectangular three-storeyed keep (French *donjon*, whence dungeon), rising to a height of ninety feet, which forms the nucleus of, and has given its name to, the conglomeration of later walls and buildings collectively known as The Tower.

In design, the original structure is said to have been inspired by a similar tower which existed at Rouen. At all events, William's builder, one Gundulf, was brought to England from that city, and his handiwork constituted an important innovation in Anglo-Norman military architecture, in that it gave rise to a number of such keeps, first at Colchester and subsequently at Norwich, Pevensey, Sherborne, and elsewhere.

With walls measuring up to twenty feet thick, these strongholds vary in height from two to four storeys. They are broadly divisible into Hall Keeps (in which the main floor is divided into entrance hall and living chamber by partition walling) and Tower Keeps (a later development, e.g. Rochester, in which the living quarters are located above the hall).

The entrance is usually located at first (on occasion at second) floor level, approached by an external flight of steps, so arranged that the fortress wall lies on the attacker's right, thus forcing him to expose his unshielded side as he approaches. From the first (or second) floor, there is access to a basement, which almost invariably contains a well, while the living accommodation above is replete with sleeping chambers and garderobes (latrines) formed in the thickness of the walls. Internal stairways lead to the upper apartments, and also to the roof, where the kitchen is often located.

Such massive structures could not be built with safety upon so insecure a foundation as that offered by the summit of a recently constructed mound of earth, and when (as was often the case) it was desired to make use of an existing castle site (originally chosen, no doubt, because it dominated an important town or river crossing), the tower was placed on the firmer ground of the lower courtyard (keep and bailey castle), either centrally (as at London) or at some strategic point on the surrounding (curtain) wall, in the manner to be seen at Corfe.[1]

[1] After allowing a century or more for settlement, a number of keeps were successfully built on the tops of mottes, e.g. the two-storey building at

The gradual transition from castles of wood to castles of stone which took place from the end of the eleventh century onwards was assisted by an alternative procedure which enabled early use to be made of the artificial mounds. This was achieved by replacing existing timber work on the summit, not by a massive tower, but by a relatively light ring wall of masonry, thereby giving rise to a structure which has come to be known as a shell-keep (though strictly, it is not a keep at all) (see Figure 3). Many such reconstructions were undertaken, as is evident from the remains which are still in evidence at Arundel, Lewes, Berkhampstead, Tamworth, Warwick, and many another site.

The royal sponsor of London's hall keep, meanwhile, did not live to see the building finished. The work required some two decades to complete, and it was still in progress when William became involved in yet another dispute with France over the proprietorship of the borderland province of the Vexin. And in 1087, after his army had attacked Mantes and left the town in flames, he was viewing the scene of destruction when his mount stepped on some burning debris and threw him to the ground. Gravely injured internally by the fall, the King was taken to the priory of St. Gervais, near Rouen, where he expired on 9 September.

An indication of how the news was received in England is to be found in the aforementioned Laud Chronicle, from which reference it is evident that, hated and feared though he may have been by his native subjects, the Norman interloper had at any rate instilled in them a wholesome respect for his laws:

> Among other things we must not forget the good order he kept in the land, so that a man of any substance could travel unmolested throughout the country with his bosom full of gold. No man dared to slay another, no matter what evil the other might have done to him. If a man lay with a woman against her will, he was forthwith condemned to forfeit those members with which he had disported himself. . . .

Hawarden, in Flintshire. But the dangers inherent in the undertaking are to be seen at York, where the stonework of a great keep (Clifford's Tower) erected on the original castle mound after nearly two hundred years of consolidation, soon developed serious fractures. The damaged structure was designed by Henry III's architect Henry de Reyns, and it has been suggested that plans to incorporate a third storey were abandoned when the unsuitability of the site made itself evident.

II

Unlike most of his notoriously wayward ancestors, Duke William II of Normandy had not only married the woman of his choice, but (so we are asked to believe) remained faithful to her until the day she died. And ironically enough, what was to prove to be his long and unblemished association with Matilda of Flanders was banned by the ecclesiastical authorities on the grounds that the couple were related to one another within the then forbidden seventh degree of consanguinity.[1] But with characteristic lack of concern, William brushed this theological technicality aside, ignored the sentence of excommunication which he and his bride thereby incurred, and subsequently bribed his way back into papal favour and a state of grace by various acts of contrition, not to mention the help of an outsize consignment of gold.

The question of a successor was thus unclouded by any suggestion of the illegitimacy of his offspring, nor was there any dearth of candidates from which to choose, for Matilda had borne her husband at least eight children, four of them sons. In order of seniority, these four were: Robert (nicknamed Curthose, because of the shortness of his legs); Richard (killed in his youth as the result of a hunting accident); William Rufus (whose ruddy complexion earned for him the sobriquet of The Red); and Henry (surnamed Beauclerc, a tribute to his reputation for learning).

Upon each of the three surviving sons a kingly inheritance was bestowed. To the eldest was bequeathed the duchy of Normandy, while the youngest received 5,000 pounds of silver, a legacy which the money-loving Henry proceeded to weigh out, then and there, in the presence of his dying father. But it was William Rufus who was nominated to succeed as King of England and who, in a matter of days, contrived to have himself crowned at Westminster.

His accession, however, was viewed with disfavour by an influential group of the great barons, most of whom were possessed of territories in both Normandy and England, and

[1] The arbitrary ruling which forbade marriage between Christians who had a common great-great-great-great-great-grandfather ultimately gave rise to such hardship among the closely inter-related members of small village communities as to render the prohibition unworkable. This hard fact received formal recognition in 1215 when, under the direction of Pope Innocent III, the Fourth Lateran Council amended the Canon Law, it being conceded that henceforth the ban should extend no further than the fourth degree.

who now found themselves owing a divided allegiance. Very soon, there was a move to depose Rufus in favour of Duke Robert, one of the leaders of the conspiracy being Odo of Bayeux. This scheming cleric had already proved his untrustworthiness by intriguing against William I, by whom he had been imprisoned some years before, and from which captivity he had only recently been released in accordance with his half-brother's death-bed wish.

The widespread nature of the plot is shown by the names of some of those who took part in it—Bernard of Neufmarché, the lord of Brecon; Robert Montgomery, with estates in Shropshire; and Robert Mowbray, the Earl of Northumbria. But the greatest threat came from the south-east, where the reinstated Odo held sway as Earl of Kent, and where, in Sussex, Robert of Mortain was entrenched in his castle at Pevensey. And it was to this region and to these traitors that Rufus gave his personal attention.

With relatively few loyal Norman forces at his disposal, the King's position no doubt seemed desperate enough, and at the onset he was deprived of the advice and support of his chief counsellor, Bishop William of St. Calais, who prudently betook himself to his See at Durham, there to sit upon the episcopal fence. The King, however, unexpectedly rose to the occasion by making an appeal to his despised and downtrodden English subjects, promising, in return for their help, to redress past wrongs, to introduce legal reforms, and even to abolish taxation in certain of its more onerous forms. He thus gained for himself the enthusiastic support of powerful remnants of the Anglo-Saxon fyrd (militia), at whose head he descended upon the rebellious followers of Gilbert de Clare at Tonbridge, and forced the surrender of that stronghold after an assault which lasted only two days.

Rufus then moved towards Rochester, intent upon seizing Odo, only to learn while *en route* that the miscreant Bishop had gone to join Robert of Mortain. Ignoring Rochester for the moment, the Norman King and his English army at once marched to the coast and there invested Pevensey Castle. But the two brothers held out stubbornly, and the attack developed into a prolonged siege which Robert of Normandy sought to relieve by landing troops at Hastings. On this occasion, however, the invaders were beaten off, whereupon the discomfited Duke retired from the scene, abandoning his uncles and leaving them to face capitulation and capture.

A seemingly contrite Odo now undertook to bring about the peaceful surrender of his castle at Rochester—and then apparently urged its defenders to continue their defiance as soon as he was safely inside! But Rufus promptly surrounded the citadel and maintained his position until lack of supplies forced the garrison to ask for terms, and with this further success the conspiracy against the King speedily collapsed. The subsequent treatment of the disloyal barons was salutary but by no means unduly severe: in the case of the worst offenders, banishment to Normandy and the confiscation of their English

FIGURE 2

Rochester Keep, viewed from the north-west. Built *c.* 1130, it stands more than 100 feet high and is an early example of a Tower Keep. (From a photograph.)

estates. Not surprisingly, both the treacherous Bishop of Bayeux and the opportunist Bishop of Durham found themselves among the dispossessed.

It would be pleasing to be able to record that for the part they played in this and subsequent episodes (including the wresting of eastern Normandy from Duke Robert in a series of retaliatory raids), the loyal English received their promised reward—pleasing, but not, alas, in accord with the unpalatable facts. Rufus, it transpired, was much given to the making of pledges which he afterwards found it inexpedient to honour. As he somewhat querulously exclaimed when reproached for his failure to fulfil some obligation or other by Lanfranc, the venerable Archbishop of Canterbury, "Who can be expected to keep all his promises?"

To the disenchantment of his lay subjects there was thus added the resentment and hostility of the ecclesiastical authorities, to whom it quickly became evident that the King had inherited his father's disinclination to regard too seriously the many privileges which they claimed as their inalienable right. The Norman invasion of England, it was true, had been undertaken under the aegis of the Church, but the Conqueror, nevertheless, had subsequently declined an oath of fealty to Pope Gregory VII in respect of his newly won kingdom, and had insisted upon retaining control, among other things, of the appointment of bishops.

Under Rufus, an even more independent and intransigent attitude towards the clergy prevailed. When the restraining hand of Lanfranc was removed by death in 1089, the royal choice of a capable but disreputable Norman priest by the name of Ranulf Flambard as his successor to the primacy was unacceptable to Rome, whereupon the vacant See was kept unoccupied and its income diverted to the King's own use. This scandalous situation was not ended until Rufus, taken seriously ill and believing himself to be dying, belatedly sought to make amends by agreeing to the appointment of the learned Anselm of Bec. But on the King's recovery, prolonged and bitter disputes arose between the two men. One irreconcilable point at issue concerned the ownership of Church property, Rufus maintaining that all such possessions were merely held in trust for the Crown, the Archbishop insisting that they must be regarded as completely free of the sovereign's jurisdiction. On this, as on other matters, neither side was prepared to give way, and the unyielding Anselm finally registered his protest by going into voluntary exile.

In these contentious circumstances, it is hardly surprising that the monkish chroniclers of the day have little that is good, and much that is bad, to say about the King. Bull-necked and excessively corpulent in appearance, he is described as being vain and capricious, ill-tempered and cynical, his conversation (accompanied by a stutter which on occasion rendered him almost inarticulate) amounting to little more than an unending series of blasphemous witticisms.[1] Every morning, we are

[1] That Rufus regarded the conflicting claims of rival theologies with a certain amount of scepticism would seem to be indicated by William of

invited to believe, he got up a worse man than he lay down, and every evening he lay down a worse man than he got up—hated by almost all his people and abhorred by God and the Saints.

The climax came at the beginning of August 1100, some four years after Anselm's self-imposed banishment, when Fulchered, Abbot of Shrewsbury, reportedly inveighed against the prevailing state of affairs in a sermon which concluded with what amounted to a thinly disguised threat against the person of the King:

> The bow of wrath from on high is bent against the wicked, and the arrow swift to wound is drawn from the quiver. It shall soon smite, and that suddenly; let every man that is wise amend his ways and avoid its stroke.

Whatever the actual substance of this St. Peter's Day tirade, the death of Rufus while hunting in the New Forest on 2 August, though outwardly the result of a highly convenient accident, inevitably gave rise to not a little rumour and speculation. Belief was widespread that the enemies of the King had resorted to a carefully planned assassination, based on the royal fondness for the chase, a deed made to look all the more plausible by the circumstance that, a few weeks earlier, a nephew of the victim had inadvertently met his end in the same vicinity in a similar fashion—struck by a misdirected arrow.

The only certainty now surrounding the event is that the facts of the matter are beyond ascertainment. Accident or otherwise, not even the identity of the killer is known, though most of the chroniclers name Walter Tirel as the person responsible, no doubt because he considered it wise to leave the country immediately after the incident. But years later, at a time when the admission could have done him no harm, Tirel strenuously denied having even witnessed, much less been the agent of, the King's death. In support of this profession of innocence, Giraldus inclines to the view that it was Ralph of Aix who loosed the fatal bolt, while there were other members of the hunting party who also came under suspicion, among them the dead man's successor, the future Henry I.

Malmesbury's account of how the King arranged a debate between advocates of Christianity and Judaism, offering himself as a candidate for circumcision in the event of a rabbinical victory!

III

Rufus died unmarried and without issue, leaving his brothers Henry and Robert to contend for the vacant throne. The last named had earlier come to an understanding with the deceased, it having been agreed that, if either of them died without leaving an heir, his realm should pass to the survivor. Robert's claim, moreover, offered the considerable advantage that the accession of the Duke of Normandy would automatically reunite the two territories, and so bring to an end the baronial quandary of divided loyalties. But when the time came for the assertion of his undoubted rights it found him in a distant land, making his way home from a Crusade, accompanied by a newly acquired Sicilian bride.

The first move was thus left to Henry, in whose mind there was no doubt as to what he must do. After gazing down at the stricken Rufus, he jumped on his horse and rode in haste to Winchester, there to take possession of the royal treasure. This accomplished, and secure in the knowledge that, as the youngest of the Conqueror's sons, it had been his good fortune to be born in Yorkshire, he coolly declared the absent Robert an alien, and had himself crowned in the presence of a handful of enthusiastic supporters.

From start to finish, the proceedings were of highly dubious legality, the more so as, in the absence of Anselm, and owing to the infirmity of his deputy Thomas of York, the act of consecration was performed by the Bishop of London. Aware of this and other irregularities, and conscious of a pressing need to gain adherents, the resourceful Henry set about increasing his following by a number of astute moves. He caused the hated Ranulf Flambard (that "son of a one-eyed witch") to be incarcerated in the Tower, and further placated ecclesiastical opinion by recalling Anselm, an invitation diplomatically accompanied by due apologies for the unseemly haste of a crowning which had unavoidably taken place in the Primate's absence. He also made a shrewd appeal to his English subjects by issuing his so-called Coronation Charter, in which he promised a return to the laws of Edward the Confessor. And lastly, he married Edith (who thereupon became known as Maud), the daughter of Malcolm III of Scotland and Queen Margaret, a sister of Edgar the Atheling. In short, he evoked a public image of himself as a native-born monarch whose half-English wife was a lineal descendant of the revered Alfred the Great.

This was the situation when the wily Flambard, with the aid of a smuggled length of rope and the timely delivery of a cask of wine for the befuddlement of his jailers, succeeded in escaping from the Tower and in making his way to Normandy, where a much aggrieved Robert was more than willing to listen to plans for yet another Norman descent upon the shores of England. The outcome was the departure of an invading army in July 1101, which, after making an uneventful landing at Portsmouth, began to march upon London. Most of the great barons stood aloof, preferring to await the outcome of the impending struggle before committing themselves to one side or the other. But Henry had the support of his native subjects, and also that of the Church (Anselm loyally took the field in person), and the King was able to set out at the head of a considerable force to intercept the invaders.

The opposing armies met at Alton, in Hampshire, where the two brothers were prevailed upon to settle their differences amicably. Among other consolations for relinquishing his claim to England's throne, it was agreed that Robert should receive from Henry an annual payment of 3,000 marks. There was also a renewal of the understanding (for what it was worth) that, in the absence of a legal heir, he who survived the other should inherit his dominions. And there was also a stipulation that each of the two rulers, within the confines of his own realm, should be free to deal with known adherents of the other's cause.

This last provision enabled Henry to revenge himself upon those barons whom he regarded as dangerous or unfriendly, though he was at pains to deal with these enemies one at a time. He was careful, too, to avoid charging them with traitorous activities, calling them individually to account for relatively minor misdemeanours which, however, were punished with the utmost severity. By the time his unsuspecting victims realized what was afoot, the opportunity for concerted action had passed, as an abortive attempt at rebellion on the part of members of the powerful Montgomery family showed. Made desperate by the knowledge that it was to be their turn next, the brothers Robert of Belleme, Arnulf of Pembroke, and Roger of Poitou began to strengthen their castles, at the same time enlisting the support of Irish friends (Murchertack, the King of Dublin, was Arnulf's father-in-law) and Welsh vassals (whose assistance was encouraged by means of lavish gifts).

Once again mobilizing his English subjects, as willing as ever to rise against their Norman oppressors, Henry accepted the challenge offered by the insurgents, investing and subduing their strongholds one after another until, having defeated them in the north, and counter-bribed their Welsh allies into neutrality, he turned with equal success to Robert of Belleme's domain in Shropshire. His first move was made against the rebel Earl's great castle at Bridgnorth, a supposedly impregnable citadel capable of accommodating a thousand men. After vainly besieging it for three weeks, the impatient Henry somewhat ungallantly brought about its surrender by announcing that, if its defenders persisted in their defiance, he would see them all hanged. At this, their absent leader, who had been awaiting news of the outcome at Shrewsbury, wisely decided to give up the unequal struggle. After making his submission, and acknowledging himself a traitor, he was allowed to retire to his estates in Normandy, though not before he and his brothers had been deprived of the whole of their English possessions.

Even the granting of Robert of Belleme his freedom turned out to be to Henry's advantage, for the rebel Earl, as soon as he reached Normandy, gathered other dispossessed barons about him, and began to plot against the English King, at the same time making private war on all who were thought to be friendly towards that monarch. Duke Robert was either unwilling or unable (he professed the latter) to exercise control over the malcontents, thus providing his brother with sufficient excuse for making a series of interventions which culminated in an open invasion of the duchy. The issue was decided by the Battle of Tinchebrai, fought on 28 September 1106, a decisive encounter which ended with Robert's capture and the conquest of Normandy by an English King at the head of a mixed force of native troops and foreign mercenaries—forty years after Hastings almost to the day.

With the two territories once again united, and with his brother held in custody (after a life-long incarceration Robert breathed his last within the confines of Cardiff Castle in 1134), Henry was now at the height of his power. As his Justiciar, or chief minister (*Justiciarius totius Angliae*) he appointed Roger, Bishop of Salisbury, an able cleric who had hitherto acted as chancellor and who, as the King's former chaplain, had commended himself to his royal patron by his readiness to expedite the saying of Mass whenever it was evident that the impatient monarch was more intent upon hunting than upon matters doxological.

Among other things, Roger of Salisbury is credited with the reorganization of that section of the Great Council (the Norman equivalent of the Anglo-Saxon Witan) which was concerned with revenue, and it was he who introduced a new and improved mode of calculation said to have been evolved in Lorraine.[1] These transactions were recorded on long sheets of parchment, which were then rolled up and stored. The earliest of these so-called Pipe Rolls which is still extant relates to 1130, for which year the royal revenue amounted to ten tons of silver.

This income was made up, in part, of regular payments due to the King from the tenants of demesne manors and towns, together with such sums, less predictable in amount, which could be extracted from his subjects under the headings of relief, wardship, escheat, and marriage. But, such were Henry's incessant demands for money, new or hitherto little used sources of income were also devised or exploited, including the first regular payments of scutage (shield-money), which bought exemption from knight service.

As the efficiency of the royal administrative machinery increased, so its scope was widened, that it might be used to curb still further the independence of the barons. To this end, servants of the Crown toured the country, not merely for the purpose of collecting taxes, but armed with powers which enabled them to inquire into the working of local and baronial courts, that abuses might be uncovered and wrongs redressed ("If a lord slay his villein blameless let him pay the were to the kindred; for the man was a serf to serve and not to be slain"). For this timely intervention on behalf of the downtrodden, the King was hopefully hailed by his long suffering subjects as that "Lion of Justice" whose coming was confidentially believed to have been predicted by the seer Merlin.

Henry was likewise concerned to consolidate his position abroad, and this he sought to achieve by making a series of alliances, aimed at neutralizing the rising power of the Capetian monarchy in France.[2] Marriages for his two children by Queen Maud had been arranged accordingly—that of his daughter Matilda to the Emperor Henry V of Germany, and that of his son William to the eldest daughter of Count Fulk V of Anjou, this last a political alignment which speedily brought the French King Louis VI to terms (Treaty of Gisors).

But in November 1120, when the successful outcome of Henry's plans to safeguard his empire and the succession seemed

[1] The difficulties inherent in the then prevailing Roman system of enumeration will be evident when an attempt is made to multiply LXXV by XXVIII. The Lorraine (or Laon) method of accounting entailed the use of counters in conjunction with a chequered cloth, an innovation now commemorated by the name Exchequer.

[2] The founder of the Capetian dynasty was Hugh, King of France from 987–996. He was called *Capet* from the cloak he wore in his capacity of Abbot of St. Martin de Tours.

assured, death unexpectedly intervened. His son William, upon whom all his hopes for the future rested, was lost at sea while making a crossing of the Channel in a vessel (the ill-fated *White Ship*) manned by a drunken crew. As a result of this disaster, the grief-stricken father was faced by the problem of finding a suitable replacement, spurred on by the knowledge that his enemy Louis of France had already shown himself ready to espouse the cause of the heir of the imprisoned Duke Robert, in the person of his son William Clito, to whom the ambitious Fulk of Anjou now betrothed his second daughter.

It so happened that King Henry was not entirely without extraneous issue. As a sparetime occupation, he had sired a score or more illegitimate offspring, the names of whose mothers make a no less impressive roll call—Ansfride, Edith, Isabel, Nesta, Sibyl. . . . The contemporary writer William of Malmesbury apologetically ascribes the royal profligacy to nothing more than a laudable desire to achieve the banality of fatherhood:

> Throughout his life he was wholly free from carnal desires, for as we have learnt from those who are well informed, his intercourse with women was undertaken, not for the satisfaction of his lusts, but from his desire for children.

However this may be, the situation in which the amorous Henry now found himself was one of some piquancy, in that, while he had succeeded in surrounding himself with offspring (a dozen or so daughters, and at least eight sons), he nevertheless still lacked an acceptable heir.

This circumstance, coupled with the fact that he had been widowed two years before, inclined him to the view that his only hope lay in arranging a second marriage. He accordingly made haste to place his services at the disposal of Adelaide of Louvain. She, however, failed to achieve her intended purpose by finding herself with child—at which juncture (1125) the timely decease of the Emperor Henry V enabled the now desperate King to designate his bereaved daughter as his successor.

The proclamation of the Empress Matilda as England's future ruler was made in the presence of the leading churchmen and barons, among those who proffered his allegiance being her cousin Stephen, a son of Count Henry of Blois and the Conqueror's daughter Adela.[1] This declaration of fealty (sub-

[1] The Conqueror had at least four daughters, the other three being Constance (who married Alain Fergant of Brittany); Adelaide (at one time

sequently twice repeated at the insistence of the careful Henry) was soon followed by news of the wedding of William Clito to the sister-in-law of Louis of France, and the renewal of the bridegroom's claim to Normandy (his earlier marriage to Fulk's daughter had been annulled).

Henry at once responded to this threat by finding another husband for Matilda, now in her late twenties, in the youthful and unenthusiastic guise of Geoffrey, a teen-age son of the House of Anjou. The alliance was celebrated in 1129, and four years later the birth of a son to Matilda was announced. But although this new Angevin arrival was eventually to attain the English throne as Henry II, he was destined to do so only after a prolonged period of civil strife, following the inevitable dispute over the succession which his grandfather had striven so hard and so ineffectually to prevent.

IV

The last years of Henry I were spent on the Continent, where he died suddenly in December 1135, reportedly from eating a surfeit of shell-fish. And with his death the inherent weakness of his plans for the succession at once became apparent. From the outset, the nomination of his daughter had been received by the barons without enthusiasm, not merely on account of her sex, but also because of her arrogant manner and uncertain temper. Nor had her subsequent marriage to Geoffrey of Anjou added to her popularity, for her husband was looked upon with all the dislike and suspicion due to a foreigner. But if the haughty Matilda was even remotely aware of the disesteem in which she was so widely held, she made no attempt to retrieve the situation by at once calling upon the English notables to honour their pledges to her father and, in the event, the delay attendant upon her failure to do so was fatal to her cause.

In Normandy, where dislike of the Angevins was deep rooted and of long standing, the choice of a new leader fell upon Theobald of Blois, a grandson of the Conqueror in the female line. At this, Theobald's brother Stephen, who was possessed of titles and estates in both Normandy and England, hastened to London, where he sought the assistance of the Bishop of Winchester, yet another member of the House of Blois. Thus

betrothed to Harold Godwinson, but who died unwed); and Cecily (who became an abbess). There may also have been a fifth (answering to the name of Gundrada).

aided, he was able to gain the support of the chief Justiciar, Roger of Salisbury, together with that of other men of influence, including the Primate, William of Corbeil, by whom he was crowned at Westminster on 22 December. When news of this *coup d'état* reached Normandy, Theobald, who held no English fiefs, obligingly withdrew his candidature in the interests of Anglo-Norman unity.

The outwitted Matilda entertained no such thoughts and, by now fully roused, her first move was to make an appeal for justice to Rome, in which she denounced Stephen and his supporters as violators of their most solemn oaths. As to their guilt there was, of course, no question. But among the perjurers were not only the leading barons of the land, but also eminent prelates and, after long and prayerful meditation, Pope Innocent II found it inexpedient to pronounce judgement. In effect, by declining to give a ruling, he condoned the offence and confirmed the usurper in office.

A resort to arms thus became inevitable and, in the long struggle which followed, the Empress was not without powerful friends and allies. Abroad, her husband sought to aid her cause by invading Normandy, while at home her uncle, King David I of Scotland, advanced into Northumberland, a move which prompted a number of sympathetic barons in other parts of England to raise the standard of revolt. One such move was made by Baldwin of Redvers, who seized Exeter Castle, only to find himself without the support of the town's inhabitants, who promptly appealed to Stephen for aid. There followed a siege of the citadel which lasted for several months, until in the end the beleaguered garrison was forced into surrender by the failure of the water supply.

The invading Scots eventually suffered a decisive defeat at the Battle of the Standard, fought near Northallerton. But in the south uprisings continued, inspired to some extent by baronial dislike of the undue reliance the King placed upon William of Yprés and his Flemish mercenaries. Foremost among the troublemakers was Robert, Earl of Gloucester, the ablest of Henry I's illegitimate brood, who now openly declared his support for his half-sister. His example was followed by other waverers, with the immediate result that Stephen found a score of their castles held against him—Dover, Canterbury, Dorchester, Wareham, Corfe, Dunster, Ludlow and Shrewsbury among them.

These strongholds he attacked with varying results, some being taken, others not. Bristol successfully defied him, but Shrewsbury, after obstinate resistance, at last capitulated, whereupon members of the garrison, including the leader, were promptly executed. This lesson was not lost upon other rebel commanders, several of whom chose voluntary submission as a preferable alternative to the compulsion of the scaffold.

It was about this time that Stephen had cause, or believed himself to have cause, to doubt the loyalty of Roger of Salisbury, with whose indispensable aid he had attained the throne. This service had naturally brought rich rewards, both to the Bishop and to several of his relatives. His son Roger of Poer had been rewarded with the chancellorship, while other members of the family had been installed in the bishoprics of Ely and Lincoln. So powerful had this quartet become that they had taken it upon themselves to fortify the royal castles under their control, ostensibly as a precaution against the jealousy of the lay baronage.

Whatever the merits of the case, the King was persuaded that the time had arrived to demand the surrender of these fortresses and, as a precautionary measure, he ordered the arrest of the culprits. Three of their number were apprehended without difficulty, but the fourth escaped and made his way to the family stronghold of Devizes, wherein dwelt Maud of Ramsbury, Bishop Roger's favourite mistress.[1] It was the presence of this lady which ensured the capture of the fugitive for, when his pursuers paraded Roger of Poer before the castle walls, and then threatened to hang him, the distraught mother insisted upon capitulation.

Although the King may have had some justification for his action against Bishop Roger and his family, it had the effect of alienating ecclesiastical support at a time when it was most needed. For it was at this juncture that Matilda reached England in person, accompanied by Robert of Gloucester and a party of knights. The Earl at once set off for his military headquarters at Bristol, leaving his companion at Arundel Castle. Here she stayed as a guest of the Queen-dowager Adelaide who, after the death of Henry I, had married William of Albini. But her husband's support for the Angevin cause now became a source of acute embarrassment to Adelaide, for it brought the King and his forces to her gates. Then, for reasons of misplaced gallantry, the unpredictable Stephen

[1] In pre-Conquest days, many of the Anglo-Saxon clergy were legally possessed of wives. But under the reforming Norman dispensation (as guided by the Synod of Rome, 1047), all such matrimonial entanglements were declared null and void, and marriage henceforth forbidden to those in holy orders. It soon became evident, however, that it was altogether too much to expect that a life of strict celibacy among clerics would necessarily result.

threw away his advantage and allowed the trapped Empress to depart under a safe-conduct!

No such mistaken sense of chivalry motivated his adversaries, however, as Stephen was soon to discover. Towards the end of 1140, William of Roumare, upon whom the King had recently bestowed the earldom of Lincoln, treacherously seized the castle of that city. He and the stolen citadel were promptly besieged, though with forces insufficient to take the place by storm. The blockade which ensued was still in progress when a fellow conspirator, the Earl of Chester, arrived on the scene with Robert of Gloucester, at the head of a large army. It was now the besiegers who found themselves in difficulties and, after a desperate encounter, the King was knocked unconscious and taken prisoner. In this capacity, he was treated with all the courtesy his sudden change of fortune warranted, and with as much consideration as the generosity of his captors would allow. Which is to say, he was loaded with chains and incarcerated in Bristol Castle.

For Matilda the way to the throne now seemed open, particularly as support for her candidacy was at once forthcoming from the disaffected ecclesiastical authorities, prominent among whom was Bishop Henry, by whom Matilda was received at Winchester. The Bishop was at pains to make it known that he was not at all disposed to sacrifice his career for the sake of his luckless brother and, in these helpful circumstances, he and his colleagues soon succeeded in coming to terms with the Empress.

It was thus an elated and coronation-minded Matilda who journeyed from Winchester to Westminster. But once in London, alas, she quickly antagonized the leading citizens by her autocratic manner, by her disregard for their rights, and by her insatiable demands upon their pockets, and popular feeling against her eventually became so widespread that an armed mob gathered and converged upon the palace. The disturbance was sufficiently alarming to persuade the royal party that it would be prudent to leave the city forthwith, and a place of safety was sought at Oxford.

The significance of these events was not lost upon Bishop Henry, whose flight from Westminster had taken him, not to Oxford, but back to Winchester, from where he lost no time in entering into negotiations with the London supporters of his brother. When word of this betrayal reached Matilda, she was so incensed by it that she promptly marched against the Bishop, whose castle at Wolvesey was soon besieged. Its owner appealed to his newly found friends for help, with the eminently satisfactory result that, as had happened at Lincoln, the investing forces were themselves surrounded.

From this predicament Matilda and David of Scotland managed to extricate themselves but, among those who failed to escape was the redoubtable Robert of Gloucester. That his capture was as severe a blow to the Angevins as had been the loss of the King to his own supporters is shown by the fact that, before the year was out, the two prisoners had been released on an exchange basis, whereafter the struggle was resumed!

In the years which followed, though the King more than held

FIGURE 3

Restormel Castle, Cornwall. A typical example, shown in plan and elevation, of a twelfth-century shell keep, built on top of a motte. The gateway dates from the preceding century. (Plan: based on a drawing in B. H. St. J. O'Neil's *Castles*; Elevation: from a photograph.)

his own in England, the whole of Normandy fell to Geoffrey of Anjou and, with the death of Robert of Gloucester in 1147, Matilda and young Henry sailed for home, leaving Stephen to entertain the hope that what remained of his realm might ultimately pass to Eustace, his heir. But even this modest ambition encountered insurmountable difficulties, in the form of the implacable opposition of the ecclesiastical authorities, with whom the King was once more engaged in bitter dispute.

The problem was tragically resolved with the untimely death of Eustace in 1153, and when, later in the same year, Henry landed in England with a token force which at once gained adherents, the disheartened Stephen agreed to confer with his young rival. At a meeting held early in November, the King acknowledged the other's hereditary right to the throne of England, while Henry, for his part, agreed that Stephen should be allowed to reign in peace for the remainder of his life—in the event, for a period of less than a year. Meanwhile, the rule of law was to be restored, and all adulterine (unlicensed) castles were to be destroyed.

These provisions promised to be an undertaking of some magnitude. Throughout the years of uncertainty and civil strife, the primary aim of the baronage had been, if not to choose the winning side, then at least to emerge from the conflict with their titles and estates intact or increased, though much, of course, depended upon circumstances which were beyond their individual control. South of the Humber the adherents of the King had been strongest in the east, while the majority of the Angevin supporters were to be found in the west. In each of these areas there resided barons whose fortunes were irrevocably linked with those of one or other of the two sides. But there were also not a few uncommitted members of the nobility who did not scruple to sell their loyalty to the highest bidder, or to whichever party seemed to be in the ascendant at any particular moment.[1] Again, some of the great lords, by an accident of geography, were able to maintain a

[1] An outstanding exponent of this policy was the notorious Geoffrey de Mandeville, whom Stephen created Earl of Essex. With the capture of the King, the Earl hastened to offer his services to Matilda, who in return granted him a more favourable charter. After Stephen's release, lavish gifts and promises lured the renegade back into the royal fold—which he promptly deserted when it seemed that the cause of the Empress was about to prevail. This final act of treachery led to the Earl's undoing for, as soon as the King felt himself strong enough, he ordered the arrest of the miscreant, and deprived him of his gains. Inexplicably, the culprit was then permitted his freedom, whereupon he forcibly occupied the abbey of Ramsey and terrorized the district of Ely until his death in 1144.

more or less neutral attitude, and even concluded pacts of non-aggression with neighbours as powerful and as independent as themselves.

In the absence of effective control by a central authority, such private arrangements undoubtedly did much to help preserve law and order in the regions to which they applied but, in less favoured parts of the kingdom, innumerable petty tyrants arose to terrorize the countryside, and a state of near anarchy prevailed, as the chroniclers mournfully record:

> For every great man built him castles and held them against the King; and they filled the whole land with these castles. . . .

In this castle-building enterprise Matilda and her supporters also joined, with the result that there were soon more private fortresses in the land than at any time before or since—Ralf de Diceto puts the number of unauthorized strongholds alone at 1,115! From the descriptions contained in contemporary accounts, however, it is evident that most of these citadels were earth and timber constructions which, once they had been surrendered, could readily be demolished, and confirmation of this would seem to be provided by the fact that few identifiable traces of these structures now remain.

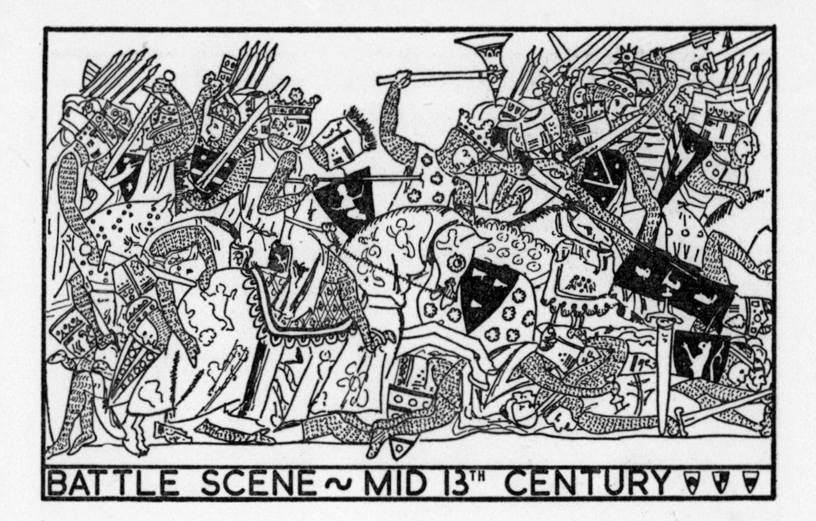

BATTLE SCENE ~ MID 13TH CENTURY

Chapter Two

Enter the Angevins

I

As members of the House of Anjou, the Angevins also came to be known as the Plantagenets, it is said, because of Count Geoffrey's habit of wearing a sprig of the broom plant (*planta genista*) in his cap whilst out hunting. At all events, it was Geoffrey Plantagenet, acting in the interests of his wife Matilda, who in due course wrested Normandy from Stephen, and subsequently bestowed the dukedom upon his son Henry.

With his father's death in 1151, Duke Henry of Normandy became the new Count of Anjou, and in the following year he added greatly to his domain by marrying Eleanor of Guienne, through whom he acquired Aquitaine, Poitou, and Gascony. The union, however, was contracted at some risk of giving affront to Henry's overlord, King Louis VII of France, whose wife this same Eleanor had until recently been. Her earlier marriage, which had endured for fifteen years, had produced two daughters, but no sons. Officially, Louis had terminated the association on the customary grounds of consanguinity. But it was no secret in Court circles that the appetent Eleanor

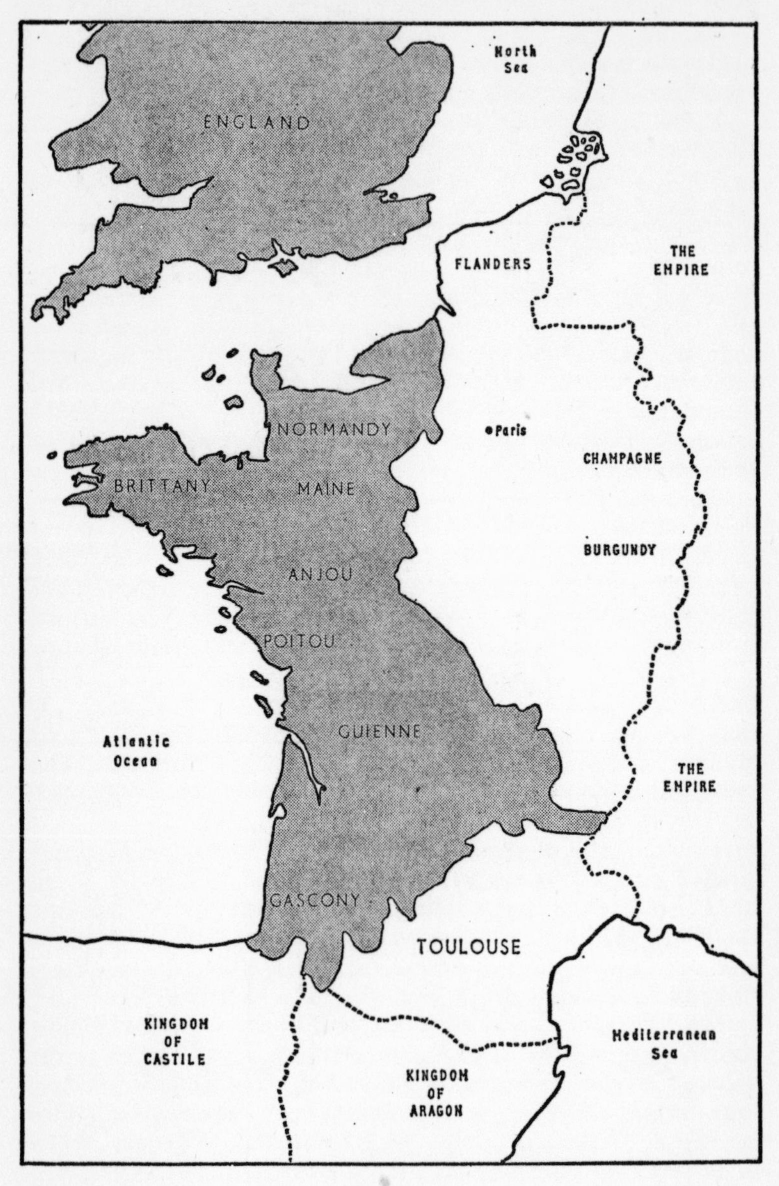

FIGURE 4

The dominions of Henry II. (A composite plan, based on William L. Langer's *An Encyclopedia of World History* and other sources.)

(who afterwards described her abstemious husband as "a monk, not a man") had become bored and dissatisfied with her neglectful partner whilst accompanying him on a crusading expedition, with results fatal to her honour.

A few weeks after her discardment, the thirty-years-old Eleanor found herself ardently courted by the teenage Count of Anjou, though it was, of course, as an heiress richly endowed with lands, not as the mother of a ready-made family, that the youthful Henry saw his unblushing bride. As for Louis, with the re-marriage of his ex-wife, he must have been made acutely aware of the fact that in the matter of territory, if of nothing else, his loss was his vassal's gain. Nor can he have been other than envious when, almost immediately afterwards, the death of Stephen brought Henry the Crown of England, making him a monarch in his own right, and establishing him as the ruler of a hybrid empire which stretched all the way from Scotland to the Pyrenees.

The extent of the Angevin realm was already greatly in excess of that governed by the French King (whose demesne lands, about the size of Normandy, were centred round Paris) when Henry II, in 1158, absorbed Brittany, a move which had the tacit approval of his liege, whom he had taken the precaution of placating with the offer of a tempting family alliance.

It happened that Louis, after ridding himself of Eleanor, had found happiness in the arms of Constance of Castile, and that his new Queen had recently presented him with yet another daughter, the now six-months-old Margaret. This baby girl, Henry suggested, should be betrothed to his infant son Henry Fitz Henry, a boy who, with the untimely decease of his brother William, had become heir to the throne of England. And despite the evident incongruities of a situation in which the mother of the groom was the divorced partner of the father of the bride, the easy-going Louis readily agreed to the proposal, sealing the bargain by offering the Vexin as his daughter's dowry.

The Vexin, in a struggle for the possession of which William the Conqueror had died, was a much-disputed buffer region situated on the right bank of the Seine, midway between Paris and the coast. At any rate nominally, the district was divided by another river (the Epte) into Norman and French spheres of interest. The entire area, however, was militarily of such strategic importance that both sides laid claim thereto, for it was recognized that whoever occupied it held the key to the Norman capital of Rouen, which in turn guarded the approach to the duchy by way of the Seine valley.

In recent years, acquiescence in French occupation of the whole of the Vexin was the price which Geoffrey of Anjou had been called upon to pay in order to ensure success in his struggle to oust Stephen from Normandy and, in promising to make restitution, the French King no doubt had in mind the very tender ages of the newly affianced couple. But although it must have seemed to Louis that he would not be required to relinquish his hold on the coveted territory for a decade or more at least, the unrelenting pressure of events was soon to prove him wrong.

Not long after Brittany had been acquired, the insatiable Henry displayed designs on Toulouse. This time, however, he went too far. The Count of Toulouse was a brother-in-law of Louis, and armed support from the French King was at once forthcoming. The interloper thus faced the prospect of warring against his overlord in person, a course he was not at all anxious to take, if only because it might set a bad example to his own vassals. A truce necessarily followed and, to add to the discomfiture of the invader, King Louis, on the sudden death of his wife Constance, promptly replaced her with Alice of Blois, thereby detaching Henry's former ally, Theobald of Blois.

Smarting under this double defeat, Henry determined to redress the balance by hastening the return of the Vexin, an enterprise in which he was assisted by the fact that the trustful Louis, as evidence of his good intentions, had placed his infant daughter in the care of her prospective father-in-law. In so doing, the French monarch presumably acted on the assumption that the ecclesiastical authorities could be relied upon not to sanction any attempt on Henry's part to bring forward the date of the wedding. In the normal course of events, such confidence would no doubt have been justified. But, unhappily for Louis, a dispute had arisen over the choice of a new Pope, in the course of which Frederick I, the masterful Emperor of Germany whom the Italians called Barbarossa (Redbeard), had forcibly intruded a candidate of his own choosing—the Cardinal Octavian, who styled himself Victor IV.

As a result, the constitutionally elected Chancellor Roland, who had assumed the title of Alexander III, had been compelled to leave Italy under duress and seek asylum in France. Henry, it need hardly be said, was not slow to make the most of this heaven-sent opportunity by demanding papal consent for the solemnization of the marriage which would gain him the Vexin. In return, he offered to recognize the fugitive Alexander as the rightful Pope, and so it came disgracefully to pass that Prince Henry Fitz Henry (aged five) somewhat prematurely became the lawful husband of Princess Margaret of France (aged two).

Despite the demands made upon his time by these continental activities, Henry did not neglect his English possessions, where a similar policy of territorial aggrandizement, brought about by the inevitable diplomatic intrigues, abrogated treaties, and open aggression, was energetically pursued.

At the onset of his reign Pope Adrian IV had benevolently made a present of Ireland to the new monarch, sanctioning a plan for the subjection of the country, that its somewhat heterodox inhabitants might be brought into the Roman fold.[1] But in part because of the opposition of the Queen Mother, the proposed conquest was delayed for several years and, when eventually the invasion began, it was undertaken on the King's behalf by Richard of Clare (alias Strongbow), assisted by other barons of the Welsh Marches.

The royal presence, meanwhile, had made itself felt in Scotland, where the accession of young Malcolm IV provided Henry with an opportunity to repudiate an agreement made earlier with King David, the boy's father. This had concerned the overlordship of Northumberland, Cumberland, and Westmorland, which districts were now reclaimed by and, perforce, surrendered to, the English Crown. Attention, too, was given to Wales, where an expedition led by Henry in person secured professions of homage from Prince Owen of Gwynedd, though local rulers in other parts of the country remained far from submissive.

Henry's determination to restore the authority and prestige of the Crown also had immediate repercussions in England, where baronial supporters of Stephen were required to surrender their lands and their castles. With few exceptions, they were prevailed upon to do so peacefully, while diehards such as Hugh of Mortimer were quickly forced to submit when they attempted to resist. At the same time, work on the demolition of unlicensed strongholds was speeded up, in conjunction with the complementary task of repairing and strengthening the royal fortresses.

This last undertaking, which occupied Henry throughout his reign, was made all the more necessary by the fact that, during

[1] The notorious Bull *Laudabiliter*. Its author, born Nicholas Breakspear, has the added distinction of being the only Englishman ever to become Pope. As Adrian IV, he presided over the destinies of Christendom from 1154 onwards, and it was his death five years later which led to the intervention of Frederick Barbarossa, and to the double election which followed.

the first century of English castle building, scant use had been made of masonry, at any rate originally. Apart from the great keeps which had been built at London and Colchester during the days of the Conqueror, a similar structure erected at Rochester by Archbishop William of Corbeil, and one or two others of less imposing dimensions, the use of materials more durable than timber had been confined to a few rocky sites like that of Richmond, in Yorkshire, where curtain walls of stone, replete with rectangular flanking towers, had been a feature of Count Alan of Brittany's handiwork from its inception (*c.* 1075).

From the beginning of the twelfth century, however, the wooden palisades of existing motte and bailey defence works were gradually replaced by ring walls, though it is not without significance that, where speed of erection was essential (as in the midst of a hostile native population), there was recourse to earth and timber constructions as late as the 1170s, as the activities of Strongbow and Company in Ireland go to show.

In England, meanwhile, Henry II made due contribution to the renovation and repair of existing structures and, among other examples, the shell keeps of Hastings, Arundel, and Windsor have been attributed to him. The characteristic feature of his rebuilding programme, however, took the form of a square (or rectangular) stone keep, of which an early and outstanding specimen is the great tower which he added to the Earl of York's surrendered stronghold at Scarborough.

Newcastle (Northumberland) was among other places similarly fortified, but the most ambitious of Henry's many reconstructions was that carried out at Dover. Begun about 1180, it entailed the building of a massive stone keep and the tower-protected walls of (what was later to become) the inner bailey, an extensive task which required a decade or more to complete. The work was entrusted to a certain Maurice the Engineer, and (so the Pipe Rolls of the period reveal) it entailed an expenditure in excess of £6,000, a stupendous sum for those days.

By contrast, Henry had earlier ordered the construction of an entirely new keep and bailey castle at Orford, Suffolk, which was built at about a quarter of the cost of renovating the great Kentish stronghold. But although a relatively modest achievement, Orford is of particular interest because, during its erection, an attempt was made to overcome an inherent weakness of the rectangular keep—the vulnerability of its sharp corners to mining.

To help defeat such activities, not only was the main tower

at Orford provided with polygonal sides, but it was endowed with a trio of projecting turrets, from which the defenders could direct flanking fire at an enemy below. Nor did the development end here. The logical outcome of a change from a rectangular to a polygonal shape was the circular tower, which offered an attacker no angles at all[1] though, by the time this was widely recognized, the keep itself was tending to become outmoded.

FIGURE 5
Conisborough Castle, Yorkshire (*c.* 1185–90). An early example of a round keep. (From a photograph.)

The first such structure to be built on a circular plan in England was in all probability that to be found at Conisborough, in Yorkshire, though here the effect was spoilt by the addition of half a dozen wedge-shaped buttresses, which rise to the full height of the tower. Its builder was Hamelin de Warenne, Henry II's half-brother, who introduced another

[1] This consideration applies equally to mural towers, though to the defenders a round, as opposed to a square, interior was not without its attendant inconveniences. With their genius for compromise, the English sought to combine the advantages of both designs by adopting the D-shape, in which a semicircular front was substituted for that side of the rectangle which faced the field.

innovation in the guise of a spreading base or talus, the sloping face of which was designed to serve the two-fold purpose of defeating the battering ram, and to act as a glissade from which stones, dropped from above, would bounce off and cause havoc among the besiegers.

Despite his long absences abroad, and his preoccupation with castle building at home, Henry also found the time to overhaul and set in motion the administrative machinery created by his grandfather and, in so doing, he produced a series of far-reaching financial, judicial, and military measures. During the troubled days of his predecessor, the royal revenues had declined catastrophically by as much as two-thirds, and the important task of reorganizing the Exchequer was given to Nigel, Bishop of Ely, whose methods of raising money assumed novel and painful forms—tallage (an impost collected from royal towns and the demesne lands of the Crown); hidage (a levy assessed on each hide of land); and even a personal property tax. Scutage, hitherto restricted to the ecclesiastical baronage, was now extracted from lay members as well, the monetary payments (at two marks = 26s. 8d. a time) received in lieu of knights' fees being used by the King to hire mercenaries. In the matter of military service he thus became largely independent of vassals who could decline to serve with him abroad, and the usefulness of whose feudal obligations was in any case limited to a period of forty days.

This deliberate weakening of the fighting monopoly of the barons was in due course followed by a compensatory reorganization of the fyrd. The Assize of Arms not only reaffirmed the duty of every English freeman to share in the defence of the realm, but it defined the military equipment with which he must provide himself. In common with knights, persons owning property or rents to the value of sixteen marks were required to possess shield, helmet, lance, and a coat of mail. For men worth ten marks, an iron skull-cap, hauberk, and lance were deemed sufficient, while lesser citizens were allowed to replace the hauberk with a quilted jacket.

Henry's legal reforms, as embodied in the earlier Assize of Clarendon, were of an even more revolutionary nature. By a process of centralization which laid the foundations of common law and the jury system, the King sought to impose a royal justice, nation-wide in its application, in place of that hitherto dispensed by baronial and ecclesiastical courts, whose arbitrary rulings, even when unprejudiced, were based on local customs which varied from one district to another.

In thus seeking to amend the law and its administration,

the King came into serious conflict with the Church, whose courts, particularly during the reign of Stephen, had contrived greatly to extend their jurisdiction. As a result of these encroachments, one of the prerogatives which the ecclesiastical authorities now claimed as an inalienable right was that they, and they alone, were entitled to sit in judgement on errant members of the clerical profession.

This so-called "benefit of clergy" had become notorious as a loophole through which such offenders were enabled to escape the rigours of the law, and its abolition was long overdue. Henry (as he thought) prepared the way for reform by using his influence to have a boon companion of his, the Chancellor Thomas Becket, elected to the primacy when that high office became vacant. As a mere deacon, Becket was not strictly eligible for the preferment but, thanks to the intervention of his royal patron, the formalities attendant upon his elevation were disposed of in a matter of hours.

The King then ventured to propose that, henceforth, those in holy orders who were found guilty of a criminal offence in an ecclesiastical court should, after their formal degradation, be handed over to the royal justices for sentence and punishment—on the face of it, a not unreasonable requirement. The new Archbishop of Canterbury, however, would have none of it and, too late, Henry discovered that when it came to making a choice between the affairs of State and the privileges of the Church, his erstwhile friend had become an unyielding antagonist.

As a result of the inevitable quarrel which followed, Becket was forced into exile, where he remained for six years. Pope Alexander III, whose own position was still far from secure, and who, though he felt bound to support the Archbishop, had no wish to lose Henry as an ally, sought to intervene. Eventually, there was an apparent reconciliation between the two men. But when at last Becket returned to England, he did so, it would seem, intent upon martyrdom. At all events, by his subsequent behaviour he so provoked the King that the exasperated monarch, in a fit of rage, gave utterance to a remark which, overheard by four of his knights, led to the assassination of the cleric within the precincts of his own cathedral.

Although Henry was subsequently absolved from any suggestion of having instigated the crime, the murder seriously weakened him in his struggle against the Church, and the abuses associated with the ecclesiastical courts continued to be a source of mounting scandal until the reign of Henry VIII. Nor was this by any means the most serious of the consequences which the King had to face as a result of Becket's death. Louis of France was quick to take advantage of his rival's unpopularity by promoting a rebellion which spread throughout the Angevin domain. It gained the support, indeed, not only of French notables (who were assisted by the Count of Blois), but also of the King of Scots and leading English barons, and even of Henry's own wife and sons.

The reason for Queen Eleanor's defection is not far to seek—a growing hostility towards her wayward spouse because of his many infidelities. After dutifully bearing him eight children, five of them sons,[1] she now found herself abandoned in favour of a succession of paramours, one of whom, if Giraldus Cambrensis is to be believed, was the intended bride of Henry's own son Richard—the Princess Alice, Louis of France's second daughter by Constance of Castile. Another of the King's mistresses, whom he afterwards openly acknowledged, was Rosamund Clifford (the Fair Rosamund), while the cost of yet a third companion somehow came to be recorded on an official expense account (Pipe Roll 30 Hen. II):

Pro pannis Regine et Bellebell, ad opus Regis' £55 17*s*.

The Queen's resentment at her treatment undoubtedly influenced the attitude of her sons, who also nurtured discontents of their own, notwithstanding that young Henry had been given the English Crown (and had received Normandy, Anjou and Maine in addition); that Richard had acquired Aquitaine; and that Geoffrey, on his marriage to Constance of Brittany, had secured the succession of the duchy (John Lackland, so-called because at the time he was too young to share in this distribution, was afterwards granted the lordship of Ireland). The trouble was that while the King had been more than generous in his territorial bestowals, the authority to rule over these domains remained firmly in his hands.

The revolt began in July 1173, when young Henry and his brothers, aided and encouraged by Louis, invaded Normandy. This move was the signal for the start of an uprising in England, where a number of discontented earls, prominent among whom were Robert of Leicester and Hugh of Norfolk, made attacks upon the castles of the King, while in the north William the Lion of Scotland (the brother and successor of Malcolm IV) made forays across the border.

These events appear to have been anticipated by a pre-

[1] These were William (died in infancy); Henry and Geoffrey (who also predeceased their father); and Richard and John (each of whom was destined to occupy the English throne briefly and in turn).

cautionary provisioning of certain of the royal strongholds, among them that to be found at Salisbury, where the garrison, "by the King's writ", was furnished with 125 measures of corn (£21), 120 bacons (£10 16s. 8d.), 400 cheeses (£8), 20 measures of beans (60s.), 20 measures of salt (30s.), and 60 measures of malt (£9 0s. 10d.), not to mention other items of equipment which included hand-mills, iron hooks, charcoal, and a cord for the castle well.

Almost from the start, things began to go badly for the insurgents. The Earl of Leicester, notwithstanding that he had an army of Flemish mercenaries at his disposal, was defeated and taken prisoner by the King's forces. So was the luckless William the Lion (who blundered into the hands of his enemies in a fog!), while Hugh of Norfolk also ended up a captive. On the Continent, too, the pattern of events was much the same and, in little more than a year, the uprising was over, leaving Henry more firmly enthroned than before.

The victor, however, used his success wisely. The rebel barons were granted an amnesty, and suffered far less than their castles, many of which were ordered to be destroyed.[1] At least some of the grievances of the members of Henry's family were met, and his sons forgiven (though not their mother, who remained under restraint). William of Scotland was granted his freedom, after he had paid homage to the English monarch and acknowledged him as his overlord. And an understanding was reached with France which kept the two countries at peace until after the death of Louis in 1180.

Louis was succeeded by Philip II Augustus, his son by his third wife. This Philip was to prove himself a strong ruler, and an implacable enemy of the Angevin empire. His aim, patiently pursued, was to bring about the disruption of that realm, and in this he was assisted by the interminable squabbles of Henry's sons, which continued unabated even after death had removed two of the disputants (the young Henry died in 1183, Geoffrey three years later). Eventually, by playing one Angevin against another, the French King induced Richard, now Henry's acknowledged heir, to further his own ambitions by joining him in declaring war against his father. In the internecine struggle which ensued Henry was driven from Le Mans to Angers, and forced to make a humiliating peace. By this time

[1] The Assize of Northampton, 1176. One of its clauses required the justices to ensure that baronial strongholds marked for destruction were utterly demolished, and the official records show that these orders were duly carried out (Pipe Roll 22 Hen. II). The work of repairing and strengthening royal castles, meanwhile, went on apace.

a dying man, one of his last acts was to request a list of those whom he was required to pardon—to find at the head of it the name of his favourite son John! Two days of bitter realization later, he was dead.

II

The romanticized picture of Richard Coeur de Lion, Richard the Lion-Hearted, as the embodiment of a chivalrous knight-errant, brave to the point of recklessness in battle, and generously conciliatory to his defeated enemies, while it undoubtedly has some substance in fact, needs to be viewed against the more sombre background of his treachery towards his father, and the manner in which he remorselessly hounded that unfortunate monarch to his death. Moreover, although this filial ingrate inherited virtually the whole of the vast Angevin domain, and was duly crowned Richard I at Westminster in September 1189, he proved to be one of England's most negligent kings, an absentee monarch who, during his ten years on the throne, spent less than ten months in the kingdom. He made, indeed, but two short visits to the country (13 August–12 December in the year of his coronation, and 13 March–12 May in 1194), and used both occasions to raise money for the furtherance of his overseas adventures.

At the time of his accession his immediate plan was to join Philip Augustus and Frederick Barbarossa in the Third Crusade, an enterprise precipitated by Saladin's (Salah al-Din's) capture of Jerusalem two years before. The German contingent was to make its way across country, via Hungary and Asia Minor (a procedure which, ironically enough, led to the accidental death of the Emperor by drowning in the River Calycadnus, in Cilicia), while the other two leaders journeyed by sea. Before embarking, Richard drew up a set of disciplinary rules for the fleet, which have since been hailed as the first official "Articles of War". These combat regulations decreed, in part, that

> Anyone who slays a man on board ship shall be thrown into the sea lashed to the corpse; if on land, he shall be buried in the ground tied to the corpse....

Progress towards the Holy Land was leisurely and, while the two monarchs were wintering in Sicily, Richard took the opportunity to free himself from his long-standing obligation to marry the Princess Alice, to whom he had been betrothed when he was three years old. The release cost him dear—a sum of 10,000 marks and certain territorial adjustments (including the Norman Vexin) favourable to France. It also earned him the enmity of King Philip who, as the reluctant suitor's continental overlord, did not take lightly this insult to his half-sister, a slight made worse by Richard's almost immediate marriage to Berengaria of Navarre.

Not surprisingly, having regard to this and other animosities which developed among its leaders, the Third Crusade achieved little enough. Thanks in no small part to Richard's energy and skill, the seaport of Acre was captured, and its garrison of more than two and a half thousand defenders chivalrously butchered in cold blood. But, despite this initial success, Jerusalem itself was not reached, much less liberated from the infidel and, in the end, all that was gained was a three-year truce which allowed the Crusaders to retain a coastal strip, that pilgrims might have access to the Holy City. Philip of France, meanwhile, had already given up the unequal struggle, ostensibly because of ill health but, in reality, to plot against his former ally.

His chosen instrument was Richard's brother, to whom he suggested marriage with the unwanted Alice, in return for French assistance to enable him to supplant the absent King. John was by no means averse to the arrangement, but word of it reached Richard, who decided that the time had come to return home. He left Acre with the intention of landing at Marseilles, but changed his plans on being warned that Philip proposed to have him arrested. Instead, he sailed up the Adriatic, with the idea of journeying across Germany disguised as a merchant. But, in making the attempt, he fell into the unfriendly hands of Leopold II of Austria, by whom he was imprisoned in the castle of Durrenstein, prior to being handed over to Frederick Barbarossa's successor, the Emperor Henry VI.[1]

Fortunately for Richard, the efficiency of the administrative system established by his father had enabled his ministers to maintain an effective rule during his absence and, when the

[1] The popular legend which relates how the troubadour Blondel de Nesle wandered through Germany, singing a song known only to his lost master and himself, appears to have arisen more than half a century after the events it purports to describe. The more prosaic facts of the matter are that, news of Richard's capture having reached England, the Abbots Boxley and Robertsbridge were sent to find him. They eventually caught up with the royal captive at the castle of Ochsenfurt, as he was on his way to join the Emperor at Spire.

Emperor demanded the enormous sum of 150,000 marks for the release of his captive, it was possible to make an immediate start on collecting the ransom. A down payment sufficed to gain the King his freedom, though not before he had been compelled to surrender England to his captor, from whom he received it back as a fief!

When at last Richard arrived at Sandwich early in 1194, it was to find that an abortive attempt on the part of John to stir up a rebellion against him was on the point of being suppressed, and that the instigator of the trouble, on receiving word from Philip to "Look to yourself, the Devil is unchained" had already fled to France in anticipation of his brother's return.

The King stayed in England for precisely two months—long enough to have himself re-crowned (in contravention of his pledge to the Emperor); to forgive John his treasonable activities (the blame for which was somewhat ingenuously ascribed to others); and to extract yet more money from his already over-taxed subjects (by way of a hidage of two shillings on lands of non-military tenure, and a scutage of twenty shillings on the knights' fee). He then set off for Normandy to settle accounts with Philip.

This, however, proved to be an undertaking which it was far easier to contemplate than to achieve and, in 1196, after two years of indecisive fighting, interrupted by a truce, Richard was glad enough to gain a further respite by signing a treaty which formally acknowledged certain territorial encroachments on the part of his enemy, including French occupation of the Norman Vexin. But no sooner was the agreement signed than it was broken when Richard, in order to guard the approaches to Rouen (and, no doubt, with the eventual recovery of the Vexin in mind), began the construction of Château Gaillard, one of the most famous fortresses of its day which, on completion, its builder referred to with affection as his *Bellum Castellum de Rupe* (Beautiful Castle of the Rock).[1]

In designing Château Gaillard, Richard was presumably influenced by the experience he had gained whilst fighting the Saracens. Whereas in Western Europe at this time the keep or donjon constituted the fortress, any outer walls being of secondary importance, in the East it was customary to erect a second line of defence within an outer enclosure or *enceinte*, thus doubly protecting the ultimate strongpoint. No less

[1] The English word "castle" is derived from the Latin *castellum*, a diminutive of *castrum*, meaning a "fortified place". *Château* is the French form.

important was the dictum that all walls must be systematically flanked by projecting towers, preferably round or multi-angular in shape.

These principles were adopted by Richard, who found a seemingly impregnable site for his fortress on the summit of the rock of Andeli, a 300-foot high promontory standing on a bend in the Seine where the waters of a tributary cut through the limestone cliffs to join the parent stream. Nor did the King allow himself to be deterred by the fact that the land upon which he intended to build belonged to someone else, or that the owner (who happened to be the Archbishop of Rouen) strenuously objected to Richard's proposal, and that at one stage of the proceedings he placed all Normandy under an interdict.

That the work of construction, once begun, was carried out with all speed is shown by the fact that the essentials of the task were completed in as little as twelve months, though in

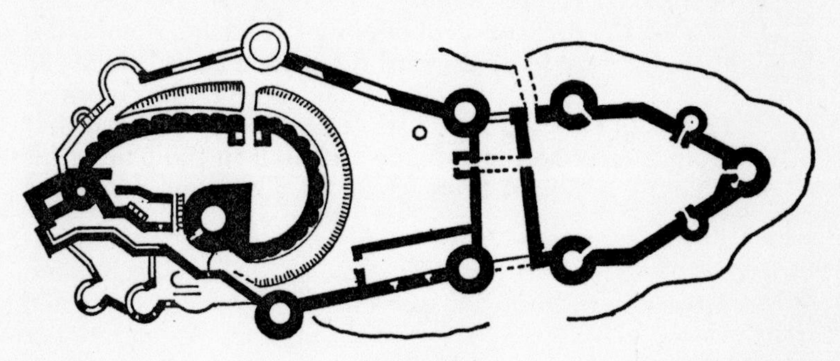

FIGURE 6

Château Gaillard, Normandy. Plan of Richard I's castle on the Rock of Andeli (based on a drawing in G. T. Clark's *Medieval Military Architecture in England*).

all, it was three years before the castle was finished in its entirety. Guillaume le Breton has described how Richard

> . . . had the summit of the hill made round and walled with strong fortifications; he cleared it of stones, and then, having flattened the interior of the enclosure, he caused a number of small habitations to be built there, to hold many people, and only kept the centre for the construction of the donjon.

Of necessity, the castle followed the contours of its restricted hill-top site, emerging as an elongated structure consisting of three baileys, arranged in line. Of these, the outer bailey was triangular in shape, with the apex facing the field, and formed a separate entity, entirely enclosed by towered walls which were encircled by a moat. The moat was spanned by a bridge which gave access to the middle bailey, which was likewise surrounded by towered defence works. This central area, the most extensive of the three wards, enveloped the moat-protected inner bailey, whose walls, in the absence of towers, took the form of a series of curved projections. And at the very edge of an adjacent precipice, partly outside the line of these corrugated battlements, stood the citadel or donjon, its entrance approached by way of a flight of steps.

The building of such a formidable fortress, in defiance of treaty obligations, constituted a challenge which Philip of France was bound to accept, and there were desultory outbreaks of fighting along the Normandy borders which continued for a year or more. Then Richard's attention was momentarily diverted by news of the discovery of a golden ornament on the lands of a vassal of his, Adomar, Viscount of Limoges. The Viscount took the precaution of offering the King a share of his find but, as his liege lord, Richard demanded the whole of the treasure, and when this was refused, laid siege to the culprit in his castle of Chalus. And it was while so trivially engaged that a bolt from a cross-bow struck the monarch in the base of his neck, inflicting a wound from which he died some days later (6 April 1199).

III

Richard left no heir, and his death was followed by a disputed succession, a circumstance which provided Philip of France with yet another opportunity to make mischief by lending his support to the candidate of his choice, as dictated by the exigencies of the moment.

The dying King had expressed a wish that his brother should rule in his stead, and this last request was respected in Normandy, where John was duly invested with the duchy at Rouen towards the end of April, and also in England, where he was crowned at Westminster a month later. By the (yet to be established) law of primogeniture, however, the dead King's successor should have been Arthur I of Brittany, the posthumous son of Richard's eldest brother Geoffrey, whose claims were acknowledged by the nobles of Anjou, Maine, and Touraine. Arthur also had the support of Philip, though, when a difference of opinion with the powerful William des Roches made it expedient to do so, the French monarch did not hesitate to recognize John's right to Anjou and Maine, and even conceded his overlordship of Brittany. But having gained this advantage, John proceeded to throw it away by two ill-considered acts, one of which entailed his re-marriage, the other the murder of his nephew.

On the customary grounds of consanguinity (which he suddenly made an issue after ten years!) John divorced his childless wife Isabelle of Gloucester, that he might be free to marry a young girl of the same name who was barely in her teens. He thereby did himself a double dis-service, for his treatment of the first Isabelle alienated many of the English barons, while his acquisition of the second made him powerful enemies abroad.

The young Isabelle was the daughter of the Count of Angoulême, and she was already betrothed to Hugo of Lusignan, the son and heir of the influential Count de La Marche. The Lusignans, mortally offended by so blatant a breach of contract, appealed to King Philip, and he, as John's suzerain, called the offender to Paris to explain his conduct. On his failing to answer the summons, John was adjudged to have forfeited all his French possessions, which were formally handed over to Arthur—with the important exception of Normandy, which Philip proposed to acquire for himself.

Having at last secured official acknowledgement of his rights, Arthur set off at the head of 250 knights to lay siege to the eighty-year-old Eleanor, who was ensconced in the castle of Mirebeau. But, luckily for the old Queen, who now found herself trapped, she was able to send an urgent request for help to her son at Le Mans. By making a series of forced marches, John reached the scene with such unexpectedness that the besiegers were caught unawares, surrounded, and compelled to surrender.

The capture of Arthur and his followers was a success which, used to advantage, might have done much to call a halt to the ambitions of the much more dangerous Philip of France. But John could see his nephew only as a rival who must be got out of the way and, after his young prisoner had been taken to Rouen early in 1203, he was heard of no more. That he was quietly disposed of there can be no doubt, and the wildest of rumours soon began to circulate concerning his fate—according to one such lurid tale, John had strangled the boy with his own hands. The probability is that the victim met a much more lingering death, as his captor was well known for his disinclination to burden the Exchequer with the cost of feeding those doomed to die.[1]

Whatever the manner of Arthur's end, his disappearance cost John the support of valuable allies at a time when Philip's invasion of Normandy, assisted by his occupation of Maine, Anjou, and Touraine, was making rapid progress. But, although antipathy towards John led to the defection of Hugh of Gournai and others, Roger de Lacy, who was in command at Château Gaillard, remained loyal to his master, and thus brought down upon himself the full force of French arms.

Of the various recognized procedures for gaining admittance to an enemy-held citadel, one was to lure the defenders from the security of their stronghold by a feigned retreat, while a method even less arduous was to rely upon the gate-opening services of an agent already located within the fortress. But, failing subterfuge or treachery, there remained either a passive policy of blockade (designed to starve the garrison into eventual submission), or more active measures involving a direct assault (necessitating the scaling or breaching of walls), or a combination of the two.

In the days of the motte and bailey, its timber palisades and wooden keep invited destruction by fire, but, with the advent of walls and buildings of stone, other methods of attacking castle fortifications came into use. Prominent among these was mining. A sap or gallery, driven under the foundations, would be buttressed with timber props as the work of excavation proceeded. On completion, the supporting struts would then be fired, causing the collapse of the structure overhead.

The mine, however, could only be employed effectively if conditions were suitable (a castle built on rock, or surrounded by a wide and water-filled moat, was virtually immune to this mode of attack) and the work, moreover, was time-consuming and laborious. A much quicker method of forcibly gaining admission to a fortress was by escalade, though the successful use of scaling ladders (sometimes made of thongs instead of wood, so enabling them to be thrown over the wall) required the swamping of the defence by the attackers without regard to loss of life.

[1] According to the *Annals of Margan*, of the many knights captured with Arthur, twenty-two were shipped to England, incarcerated in Corfe Castle, and there allowed to starve to death. A similar fate at the hands of John subsequently befell the wife and son of William de Braose. The two victims, locked together in a cell, were found to be dead after eleven days of suffering, in the course of which the demented mother had sought to relieve her hunger by gnawing the cheeks of her companion.

A development of this form of assault employed the belfry, a moveable timber tower made sufficiently tall for it to top the enemy battlements, on to which, as soon as the edifice had been wheeled alongside, it would disgorge its occupants. Similar platforms, judiciously sited, served as look-out posts, from which archers could harass the defenders with a high level fire, and so provide cover for those engaged in other operations.

These might be no more than an attempt to open a hole in a wall by prising loose some of its stones with the aid of an iron-pointed instrument known as a bore. But a much more effective way of making a breach was by ramming. The conventional ram (mouton) consisted of a heavy tree trunk, suspended by ropes or chains from an overhead cross-beam. When pulled back to its fullest extent, the metal-capped pole would swing forward on being released, and so batter the offending masonry, an operation which could be repeated indefinitely.

Such activities, of course, did not remain unnoticed by the defenders who, in response, would seek to interpose some form of buffer between the ram and its target. Those in charge of the machine would also receive attention and, in order to afford them protection, the so-called penthouse was evolved. This was a timber shelter, either moveable or built *in situ*, strong enough to enable it to withstand the rocks and other missiles which would be showered upon it from above. By reason of the slow and often stealthy approach associated with the mobile version, it became known as a "cat" or "tortoise", this last reference a reminder that the device was an elaboration of the Roman *testudo*, the cover legionaries used to form by overlapping their shields above their heads when attacking a wall.

Bombardment from a distance was contrived by means of engines of war which likewise had their origins in classical antiquity. These were the *petrariae*, outsize stone-throwing machines such as the mangonel (essentially a long arm with a cup or sling at its free end, motivated by a skein of twisted rope) and the trebuchet (worked by a system of springs and counterweights), this last a particularly powerful hurling device, used on occasion to heave the bodies of dead horses over castle walls. The Roman ballista, which fired a javelin-like missile, was also much used by besiegers and, during the twelfth century, it achieved notoriety, in miniaturized form, as a hand weapon.

As such, the cross-bow consisted of a wooden stock, with a bow fixed at one end, the string of which was stretched by a lever or a small windlass. Release was by means of a trigger and, as the device was capable of firing a bolt (quarrel) twice as far (up to 450 yards) as the lighter missile discharged by the conventional bow and arrow, it rapidly supplanted the older form of the weapon, at all events in Europe.[1] This was notwithstanding its denunciation, in a Papal Bull issued in 1139, as an instrument too barbarous for one Christian to use against another, albeit with pious disregard for the welfare of the unbeliever, the infidel was thoughtfully exempted from this charitable dispensation.

But, although a formidable array of these artillery and other devices were now ranged against Château Gaillard, such was the reputed strength of its defences that at first Philip was content merely to invest the fortress, in the hope that he might eventually starve its defenders into submission, or at any rate considerably weaken their powers of resistance.[2] The French King was encouraged in this belief by the fact that, on his approach, the inhabitants of a nearby village had fled to safety within the castle walls, thus providing its commander with many extra mouths to feed. When it became evident that the siege was likely to be unduly prolonged (an attempt on John's part to relieve the fortress having failed), these unfortunates were expelled, several hundred of them to perish miserably of cold and hunger between the opposing lines.

The siege, which began in the late summer of 1203, was rigorously maintained throughout the winter and until the following spring, when a sustained assault was begun by means of mangonels and other *petrariae*. At the same time, under the protection of a long penthouse, part of the outer moat was filled in, so enabling the salient tower of the outer bailey to be undermined, strutted, and fired. The ground attackers then turned their attention to the middle bailey, and this, too, was eventually occupied, thanks to a feat of daring on the part of

[1] Manipulating the heavy crossbow from behind the protection of a fortification was one thing; using it in open warfare another. In the field, the English retained a preference for the long-bow (which in expert hands could discharge its arrows five times as fast as the more cumbersome mechanism) until as late as the second half of the fifteenth century. The capabilities of this national weapon (which was of Celtic origin) were brought forcibly to notice during the reign of Henry II, when a knight fighting the Welsh found himself pinned to his horse by an arrow which had penetrated his armour, his thigh, and his saddle!

[2] In days gone by, such a move would have ended in failure if the members of the garrison had sufficient food and water to enable them to hold out for forty days, after which period of obligatory service, a feudal host tended to melt away. But this was a vexatious limitation which vanished with the advent of the hired soldier, who would normally continue fighting so long as he received his pay of 1d. per day.

several soldiers who gained access to it by way of the castle sewers. The wall of the inner bailey next received attention, the pounding and mining it received causing a portion of it to collapse, thus allowing the keep to be reached and stormed. This final strongpoint was taken on 6 March, some six months after the affray began.

The effect of the fall of Château Gaillard was immediate and profound, for it led to the loss of Rouen and, with it, the rest of Normandy. Philip was thus left in undisputed ownership of the whole of John's continental possessions to the north of the Loire, the Angevin retaining little more than his mother's inheritance of Aquitaine. Nor did his gross mismanagement of affairs end at this for, in the course of the next decade, he forfeited (at any rate nominally) his English kingdom in addition!

This came about as the culmination of a long and bitter dispute with Pope Innocent III over the election of a new Archbishop of Canterbury. John had one suitably pliant candidate in mind, the ecclesiastical authorities wisely chose another. The Pope decided to settle the argument by appointing yet a third, in the person of Stephen Langton, whom John obstinately declined to accept. As a result, all England was placed under an interdict, after which the King, still as defiant as ever, was first excommunicated and then declared to have been deposed.

According to all the rules of anathematization, John should by this time have been reduced to monarchical impotence. But in fact, not only did he retain command of the situation, but he remained as aggressive and as uncompromising as before—until, as a last resort, the Pope authorized Philip of France to intervene. At this, John finally took alarm, rightly fearing that an invasion from abroad would be assisted by widespread revolt at home, thanks to his many violations of feudal customs and his never-ending extortions of money from the barons. To ward off this double threat, and at the same time to regain ecclesiastical recognition of his occupancy of the throne, the King made instant submission to Rome, and voluntarily surrendered England to Innocent III, from whom he received it back at a rent of 1,000 marks. It was an inspired move, for the disgruntled Philip was at once warned that on no account must he invade what was now a papal fief!

John's next step was to evolve a grandiose scheme aimed at the recovery of his lost empire. For their part, the English nobles were distrustful and not disposed to help, but the King formed a coalition with his nephew Otto IV of Saxony and others who were hostile to Philip of France. Their intended victim, however, proved to be more than a match for the allies, upon whom he inflicted a crushing defeat at Bouvines. Much discouraged, John returned home. But when he tried to raise money to pay for his costly failure by demanding scutage from those who had denied him their services, many of the barons united against him, and called for confirmation of the charter earlier granted by Henry I.

Though he did so with extreme reluctance, John was eventually induced to set his seal to a document which has since become renowned as Magna Carta—the Great Charter.[1] But, having done so, he spent the next two months recruiting mercenaries from Flanders and elsewhere, in the meantime having prevailed upon the Pope to annul the concessions which he had been compelled to sign under duress. Civil war soon followed, the King relying upon his hired troops, the barons seeking the aid of Philip of France by offering the Crown of England to his son Louis.

The first trial of strength took place at Rochester Castle, which Reginald of Cornhill had handed over to the rebels. Two weeks later (in mid October) the King arrived to reclaim his lost fortress, which was placed under strong and continuous attack. A serious breach having been made in the bailey wall, the defenders retired to the great stone keep built by William of Corbeil, and there continued their defiance. Mining operations were then decided upon, a reference to which is to be found in a royal writ dated at Rochester on 25 November 1215, and addressed to the Justiciar, Hubert de Burgh:

> We command you that with all haste, by day and by night, you send us 40 bacon pigs of the fattest and those less good for eating to bring fire under the tower.

The siege came to an end a few days later, when a corner of the great keep was brought tumbling down and the forces of the King at last gained admittance. John was for hanging all who were taken prisoner forthwith, but more humane counsels prevailed. Even so, the capture of the fortress had a most disheartening effect upon the rebels, many of whose strongholds were left undefended on the King's approach while making a

[1] Couched in Latin, somewhat vaguely worded, and designed, in the main, to safeguard baronial privileges (the rights of villeins and others scarcely find mention), the fame of Magna Carta derives not so much from the actual contents of its sixty-odd clauses as from the rather wide interpretations which came to be placed on them in later reigns, particularly in the days of the Stuarts.

show of force which took him as far as Scotland. After the fall of Rochester, as one chronicler remarks, few of the barons were disposed to put their trust in castles.

But May 1216 saw the arrival in England of Prince Louis, accompanied by 1,200 knights, and, with his coming, so many waverers deserted the King's cause that it seemed his overthrow was merely a question of time. The end came in the following October when John was in Norfolk, intent upon making his way to the adjacent county of Lincolnshire. He and his army took a circuitous inland route, while his baggage train, loaded with stores and equipment, including the royal treasure, essayed to make a short cut across the estuary of the Wellstream (modern Nene), only to be engulfed by the incoming tide.

Worn out and suffering from fever, John eventually reached Newark Castle, where he developed a voracious appetite for peaches and new cider. Two days of biliousness later he expired, leaving behind him a memory so hated and reviled that no member of the English monarchy has since been burdened with his name.

IV

Four years after the death of her husband, Queen Isabelle married Hugo X of Lusignan, a son of the first love from whom she had been so cruelly parted by the ambitions of her father. She had in the meantime borne John five children, two of whom were sons—Henry, who succeeded, and Richard, who became Earl of Cornwall. By his many mistresses, the late King had also provided himself with numerous other offspring, among them Joan, Geoffrey, John, and Oliver, though the full extent of his procreational irresponsibilities is not known with any precision.

Henry III was but nine years old when he came to the throne, to find the kingdom torn by civil strife and much of the country (including its capital) in the hands of a foreign Prince. But the boy King, as a papal ward, had the backing of the Church, and he was also supported by some of the barons, including the influential William Marshall, Earl of Pembroke, who acted as regent. The royal cause was greatly assisted, too, by the fact that the formidable Dover Castle, which lay astride the French lines of communication between London and Paris, continued to be held for the Crown by Hubert de Burgh, who successfully resisted all attempts to dislodge him.

The situation was eventually resolved when Prince Louis was decisively defeated at Lincoln in 1217, an encounter which led to his withdrawal from the country, speeded on his way by a parting gift of 10,000 marks. Thereafter, with the subsequent death of William Marshall, the government of the realm devolved upon Pandulph (the papal legate), Hubert de Burgh (who acted as chief Justiciar), and Peter des Roches (an adventurer from Aquitaine who had found high favour under John).

One of the immediate aims of the administration was to ensure that the rebel barons gave no more trouble, and, as a precautionary measure, the destruction was ordered of any private strongholds which were newly arisen or had recently been rebuilt. This move was followed by a demand for the surrender of all royal castles not garrisoned by forces of the Crown, an injunction which, though generally obeyed, led to a number of incidents.

Falkes de Breaute, who had gained wealth and prominence in the service of Henry's father as the leader of his mercenaries, took the greatest exception to a proposal aimed at depriving him of his hard-won strongholds and his lucrative sheriffdoms. The impending trouble came to a head when the followers of Falkes's brother William captured and held prisoner in Bedford Castle one Henry de Braybroke, a royal judge who had recently pronounced against the pretensions of the de Breautes at Dunstable Assizes, held nearby. This violence to the person of a high officer of the Crown constituted an outrage which most certainly could not be allowed to go unnoticed, and the culprits quickly found themselves surrounded by royal troops, with the King at their head. But when commanded to deliver up their prisoner and to surrender their stronghold, the rebels rashly chose to continue their defiance.

Bedford was ultimately taken by storm, after being closely besieged for about eight weeks, and it so happens that the events leading to its capture find mention in a number of contemporary accounts. It is possible, moreover, to couple these descriptions with incidental references to the affair which occur in official documents of the period, so that an unusually instructive glimpse is obtained of the exponents of medieval siegecraft at work.

Some idea of the extensive nature of the preparations required, and of the administrative effort entailed, may be gathered merely from a perusal of ancillary listings of men and materials. We learn that miners were summoned from Hereford and the Forest of Dean, carpenters from Windsor and

Lincoln, stonecutters from Bedfordshire and Northamptonshire ("to work stones for mangonels and *petrariae*"), and detachments of cross-bowmen from London and elsewhere, all of whom needed to be provided with transportation for themselves and their gear, so that, in the words of the King's writ addressed to local sheriffs and constables, "they shall be able to travel to us by day and by night as swiftly as they can and not tarry". Materials and equipment were likewise requisitioned from near and far—timber from Northamptonshire (accompanied by bitter complaints from the monks of Wardon, whose woods had been denuded of trees by the King's men), tallow from London, ropes and cables from Cambridge and Southampton, siege engines from Lincoln and Northampton, bolts and quarrels by the thousand from Corfe Castle.

The actual attack, thus mounted, was preceded by a spiritual assault designed to deprive the defenders of any assistance from On High: under the able direction of the Archbishop of Canterbury and his associates, the rebels were first solemnly excommunicated. This formality having been observed, the siege engines, among them half a dozen mangonels, began their bombardment of the castle walls, their fire directed by the occupants of two belfries. Mining operations were also started, under the cover of a penthouse.

According to the author of the *Annals of Dunstable*, the reduction of the fortress took place in four stages. First, the barbican (outwork) was taken. Then the external bailey was occupied, a success which deprived the defenders of much equipment and livestock. In the third assault, the wall of the inner bailey was breached, so that the attackers at last found themselves at the foot of the main tower, through the entrance to which ten of their number rushed, only to be trapped inside and cut off from their companions. At this, sapping operations were at once begun, as a prelude to the final assault, which took place on the vigil of Assumption (14 August) when

> . . . fire was put under the tower by the miners, so that smoke broke through into the dwelling place of the tower where the enemy were; and the tower was split so that cracks appeared. Then the enemy, despairing of their safety, allowed Falkes' wife and all the women with her, and Henry, the King's justice, with other knights whom they had shut up before, to go out unharmed, and they subjected themselves to the King's command. . . .

Unluckily for the culprits, although they were magnanimously absolved from their excommunication, the King's command was that they should pay for their temerity with their lives, and soon eighty and more of the rebels were dangling from a row of newly erected gallows. Falkes de Breaute, who had taken no active part in the affair, was allowed to depart for Rome, while what remained of Bedford Castle was handed back to a former owner, though not before it had been rendered incapable of defence by the destruction of its tower and outer bailey. The valuable building stone thus made available was shared by the canons of Newenham and Caldwell, and by the Church of St. Paul of Bedford.

It was three years after this incident that Henry declared himself to be of age. But while his reign saw the development of such typically English institutions as that which came to be known as Parliament (in effect, an extension of the meetings of the Great Council, whereat the King was wont to "parley" with his leading subjects), it also witnessed an unprecedented influx of foreigners, who were given well paid posts and who came to exercise considerable influence.

The first of these intruders were fellow Poitevins brought over by Peter des Roches, and when, in 1236, the King married Eleanor of Provence,[1] there was an immediate arrival of the Queen's needy relatives, including four of her uncles, one of whom was prevailed upon to accept the Archbishopric of Canterbury. Another family group made welcome by Henry consisted of his Lusignan half-brothers, his mother's children by her second husband, while yet a fourth and still more numerous parasitic horde was made up of Italian clerics, sent in droves by a succession of Popes to fill the ecclesiastical offices of a kingdom which was still looked upon as a dependency of Rome.

The presence of these aliens was all the more resented because, with the loss of their fiefs in Normandy and elsewhere, a national consciousness had begun to manifest itself among members of the English baronage, whose mounting discontent at last found expression in the Provisions of Oxford (1258), an attempt to restore the Charter. Henry at first accepted, but later repudiated, these and subsequent demands, and in 1263 there was a resort to arms.

The barons found an able champion in Simon de Montfort, Earl of Leicester and brother-in-law of the King. Under his leadership, not only did victory go to the reformers at the ensuing Battle of Lewes, but Henry and his eldest son Edward were taken prisoner, thus preparing the way for the famous

[1] By whom he had the future Edward I, Edmund, Earl of Lancaster, Margaret (who married Alexander III of Scotland), and Beatrice (who married the Duke of Brittany), among others.

de Montfort parliamentary gathering of 1265, at which, for the first time, burgesses as well as knights of the shire were invited to be present.

But de Montfort, with his rise to power, indulged in the ill-considered luxury of quarrels which made powerful enemies of one-time friends, at which juncture Prince Edward, who was being held as hostage, escaped from his guards and found safety with Roger Mortimer at Wigmore Castle. Here, the royal banner was raised and at once attracted adherents, notable amongst whom was Gilbert de Clare, hitherto a supporter of the opposition. Within three months of regaining his freedom, the young Edward was able to gather about him an army sufficiently strong to challenge and utterly defeat his enemies at Evesham (4 August 1265), where Simon de Montfort himself was slain.

De Montfort had been trapped at Evesham while on his way to join a large body of supporters stationed at Kenilworth, some forty miles away. These and other hostile groups remained to be dealt with, and as a first move a meeting of the Great Council was convened, at which the rebels were declared to be disinherited. Attempts were then made to induce Henry de Hastings and his followers at Kenilworth to lay down their arms, but the terms offered were dismissed as unacceptable, and for the moment the royalists lacked the strength to enforce them. This deadlock was not ended until the following year when, in June, Prince Edward appeared before the castle gates in some force.

Kenilworth, set in the midst of a now vanished lake, a feature which defeated attempts at mining, was admittedly a difficult place to assault. But if its fall was unduly delayed, it was because the conditions necessary to bring about its surrender were met only in part. Although there was little prospect of the garrison being relieved, its members did not find themselves seriously outnumbered, and so were able to make periodic sorties, and even engage in foraging expeditions.

As at Bedford forty-two years earlier, the Primate of England was called upon to perform the rites of execration—only to discover, greatly to his indignation, if not to his dismay, that he had a rival in the guise of a resident chaplain, who mounted the fortress walls and formally pronounced sentence of excommunication upon the Archbishop! These hilarious exchanges over, there then began an artillery bombardment which reached such an intensity, maintained from within as well as from without, that (according to one eye witness) there were constant collisions between the flying boulders overhead, which shattered one another in mid-flight and bestrewed the countryside with their fragments.

Much has been made of the fact that, despite the fierceness of the attack, the castle was not taken by storm, that the defenders succeeded in holding out for nearly six months, and that, when they eventually condescended to lay down their arms, it was on conditions much more favourable than those originally offered to them. Even so, by the time agreement was reached, the members of the garrison were desperately short of food, and their tenacity in no way invalidates the lessons of Château Gaillard—that however strong a fortress might be, it would sooner or later be compelled to capitulate, given that the attackers outnumbered the defenders, that a tight blockade was maintained, and that the proceedings were not interrupted by the arrival of relief forces.

As if to emphasize the inevitability of this conclusion, it was about the time of the siege of Kenilworth that a certain Roger Bacon unwittingly heralded the coming eclipse of the medieval stronghold when he penned a strangely prophetic reference to the

> . . . noise and fire which are made in various parts of the world by the powder of saltpetre and sulphur and hazelwood charcoal. If this powder is enclosed in a tube of parchment as thick as one's fingers, it makes such a noise as greatly vexes the ear, especially of one who does not understand it, and the terrible flash is also very alarming. Now if a tube of great size were made, nobody would be able to bear either the shock of the noise, or the flash; and if the instrument were made of solid substance, then the violence would be far greater.

CAERNARVON CASTLE

Chapter Three

The Edwardian Era

I

EDWARD I (the numbering of England's monarchs began with the Conquest) was named by his father after the Confessor, for whom the devout Henry III evidently entertained a high regard. The fond parent subsequently bestowed upon his eldest son all the outlying dependencies of his kingdom, including Wales, Ireland, and such territories as still remained to him in France. And in 1253, after conferring the duchy of Gascony upon the Prince, the King proposed that Edward, having attained the responsible age of fourteen, should take to wife Eleanor of Castile, a union which was duly celebrated in the following year.

A decade or so later, having shared his father's defeat at Lewes, and thereafter retrieved the family fortunes at Evesham, Prince Edward became ruler in all but name until he formally succeeded to the throne with the passing of the enfeebled Henry in 1272. At the time of the death of his father, however,

Edward was absent on a Crusade, and his coronation could not take place until his return nearly two years later. In this leisurely fashion there began the notable reign of a monarch who, unlike his Norman and Angevin predecessors, may be regarded as being more English than French, a domesticated ruler popularly and variously known as "Longshanks" (he was over six feet in height and possessed of a magnificent physique), as "the English Justinian" (a tribute to his constitutional reforms), and as "the Hammer of the Scots" (in acknowledgement of an aggressive northern policy).

Of the far-reaching legislative activities which characterized the new administration, these were to no small extent inspired by, and an extension of, the reforms introduced by Henry II. Edward had resort, however, not merely to the customary Ordinances (made in Council), but also to the Statute, a relatively new device which came eventually to require the assent of both King and the Members of the representative assembly. But although the writs summoning the famous Model Parliament of 1295 contained the momentous phrase "*quod omnes tangit ab omnibus approbetur*", the monarch's purpose in convening this particular gathering was not so much to ascertain the wishes of his subjects as to make known to them his own desires and intentions.[1]

Meanwhile, prior to his prolonged and not altogether effectual hammering of the Scots (an operation which, in 1295, was about to begin), the King had achieved a noteworthy success in bringing about the subjection of Wales. During the previous two centuries, the turbulent Celts had managed to

[1] There was as yet but one assembly, the forerunner of the House of Lords. The House of Commons (*vide infra*) subsequently came into being as a result of unofficial gatherings of knights and burgesses, who met in private to discuss what their attitude was to be towards the anticipated demands of their betters. A remarkable aspect of the process of separation, as G. M. Trevelyan has noted, is that unlike analogous bodies in Europe, the English Parliament divided, not into the three estates of nobles, clergy, and *bourgeoisie*, but into an Upper and a Lower House (the clergy preferred to discuss their own affairs in Convocation, and left it to the great prelates to attend Parliament in a baronial, rather than an ecclesiastical, capacity).

As for the (perhaps inadvertent) use of the injunction "*quod omnes tangit ab omnibus approbetur*" (let that which toucheth all be approved by all), no doubt this voiced a sentiment which could be relied upon to appeal to knights and burgesses, if not to barons and bishops. But however this may be, that the wording in question was not intended to be given too literal an interpretation is evident from the fact that it did not concern members of the lowly villeinage, who comprised some four-fifths of the country's inhabitants. In the event, the enfranchisement of England's rural population did not take place until the nineteenth century, while votes for women on the same terms as men was not achieved until as recently as 1928.

retain a considerable measure of freedom, notwithstanding the efforts of the Norman monarchs to conquer them, both in person, and indirectly through the Marcher Lords, whose troubled border fiefs centred round such strategic outposts as those of Chester, Shrewsbury, Hereford, and Gloucester.

Ultimately, the unpacified inhabitants of the mountain fastness of Wales had attained near-independence under Llewelyn the Great (1194–1238), whose grandson, Llewelyn ap Gruffyd (Griffiths) even ventured to meddle in English affairs to the extent of entering into an alliance with the rebellious Simon de Montfort. Despite this and other provocations, with the defeat of his ally at Evesham, Llewelyn was recognized as the leader of his people in return for an acknowledgement on his part of the overlordship of Henry III.

Seemingly, this conciliatory and by no means ungenerous treatment was mistakenly regarded by Llewelyn as a sign of weakness on the part of the English Crown. At all events, in 1274 he pointedly declined to attend the coronation of Edward I, or to render him homage. There could be but one response to so deliberate an affront, and three years later, supported by seaborne landings, Edward marched into Wales, first confining his antagonist to the precipitous slopes of Snowdonia, and then threatening him with starvation by occupying the island granary of Mona (Anglesey). Llewelyn perforce submitted, and was reduced to the status of a local chieftain. Even so, he might well have fared worse for, although he found himself deprived of all lands to the east of the River Conway, he was allowed to retain the Principality, as the territory to the west of that waterway was termed.

Having thus exerted his authority, Edward ordered an immediate start to be made on the construction of a series of castles, designed not only to enable him to maintain his hold on the region, but also to counter-balance the building activities of the Marcher Lords, some of whose strongholds were being strengthened in accordance with the latest ideas imported from the East. One such measure was the incorporation of concentric lines of defence, so arranged that the high curtain wall of an inner ward was completely enveloped by a much lower outer wall, thus allowing archers stationed behind the one to discharge their arrows with safety over the heads of companions manning the other.

An outstanding example of this and other trends in military architecture was already to be observed at the Clare castle of Caerphilly in Glamorgan, seven miles or so to the north of Cardiff. The original structure, built in 1266 or thereabouts by

Richard Clare, Earl of Hereford and Gloucester, seems to have been an unpretentious stronghold which was attacked and destroyed by Llewelyn, without too much difficulty, almost as soon as it was completed. Work of a much more ambitious nature was then begun, and it was this replacement which eventually emerged as the largest of all English fortresses, and one of the mightiest.

In its final form, an inner bailey, replete with hall, living rooms, and domestic offices, was surrounded by a quadrangular enclosure, the external wall faces of which were commanded by four round and boldly projecting towers. The area thus protected was completely enveloped by a second line of defence,

FIGURE 7

Caerphilly Castle, Glamorgan. One of the largest and most powerful strongholds of its time. (From a photograph.)

consisting of a lower and less massive stone curtain, in which corner towers were replaced by circular bulges in the wall.

There were also other innovations. A serious defect of earlier strongholds had proved to be the absence of an emergency exit—if the single entrance to the Norman keep was carried by assault, the defenders found themselves trapped for the want of an escape route. Even when the keep ceased to be an essential feature of castle design, the problem remained, and it had been met by the introduction of the postern gate. Experience then showed the desirability of providing a multiplicity of exits and entrances, that an investing force might have no way of knowing from which of several sally-ports an attack from within might come, or by which particular avenue supplies of food might contrive to reach the beleaguered garrison.

The designer of Caerphilly was fully alive to this vestibular requirement. Not only did two main gateways pierce the east and west walls of the inner bailey, but in addition there were no less than three posterns, one on the south side, and two on the north. The outer curtain was similarly endowed, except that there was but a single secondary door on the northern perimeter. For the rest, the main western gates gave access, over a drawbridge, to an extensive outwork, while the eastern gates led, again by way of a drawbridge, to a barbican, in the shape of a screen wall, some 300 yards in length. The purpose of this barrier was to retain the contents of an artificial lake, on islands in the midst of which the castle and its western outwork stood. The level of the lake, whose waters were fed by a stream, was regulated by a trio of sluices formed in the retaining wall.

By comparison with this formidable stronghold, the first of the castles which Edward caused to be built in North and Mid-Wales (two in each region) were relatively modest affairs. Work on all four was begun in 1277, in July of which year the *Brut-y-Tywysogyion* (Chronicles of the Princes of Wales) placed on record that:

> On St. James' Day Edmund the King's brother accompanied by an army, came to Llanbadarn, and began the building of Aberystwyth Castle.

Little of this structure now remains, while the masonry of its associated building at Builth has disappeared to such an extent that it is no longer possible to trace the castle's original outlines. That the vanished fortress cannot have been very large, however, is suggested by the available accounts, which indicate that the cost of the work amounted to £1,666 9s. 5¼d.—less than half the sum spent on Aberystwyth.

In the north, more extensive strongholds were built at Rhuddlan (at a cost of some £10,000) and at Flint (about £7,000). Of these, Rhuddlan exhibits a simple concentric design, though an unusual feature is the location of its two gatehouses, which are placed diagonally opposite to one another at two of the angles of the inner enclosure. By contrast, the arrangement at Flint is altogether different. Here, the designer has provided what amounts to a replica in stone of the old motte and bailey plan, in which the motte is represented by a massive round keep, standing in isolation at one corner of the bailey, the curtain wall of which has circular towers at each of its three remaining corners. A drawbridge originally connected the two components, which were so sited and ditched that they were surrounded by the tidal waters of the Dee estuary.

Work on at least one of these strongholds had still to be completed when Llewelyn's brother David made a surprise attack on Hawarden Castle, taking prisoner the Lord Chief Justice of Wales, Sir Roger de Clifford, after severely wounding him as he lay abed (Palm Sunday 1282). This assault was the signal for a general uprising, and while Rhys, the son of Maelgwn, stormed and captured the unfinished fortress of

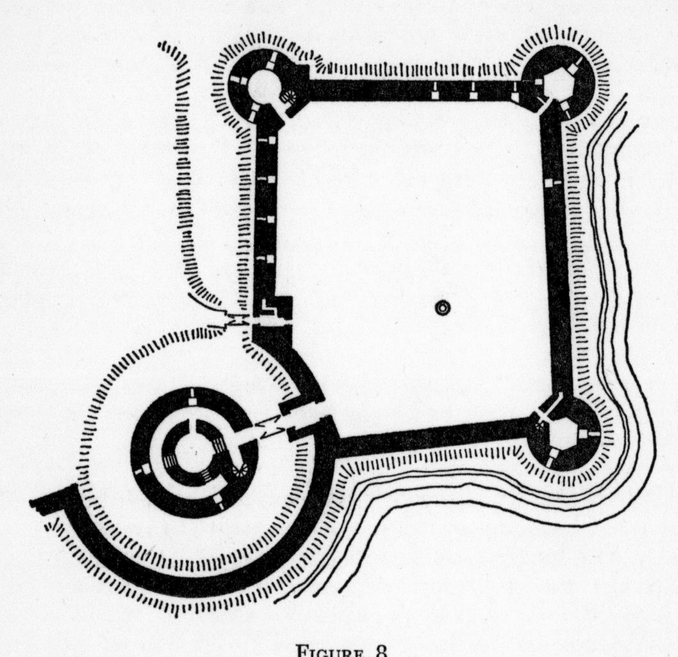

FIGURE 8

Flint Castle. Plan, showing the inner bailey and isolated cylindrical keep (based on a drawing in S. Toy's *A History of Fortification*).

Aberystwyth, Llewelyn joined his brother in laying siege to the strongholds of Rhuddlan and Flint.

An angry and determined Edward again led his troops into Wales, and the valiant Llewelyn, in an encounter with some of his enemies in the vicinity of Builth, was slain. After this disaster, the Welsh forces began to disperse, with the result that David eventually found himself deserted except for his wife and family, at which juncture a countryman, one Einion ab Evan,

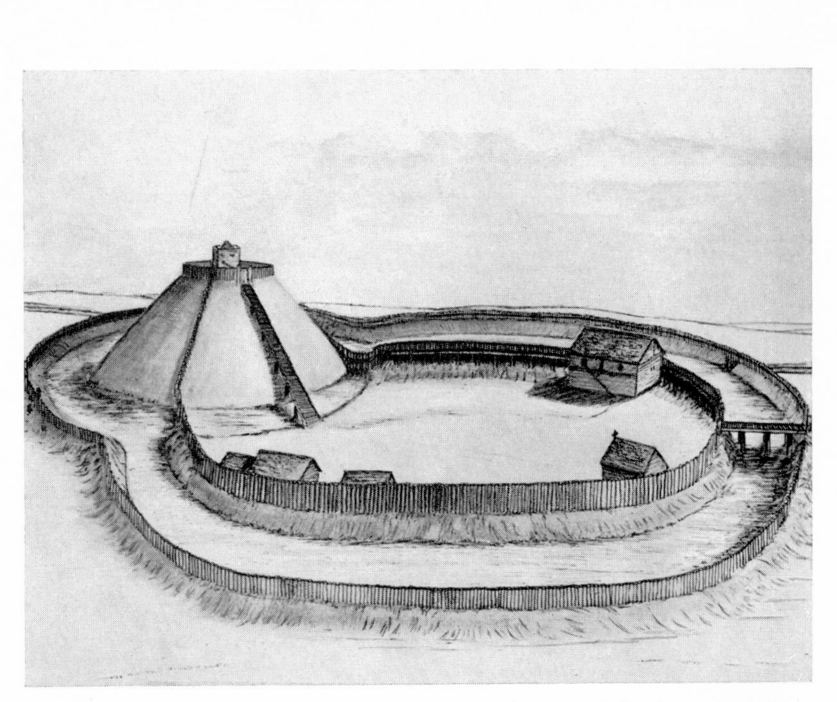

The Norman motte and bailey, then and now: (*above*) an artist's reconstruction (*photo:* B. T. Batsford Ltd.); and (*below*) an aerial view of remains at Berkhampstead, Hertfordshire (*photo:* Aerofilms and Aero Pictorial Ltd.).

The White Tower, London: the massive stone keep begun by William the Conqueror and completed by his son and successor in 1098 or thereabouts. (*Photo:* Crown Copyright)

disclosed the fugitive's hiding place to the English, by whom he was tried and executed as a traitor.

With effective resistance once again at an end, the King decided to annex the erstwhile Llewelyn Principality to the Crown, thereby ensuring that the Gwynedd region of Wales was not added to the Powys and Dinefawr domains of the Marcher Lords. Accordingly, a second and more ambitious programme of royal castle building was at once inaugurated, much detailed information concerning which has been brought to light by the documentary researches of J. G. Edwards.[1]

The work of construction (necessarily a seasonal occupation) was undertaken simultaneously at the three sites of Harlech, Conway, and Caernarvon, a task of sufficient magnitude to require a labour force of several thousand men, numbered among whom were many artisans unwillingly recruited from all over England (and thoughtfully provided with armed guards to deter them from absconding!). And as in the case of the four earlier Edwardian castles, the architect and supervisor of the Harlech and Conway undertakings, if not that of Caernarvon, was St. George d'Esperanche, a master-mason from the Department Isère, France, whose services, there is reason to believe, were loaned to the King by his kinsman, Count Philip of Savoy.

Harlech, set on the summit of a rugged headland, emerged as a grim, rectangular structure which boasted a self-contained strongpoint (the equivalent of the twelfth century keep) in the form of a massive gatehouse. It was also replete with inner and middle baileys enclosed by a double line of walls, not to mention an outer bailey which extended down precipitous slopes to the north and west. But although this elevated fortress was built on the prevailing concentric plan, the acknowledged "master of the King's works in Wales" was by no means indissolubly wedded to such an arrangement, as indeed he had already demonstrated at Flint.

At Conway, he chose a site which was already admirably adapted by nature for defence—a narrow, rocky peninsula, whose almost sheer sides were washed at their foot by the tidal waters of the River Conway and its tributary the Gyffin. Along the edges of this isolated platform was built a single, lofty stone curtain, its top equipped to take projecting timber fighting galleries (hoards) as an additional defensive aid. The wall was also protected by eight flanking towers, standing in two lines of four, those containing the royal apartments displaying high turrets. Main gateways were placed at either end of the

[1] *Edward I's Castle-Building in Wales* (The British Academy, London, 1944).

enclosure, and a small inner bailey was served by two posterns, one of which, evidently intended for rope-assisted emergency use only, opened high above the river in the south face of the curtain wall. At Conway, there was thus provided an edifice of great military strength which (at any rate in the opinion of some) also constitutes the most aesthetically satisfying of all England's castles that have survived.

As at Conway, the castle erected at Caernarvon also conforms to its site, a location important in that it commands the entrance to the Menai Strait. This fact was evidently not lost upon the early Normans who, in the person of Hugh of Avranches, established a fortified mound here towards the end of the eleventh century. But, unlike its companion structures, Caernarvon Castle was built in three stages, over a period of

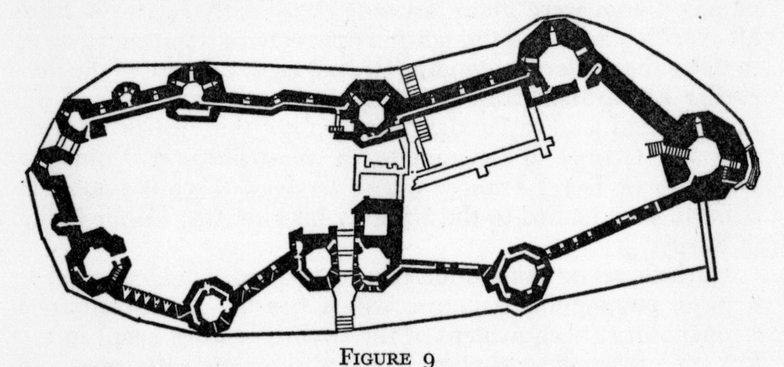

FIGURE 9

Caernarvon Castle, 1283–1323 (based on a plan published by H.M. Office of Works).

forty years, and much of the work appears to have been carried out under the supervision of Walter of Hereford, whose design took the form of a single defended area, divided into two by an internal partition. Five entrances were provided (three of them posterns), and the curtain wall was strengthened by nine polygonal towers, variously displaying six, eight, and ten sides.

In 1284 the future Edward II was born at Caernarvon, and at the turn of the new century his father bestowed upon him the title of Prince of Wales.[1] But in between these two events, a

[1] The story that the King was moved to make one of his rare jokes by introducing his infant son to his newly conquered Welsh subjects as the promised native-born Prince who could speak no English, would seem to be unfounded. Young Edward, at all events, was seventeen years of age when he became Prince of Wales. Similarly, the popular tradition that he first saw the light of day in one of the rooms of the Eagle Tower takes no account of the inconvenient fact that in 1284 this part of the castle had yet to be built.

series of native uprisings occurred, one of which was led by Madog, an illegitimate son of Llewelyn, who in 1294 took the town of Caernarvon and its partly-built castle by assault. The revolt, however, was soon put down, and in the following year the task of repairing and extending the damaged fortifications was begun. At the same time, the building of yet another Welsh stronghold was decided upon, the chosen location being at Beaumaris, in Anglesey, where a marshy flat provided a site

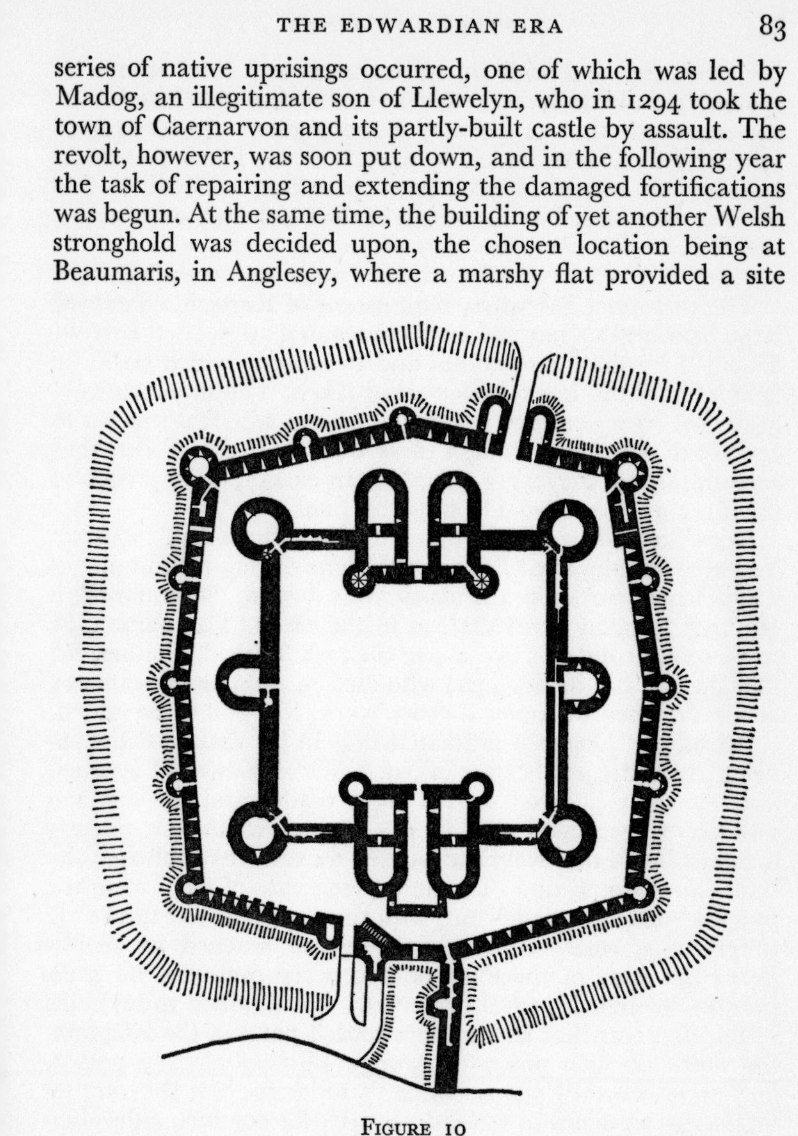

FIGURE 10
Beaumaris Castle, Anglesey (based on a plan in S. Toy's *The Castles of Great Britain*).

possessed of few natural advantages, apart from its close proximity to the sea. Thanks to this circumstance, the castle was encircled by a water-filled moat, and was even provided with a small dock.

St. George d'Esperanche was responsible for the design of

the structure, and with an unrestricted and level stretch of ground to build on, he produced a symmetrical plan incorporating concentric lines of defence. A rectangular (almost square) inner ward was surrounded by massive walls, fifteen feet thick, guarded by a pair of gatehouses (standing opposite to one another, and placed in the middle of the north and south walls), two D-shaped towers (similarly projecting from the face of the east and west walls) and four drum towers, one at each corner.

The two inner gateways, reminiscent of Harlech, contained large halls and rooms, and each constituted an isolated fortress, defended by three portcullises and two doors, which could be held even if the inner bailey were taken. The outer curtain, protected by a dozen or more wall towers, also featured north and south entrances, though these were built out of line, thus ensuring that if they were forced by an enemy, his approach to the inner gateways would expose his flank.

Notwithstanding that as many as three and a half thousand men were employed at this one site alone during the summer of 1295, when work on the castle was begun, its completion required so many years that, as in the case of Caernarvon, its royal sponsor did not live to see the task finished. Neither, for that matter, did its designer, who died in 1309 or thereabouts, at a time when the outer defence works had still to be added.

All told, it has been estimated that in his determination to bring about the pacification of North Wales, Edward I lavished not less than £80,000 on his eight castles and the fortified settlements associated with them[1]—an enormous sum when it is remembered that wages accounted for some two-thirds of the total expenditure, and that the average rate of pay amounted to a few pence per day—and, with the completion of this costly programme, castle building in England reached its zenith. From the start of the fourteenth century onwards, no comparable stronghold, royal or private, was destined to be built.

The fact was that in the more settled parts of the kingdom, the need for such powerful strongholds had already passed, and architecturally the nobleman's residence was showing an increasing tendency to sacrifice security for comfort, a development which found its ultimate expression in the manor house. Even in border areas and coastal regions, such private residences could always be fortified if the need arose, as is shown by the terms of the licence issued to Sir Edward Dalyngrigge, less than

[1] Harlech, which stands alone, is an exception in this respect. At Conway and Caernarvon, however, not only are the main strongholds still in a remarkable state of preservation, but the town walls are also to be seen much as they were when they were built.

half a century after the completion of Caernarvon and Beaumaris. It was specifically allowed that the owner

> . . . may strengthen with a wall of stone and lime and crenellate and may construct and make into a castle his manor house of Bodiam, near the sea, in the county of Sussex, for the defence of the adjacent country and the resistance of our enemies.

The enemies in question were the French. But although Bodiam Castle emerged as a massive rectangular structure, replete with a round tower at each corner and set in the midst of a wet moat, with an approach guarded by isolated outworks connected by a series of drawbridges, internally its defences

FIGURE 11
Bodiam Castle, Sussex (from a photograph).

were weak, as none of its buildings could be defended against an attacker once he had gained admittance—a serious defect in an age in which treachery was rife. But Bodiam Castle incorporated one novel feature which its earlier and more formidable predecessors lacked: its gatehouse displayed gunports for cannon.

In the meantime, no sooner had Edward succeeded in imposing a peace of sorts on the Welsh, than he was faced by an outbreak of rebellion in Scotland. This trouble had its beginning in the disputed succession which arose when, riding in darkness, Alexander III and his mount followed a track which led to the edge of a cliff. His heir was a motherless grandchild, the three-year-old daughter of King Eric of Norway, and it was arranged that this infant should marry the young Lord Edward of Carnarvon. But, unhappily for the prospects of a peaceful Anglo-Scottish unification thus opened up, the Maid of Norway did not survive the journey the plan entailed, and the English King then had the thankless task of choosing between more than a dozen rival candidates for the vacant throne, prominent among them being Robert Bruce, the aged Lord of Annadale, John Hastings, and John Baliol, all three of whom were descendants of nieces of Scotland's King William the Lion. The nomination was secured by John Baliol, but Edward's subsequent treatment of him as a subordinate gave rise to much resentment. It also led to a Scottish alliance with England's enemy Philip IV of France, in effect a declaration of independence which was accompanied by forays across the Tweed.

In the inevitable war which followed, Edward made good use of the lessons he had learned while fighting the Welsh. Among other things, his campaigns in Snowdonia had revealed the inadequacy, both as regards numbers and equipment, of the traditional feudal levy. As a result, these forces had been augmented, not by groups of foreign mercenaries (a course forbidden under the terms of Magna Carta), but by companies of free compatriots who contracted to fight for pay. Experience had also shown the importance of maintaining command of the sea, and had demonstrated the tactical advantage to be gained by interspersing mounted archers with troops of cavalry—the bowmen, having pursued and caught up with their quarry, then dismounted and let fly a shower of arrows, inflicting sufficient losses to enable their still-mounted companions to ride the weakened enemy down.

The English stormed the frontier town of Berwick, and then met and defeated John Baliol at the Battle of Dunbar, whereupon Edward confidently proclaimed himself King. The Scots, however, obstinately declined to agree with him, and a seemingly endless series of uprisings followed, at first led by William Wallace, and then by Robert Bruce, a grandson of the claimant against Baliol. Edward responded by making one armed intervention after another, in the course of which Wallace was captured and executed, and reprisals were taken against his successor's wife (she was deported) and his brothers (who were hanged). Bruce himself, however, remained at large, and it was while leading another campaign against him, in 1307, that the indefatigable Edward, then approaching seventy years of age, reluctantly breathed his last at Burgh-on-Sands, while *en route* from Carlisle to the Scottish border.

II

Like his father, Edward I had been unusual among English monarchs in that, throughout his long life, his amatory inclinations were reserved exclusively for his lawful spouse, and in view of this monogamic idiosyncrasy the wonder is, perhaps, that the obliging Eleanor of Castile contrived to bear no more than the thirteen children with which she presented him. As it was, a high proportion of these offspring died in infancy, and the namesake who succeeded to the English throne was the fourth and last of his sons by her, though in later years Margaret of France, his second wife, provided him with a couple more.

Edward II inherited his father's stature and his striking good looks, but not his ability, determination, or strength of character. And although, in the year of his coronation (1308) he dutifully married a girl half his age (the twelve-year-old Isabella of France) in fulfilment of a contractual obligation, it soon became apparent that the new monarch much preferred a life of pleasure to the responsibilities of kingship. A restless baronage, freed at last from the strong and restraining hand of his predecessor, noted the fact and duly saw to it that, while the King reigned, others ruled.

For his part, Edward II early displayed an inclination to rely upon favourites for companionship and advice. The first of these intimates was Piers Gaveston, a Gascon knight whose high-handed ways made him many powerful enemies. Led by the King's cousin, Thomas, Earl of Lancaster, the baronial party compelled Edward to send his friend to Ireland, a banishment from which the exile received a royal recall in the following year. The barons replied to this act of defiance by entrusting the affairs of state to a committee of twenty-one (the Lords Ordainers).

This was the situation when the King and Gaveston, who were at Newcastle together early in 1312, learned with alarm of the approach of Lancaster at the head of a large force. The two managed to make their escape and afterwards parted company, Edward going to York and Gaveston taking refuge in Scarborough Castle. Here, he was closely besieged by the Earls of Surrey (John de Warenne) and Pembroke (Aymer de Valence), with whom, thanks to a lack of supplies, he was soon forced to come to terms. On his receiving a most solemn assurance that his life would be spared, Gaveston surrendered, to be escorted southwards by Aymer de Valence, who intended to place the prisoner in his own castle of Wallingford. But, in the course of the journey, Guy Beauchamp, Earl of Warwick, intervened. Gaveston was forcibly seized, taken to Warwick Castle, and executed nine days later.

Edward, helpless to save the life of his friend, vowed to avenge his murder. But for the moment his attention was distracted by events in Scotland, where Robert Bruce had been engaged in reducing one stronghold after another, until at last only Stirling Castle remained in English hands. Despite the refusal of many of the barons to assist him, the King set out to relieve the threatened fortress, only to suffer at nearby Bannockburn a defeat so crushing that Scottish independence was thereby assured for centuries to come.

This disaster placed Thomas of Lancaster more firmly in control than before, and Edward found solace in the company of new favourites. These were the Hugh Despensers, father and son, whose insatiable greed for land and titles was such that it quickly brought them into open conflict with some of the Lords Marcher. The expulsion of the King's companions followed, whereupon the indecisive Edward was goaded into activity at last by the insulting refusal on the part of Lady Baldesmere to offer the Queen the hospitality of Leeds Castle (Kent). Bartholomew de Baldesmere, the lady's husband, was an outspoken enemy of the Despensers, so that the King was afforded a double satisfaction when he attacked and captured the stronghold. Not content with this, he then demonstrated the extent of his displeasure by hanging Sir Thomas Colepeper, the castellan, and eleven members of the garrison and, when baronial friends of the owner tried to intervene, drove them off.

The Despensers were now recalled, and in thus challenging the authority of his self-appointed overseers, the King received encouragement and assistance from the disillusioned Aymer of Valence and other notables who, though they had no time for the royal favourites, had grown to detest the Earl of Lancaster and his associates even more. These not-so-worthy gentlemen responded by taking up arms, only to allow themselves to be outmanœuvred and forced to surrender at Boroughbridge, in Yorkshire. This misfortune of war cost Lancaster, de Baldesmere and others their heads and, with the peaceful submission of the powerful Roger de Mortimer, the eighth baron of Wigmore (another implacable antagonist of the Despensers), effective opposition to the King and his friends came to an end, at any rate for the time being. But to his great cost, as Edward was soon to learn, he made what was to prove to be the fatal mistake of consigning Mortimer to perpetual imprisonment in London's Tower, instead of ordering his demise forthwith.

The King, or rather the Despensers, now ruled the country, and in so doing earned for themselves the undying enmity of the Queen—Edward, by his shameful neglect of her for his friends, the Despensers, by their scarcely-concealed designs upon her income and her property. Isabella, however, did not make known her feelings until she was safely abroad, ostensibly on a diplomatic mission to her brother who, early in 1322, had succeeded to the French throne as Charles IV. On his accession, the new monarch had waited patiently, but in vain, for Edward to render due homage in respect of his continental possessions. There had also been a dispute with the English seneschal overseas concerning the sovereignty of some territory at St. Sardos, and in July 1324, no satisfaction having been obtained on either count, King Charles had announced the confiscation of Gascony and Ponthieu, which he invaded forthwith.

It was in a belated attempt to retrieve this situation that Edward allowed Isabella to journey to Paris, only to learn of her disinclination to return to his Despenser-dominated household. But worse tidings were to follow for, at the French Court, Isabella met and made common cause with a group of disaffected members of the erstwhile baronial party. Prominent among these exiles was a fugitive English nobleman who had recently contrived to escape from life imprisonment in the Tower—Roger de Mortimer, no less, with whom the susceptible Isabella was soon living in open adultery!

Edward had for some time been entreating his wife to return home when, in 1326, she at last condescended to do so—accompanied by her lover and a contingent of foreign troops. On arrival, the invaders were welcomed as liberators, and the King and his supporters put to flight. The elder Despenser was caught at Bristol and promptly hanged, a fate which overtook his son a month later, when he and the King were captured in Wales. Not content with demanding the abdication of her husband in favour of their eldest son, the vengeful Isabella had the unfortunate Edward confined to Berkeley Castle, on the Severn. Here, so the chronicler Jean Froissart was informed by a local squire a few years after the event, the royal prisoner soon died, "for his days had been shortened". The precise manner of his end is not known (according to one account, a red-hot iron was plunged into his bowels), but it may be surmised that, after months of ill-treatment and semi-starvation had failed in their intended purpose, there were heard

The shrieks of death, through Berkeley's roofs that ring—
Shrieks of an agonizing King!

III

Isabella's son was but fifteen years of age when he was crowned as Edward III in January 1327, and, in view of his youth, Henry, Earl of Lancaster (brother of the executed Thomas) was appointed as guardian. The government of the country, meanwhile, remained in the hands of the Queen Mother and her paramour, and the latter, in making the most of this unique opportunity to amass a fortune, also had himself created the first Earl of March, a title inspired by his extensive territorial possessions on the Welsh border.

Mortimer also busied himself with affairs of state. One of his first steps was to come to an understanding with Charles IV of France who, in return for the payment of a heavy indemnity, agreed to relinquish his hold on most of the English lands he had seized. But no sooner had this been arranged than Charles died, leaving no heir to succeed him, a circumstance which, as Isabella was quick to perceive, gave the young Edward a strong claim to the French throne as the eldest son of the dead monarch's sister.

The matter, however, was not pressed at this time, though it was to be raised on more than one occasion in the years ahead. The French barons, meanwhile, found a candidate more to their liking in a member of the royal line of Valois, a cousin of the dead Charles. He attained the throne as Philip VI, and justification for the success of a male claim in a junior line against a female claim in the senior line was conveniently found by making reference to Salic Law, as formulated centuries earlier by the Frankish conquerors of Gaul:

> . . . but of Salic land, no portion of the inheritance shall come to a woman; but the whole inheritance of the land shall come to the male sex.

Mortimer also reached agreement with the Scots by the realistic expedient of abandoning England's claims to sovereignty over them, and by acknowledging the kingship of Robert Bruce. It was a decision which earned its author much unpopularity, and this and other moves (not the least his acts of self-aggrandizement) led to his attempted overthrow. One outcome was the execution of the King's uncle Edmund, Earl of Kent, after his implication in a futile plot to reinstate Edward II, in whose survival he had been induced to believe. Henry of Lancaster, in another conspiracy, then enlisted the support of his ward by imbuing the young monarch with a desire to assert his rights. Thus it came about that in October 1330, William Montague, on instructions from the King, forcibly seized Mortimer in his bedchamber at Nottingham Castle, where he and Isabella were staying.

With his mother (confined at Castle Rising) and her lover (hanged at Tyburn) out of the way, Edward III now began to rule. He was, by this time, both a husband and a father, his wife Philippa of Hainault having recently presented him with a son and heir (later to achieve renown as the Black Prince),[1] the first of half a dozen or so offspring she was to bear him. Of this brood-to-be, six others were sons, four of whom were destined to establish a line of rival claimants to the throne—Lionel of Antwerp (Duke of Clarence); John of Gaunt (Duke of Lancaster); Edmund of Langley (Duke of York); and Thomas of Woodstock (Duke of Gloucester).

Edward III proved to be a popular King, as generous as he was handsome. Unlike his father, he managed to remain on good terms with the barons, in part because he was careful not to provoke them unduly, but also because his own liking for war provided them with ample opportunity to dissipate their martial instincts on the field of battle.

The King's interest in military matters was reflected in the equipment with which his armies were provided. Although it is not known who first conceived the idea of using the pyrotechnical mixture, as described by Roger Bacon, to bring

[1] To his contemporaries, he was Edward of Woodstock, and the first known reference to him as the Black Prince does not occur until Elizabethan times (Grafton's *Chronicle*, 1569). The origin of this popular title is uncertain. According to one theory, it derives from the colour of the Prince's armour, to which the objection has been raised that he was given to wearing a gilt suit of mail. Perhaps a more likely explanation is that it commemorates the part he played in the Hundred Years' War, with particular reference to his acquiescence in the massacre of the inhabitants of Limoges. At all events, the terror inspired by his campaigns in France appears to have prompted his hapless victims to refer to him as a "Prince of Darkness".

At the age of three, the Black Prince was made Earl of Chester, and four years later, as the Duke of Cornwall, he became the first member of a new rank in the English nobility. In 1361, with the connivance of Pope Innocent VI (who obligingly set aside the difficulties of the prohibited degrees) he married his cousin Joan, by whom he had two sons, Edward of Angoulême (who died in 1371) and Richard of Bordeaux. Joan, otherwise known as the "Fair Maid of Kent", was the widow of Sir Thomas Holland, by whom she also had two sons, Thomas and John.

about the forcible ejection of a missile from a hollow tube, it appears that in an encounter with the Scots in 1327, the English employed certain "crakys of war". Six years later, this was followed by the rumoured use of "gonnes" against the same enemy at Halidon Hill, a report seemingly confirmed by official records of the period, which contain references to the purchase of sulphur and saltpetre on the King's behalf. No doubt these early firearms were small in size and not very efficient in use, but their development into powerful weapons of offence, capable of hurling stone (and later iron) balls (hence "rounds" of ammunition) was clearly only a question of time.

Meanwhile, the result of the Battle of Halidon Hill (an English victory) was of crucial concern to the Scottish succession. At his death, Robert Bruce had been replaced by his five-year-old son David II, but a rival claimant had arisen in the person of Edward Baliol, who received English support. Halidon Hill was the outcome, and, with his defeat, David fled to France, leaving Baliol to occupy the vacant throne.

Scotland now had two rulers, the one a puppet of England and the other an ally of France and, in championing the cause of the boy David, Philip of Valois diverted Edward's attention from the young fugitive to himself. His purpose, no doubt, was that of deliberately provoking a quarrel, for he already regarded askance England's possession of Aquitaine, and he was also jealous of her flourishing wool trade with Flanders. If this was in fact his intention, his plan succeeded, for relations between the two countries rapidly deteriorated and soon led to the outbreak of the so-called Hundred Years War (actually a series of wars, in the course of which the English strove to maintain their foothold in France, and their opponents to expel them).

When hostilities began, Edward proclaimed himself King of France in the right of his mother, a politic move which enabled his Flemish allies to continue to support him without violating their oaths as vassals of the French monarchy. There ensued several years of indecisive fighting, interrupted by periods of truce, which culminated in the Battle of Crécy, at which the English long-bowmen, supported by dismounted cavalry, stood their ground and broke the headlong rush of the much more numerous French knights and Genoese mercenaries who sought to overwhelm them.

This outstanding victory was followed by a successful attack on Calais, which surrendered to the English after a long siege. The fall of the town preceded a lull in warlike activities, which was broken at last when the Black Prince arrived at Bordeaux, in turn by an external moat, crossed by bridges leading to a gateway on the west and a postern on the east. Walled passageways extended from these entrances to the inner citadel, thus dividing the outer bailey into two compartments. The symmetry of outline has been ascribed to the architect Henry of Yevele.

Queensborough Castle was so named by Edward in honour of his consort, though this gesture did not deter him, five years later, from having an affair with a member of the royal household. Alice Perrers, the lady concerned, was the wife of Sir William de Winter, and with the death of Queen Philippa in 1369, she came completely to dominate the King, now in his

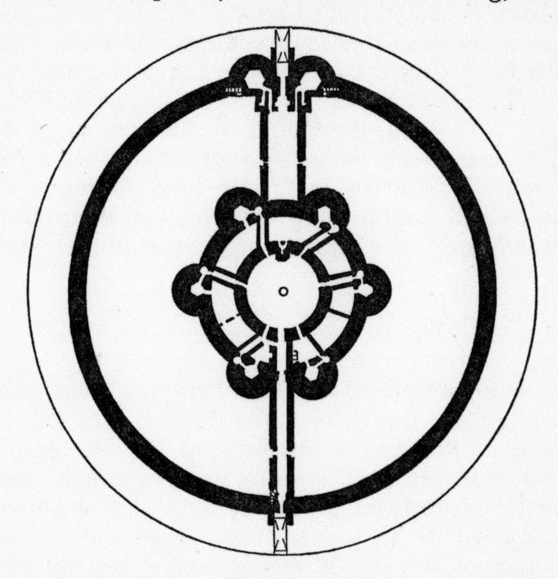

FIGURE 12

Queensborough Castle, Isle of Sheppey. Built 1361–77 to a concentric design, it was destroyed in the seventeenth century. (From a drawing in the Hatfield MS.)

dotage. The ambitious John of Gaunt (i.e. of Ghent, his birthplace) sought to further his own interests by coming to an understanding with his father's mistress, and thereby usurped the functions of his eldest brother by making himself the acting head of state.

The Black Prince, though aware of the threat to his authority, was a dying man. He attempted to counter his brother's move by giving his support to the reforms demanded by the so-called Good Parliament of 1376. The knights and burgesses present at this gathering were determined that before they would agree to provide any financial assistance, the "redress of grievances must precede supply". These sentiments found an able exponent in Peter de la Mare who, acting as Speaker, insisted that certain fraudulent officers of the Crown must be punished and royal expenditure curbed. By resolutely standing their ground, the members of the Commons finally got their way. Richard Lyons and William Latimer, two aristocratic war profiteers, were called to account—the first such impeachment in English parliamentary history. More surprising still, it was actually agreed that the notorious Alice Perrers was one extravagance which the King could no longer afford, and the lady in question found herself banished from Court.

But in the midst of these proceedings, the Black Prince died and, with his going, the reforms he had sponsored were soon undone. John of Gaunt, in the name of the senile Edward III, summoned a Council dominated by his own supporters, and the earlier enactments were declared invalid. As a result, the King's mistress returned to favour (and to her accustomed bed), Lyons and Latimer were set free, and the presumptuous Peter de la Mare found himself imprisoned in their stead.

IV

With the death of Edward the Black Prince, it must have seemed that a malign fate was determined that Edward III should on no account be followed by an Edward IV. Not only had the King's heir forfeited the Crown by predeceasing his father, but he himself had outlived his eldest son, who would otherwise have succeeded in his place. Thus, when the throne at last became vacant in 1377, it was occupied, not by Edward of Angoulême, but by his younger brother, Richard of Bordeaux.

It would have been a difficult inheritance for a grown and experienced man, let alone a mere boy of ten. The calamitous effects of the Black Death were still in evidence, while a new and more general form of taxation, recently introduced, had led to much discontent among the poorer sections of the community.[1] The country's enemies, too, were becoming increasingly aggressive. In the north, the Scots were again making raids across the border, while in the south the French, who had

[1] The cause of the unrest was the poll-tax, otherwise known as the "tallage of groats", which called upon every person over the age of fourteen to subscribe the sum of one groat (4d.). Until the introduction of this novel impost by John of Gaunt's packed assembly of 1377, the villeinage had been immune from direct taxation.

Clifford's Tower, York. This stone keep, which stands on an eleventh century motte, dates from the time of Henry III (1216–72). (*Photo :* Crown Copyright)

Caerphilly Castle, Glamorgan. It was this massive fortress, with its concentric lines of defence, which marked the beginning of a new epoch in English military architecture. (*Photo :* Aerofilms and Aero Pictorial Ltd.)

Conway Castle, Caernarvonshire—as it is, and as it was: (*above*) as seen from the north-east; and (*below*) an artist's impression of its appearance when newly built, viewed from the south-west. (*Photos:* Crown Copyright)

gained command of the sea, were attacking and burning coastal towns with impunity. They even succeeded in overrunning the Isle of Wight, and, such was the unsettled state of affairs, England itself might well have been occupied, had an invasion from across the Channel been attempted in force.

To add to the uncertainties of the times, in 1378 an hierarchical dispute gave rise to the Great Schism, a rift marked by the election of two Popes, the one stationed at Rome, the other entrenched at Avignon, whereafter a wondering world was treated to the unedifying spectacle of each of the rival pontiffs denouncing the other as an interloper and a fraud. This division of Western Christendom into two obediences (later in the quarrel to become three) inevitably weakened still further the authority of a Church already under censure because of the wealth and worldliness of some of its leading practitioners, one of whom had contrived to amass a personal fortune of 25,000,000 crowns, while, in the days ahead, it was to be the proud boast of another[1] that in his time he had raped at least 200 women, the wife of his brother among them.

In England, a cleric by the name of John Wycliffe had already set his feet on the path of reform, and was calling for an end to such manifest abuses as those associated with the system of enforced confession, penances, and indulgences. Nor did he stop at denying the priestly power of absolution. His attacks were also directed against such cherished notions as the phenomenon of transubstantiation, while even the credentials of the Bishop of Rome himself did not go unchallenged. But what made the greatest appeal to his ever-growing following of so-called Lollards, it may be supposed, was not so much his voicing of these and other heresies as his advocacy of sacerdotal frugality and his pointed contrasting of the luxurious way of life of many prelates and monks with the abject poverty of the majority of their lay customers.

Although, more than forty years after his death, Wycliffe's body was exhumed and burned by express orders of the Pope, the ecclesiastical authorities failed in all their attempts to silence him during his long lifetime. Summonses to Rome he wisely ignored, while at home powerful friends shielded him from prosecution in the sacred courts. Prominent among those by whom he was protected was John of Gaunt, who likewise deplored the Church's possession of great wealth and vast estates, though for a somewhat different reason—he thought to obtain these riches for himself. But this is not to suggest, as his enemies did not hesitate to assert, that Gaunt also had

[1] The Schismatic Pope John XXIII (1410–15).

designs on the throne. During the early years of the new reign he was careful to remain discreetly in the background, and neither he nor his brothers were directly represented on the advisory Council which was appointed to act on the boy King's behalf.

The first Parliament of the new reign gathered at Westminster in October 1377, to hear members of the Council make the inevitable demands for money, urgently needed to supplement the royal revenues. Within the space of two years, so desperate had the need become, that there was again resort to the unpopular poll-tax, though with variations: a graduated scale of payments was introduced, with the liability of Dukes and Archbishops set as high as ten marks apiece. But in terms of revenue, the result of the experiment was disappointing—a yield (£27,000) of little more than half that estimated (£50,000)—and in the following year there was a return to a flat rate, which was now increased threefold to 1s. per head.

The outcome of the mounting unrest caused by this and other grievances was the Peasants' Revolt of 1381, a popular uprising which in southern England led to the widespread burning of manors and culminated in the march of 100,000 of the malcontents on London, with Wat Tyler, Jack Straw, and other leaders at their head. Within a matter of days, control of the capital was in their hands, with every road out of the city closely guarded.

The insurgents would treat only with the King who, with his retinue, was trapped in the Tower. In the course of a dramatic meeting with their fourteen-year-old monarch, Tyler and Company were given the solemn assurance that their demands would be met, including the abolition of serfdom and a free pardon for all. Richard's plan was to persuade the rebels to return to their homes, where they could be dealt with individually and at leisure, and his real intentions were made plain enough at a later encounter, at a time when order was in the process of being restored. To members of a deputation who hopefully inquired as to the validity of their newly won liberties, he coldly intimated that "Villeins ye have been and are, and in bondage ye shall remain—not as heretofore, but incomparably worse".

Not long after this exhibition of royal courage and dissimulation, Richard once again came under the authority of his elders, and for the next few years the government of the country remained in the hands of a small group of courtiers, notable amongst whom were Michael de la Pole and Robert de Vere, a favourite companion of the King. Unluckily for these gentlemen, their handling of affairs proved to be inept, particularly in the foreign field, a circumstance which enabled a group of political enemies to bring about their downfall. The Duke of Gloucester, the youngest of the King's uncles, supported by the Earls of Arundel, Derby, Nottingham, and Warwick, formally "appealed", i.e. charged, the responsible ministers with treason, and, in the Merciless Parliament of 1388, secured the death or exile of them all.

Understandably enough, this forcible intrusion of the five Lords Appellant did not endear them to their resentful sovereign, and, after they had ruled for about a year, Richard, who was now twenty-two, declared himself to be of age. This assumption of personal control was followed by eight years of uneventful government, during which the King came increasingly to rely upon the advice and support of the most powerful baron in the land: the avuncular John of Gaunt.

Richard's uncle was by this time a much married man. His first wife, Blanche, through whom he had become successively Earl (1361) and Duke (1362) of Lancaster, had duly provided him with a son and heir—the (in his royal cousin's eyes) miscreant Henry Bolingbroke, Earl of Derby. A second marriage to Constanza of Castile, contracted in 1369, had produced a daughter, since when an extra-legal association with Lady Catherine Swynford had made him the father of four more offspring. In 1394 Constanza died, and two years later, after having somewhat tardily transformed his mistress into a wife, John of Gaunt sought to legitimize his children by her under the name of Beaufort, a proposal to which the obliging Richard readily gave his consent—and thereby helped to found the royal line of Tudor.

The King, meanwhile, though he was much beholden to John of Gaunt, was no friend of that nobleman's unscrupulous brother Thomas, and in 1397 a serious quarrel broke out between the Duke of Gloucester and himself. Both sides appear to have decided that matters could not remain as they were, and it was the Duke who moved first. In August, he called a meeting of the Lords Appellant at Arundel Castle, there to discuss how to bring about the overthrow of the King. But news of the plot was promptly relayed to the intended victim by one of the conspirators (Thomas Mowbray, Earl of Nottingham).

John of Gaunt's son, Henry Bolingbroke, escaped immediate retribution. So did Thomas Mowbray, whose act of betrayal condemned his other companions to banishment or to death—the Duke of Gloucester was shipped to the fortress of Calais, and was not heard of again; the Earl of Arundel was tried, convicted, and executed on Tower Hill; while the Earl of Warwick, after making an abject confession of guilt, was sent into exile.

Richard celebrated the downfall of his enemies by making a distribution of honours and titles from which the two surviving conspirators were pointedly not excluded—Thomas Mowbray became Duke of Norfolk and Henry Bolingbroke Duke of Hereford. But the King was merely biding his time, and his chance came in 1398, when Bolingbroke (who apparently regarded the informer as responsible for the death of his uncle Thomas) taxed Mowbray with treason, citing as evidence a recent conversation which had taken place between them. Mowbray denied the accusation and made counter charges, whereupon the two men, having thus played into Richard's hands, were both arrested. Thomas Mowbray, Duke of Norfolk, suffered the confiscation of his properties and was exiled for life. Henry Bolingbroke, Duke of Hereford, was banished for a period of ten years (afterwards reduced to six, on his aged father's pleading), added to which his punishment was further tempered by the assurance that the family estates would fall to him, should he succeed to them during his enforced absence abroad. As to this, if Richard had no intention of keeping such a promise, his making it was a grave mistake. On the other hand, having pledged his word, not to keep it was a still greater error of judgement, as became evident soon enough.

John of Gaunt died at Leicester on 3 February 1399, and his passing brought with it the belated realization that in a few years the exiled Henry Bolingbroke would be entitled to assume control of more than thirty castles, and resources so vast as to rival those of the King himself. In the face of this intolerable, not to say highly dangerous, prospect, Richard's desperate answer was to resort to an act of sequestration, which he clumsily attempted to legalize by forgery. And having thus contrived to cheat the unsuspecting Henry of his inheritance, he extended his cousin's sentence to one of perpetual banishment.

These acts of injustice and folly, perpetrated with the connivance of the Council, were not publicly proclaimed until the end of May, at a time when the King was on his way to Ireland, intent upon subduing an outbreak of rebellion. He was still so engaged when news was received that Henry Bolingbroke had landed in England. He had arrived, the report said, in the company of Thomas Arundel, the dispossessed Archbishop of Canterbury, and it appeared that he and his cause were gaining enthusiastic and growing support. The account did not exaggerate the position. So far as Richard was concerned, widespread desertions had been accompanied by the treachery of supposed friends and, when the King reached Milford Haven towards the end of July, it was to find that most of the country had declared for his enemy, and that the army of supporters he had expected to find awaiting him on his return from Ireland had melted away.

These hard tidings were confirmed when he arrived at Conway Castle, where information awaited him that his further progress had been blocked by Henry's capture and occupation of Chester. It was from here that Archbishop Arundel and Henry Percy, Earl of Northumberland, arrived at the castle as emissaries, the bearers of deceptively reasonable demands: the return of the Lancastrian estates to their rightful owner; the surrender and trial of five of the royal councillors; and an unfettered Parliament. On his receiving the additional assurance, sworn on oath, that his cousin had no treasonable intent, and that his throne was in no way endangered, Richard agreed to accompany his visitors, and so walked into the trap which had been prepared for him. He reached London a prisoner, where he was confined to the Tower.

His enforced abdication followed, and on 20 October 1399, disguised as a forester, the ex-King was taken to Henry Bolingbroke's castle at Pontefract. And not long after his arrival there, the royal captive died, allegedly of starvation, supposedly self-imposed. With his death, the direct Plantagenet line came to an end, for the deposed Richard, though twice married, was without issue.[1]

Of the five great English Houses established by Edward III, the fifth line, like the first, also became extinct when the solitary male heir of Thomas of Woodstock died in 1399. But representatives of the other three lines remained. Of these, the second son,

[1] His first wife was the Princess Anne, sister of King Wenceslas of Bohemia, whom he married in 1382, at the age of fifteen. Queen Anne (who was then sixteen) died twelve years later, without having produced an heir, and in 1396 Richard took to wife Isabella of France, though hardly with any immediate view of making good this filial deficiency—his new bride was a child of eight!

In the meantime, the succession to the English throne was invested in Roger Mortimer, the fourth Earl of March, who was Richard's heir by virtue of his mother, Philippa of Clarence. But in 1398, Roger Mortimer, then *Seigneur d'Irland*, was killed whilst warring against Art Oge MacMurrough, the rebellious King of Leinster. It was the untimely death of his Lieutenant which took Richard on his fateful journey to Ireland in the following year.

Lionel of Antwerp, was survived by a daughter, Philippa, who married Edmund de Mortimer, third Earl of March. Though the male line of March was destined to end with the fifth Earl, his sister Anne in due course espoused Richard of Cambridge, head of the House of York and son of Edmund of Langley, thus uniting the second and fourth Edwardian lines, while the third line, that of John of Gaunt, was carried on by Bolingbroke as Henry of Lancaster. In effect, by the end of the first decade of the fifteenth century, death and inter-marriage had reduced the five Edwardian lines to two, represented by descendants of the Houses of Lancaster and York.

SIEGE OF A TOWN ~ LATE 15TH CENTURY +

Chapter Four

Lancaster versus York

I

ON THE DEATH of Roger Mortimer in Ireland, Richard II had at once recognized the eight-year-old offspring of his lieutenant as heir presumptive to the English throne. But after Henry Bolingbroke's decisive intervention, the prior claim of the young Edmund Mortimer, fifth Earl of March and third Earl of Ulster, was passed over by a compliant Parliament in favour of the head of the House of Lancaster, and the eldest surviving son of John of Gaunt thus became Henry IV.

It seemed to at least one contemporary observer that the prize had been obtained

> For hatred more of Kyng Richardes defection
> Than for love of Kyng Henry

and that the position of the newcomer was far from secure. Archbishop Thomas Arundel proposed to legalize the usurpation by prevailing upon Richard to agree to abdicate and at the same time to recommend that Henry should take his place. But Henry was not disposed to be content with this. He wanted to establish that the Crown was his by hereditary right, even though the making of such a claim implied the seniority of Henry III's second son (Edmund of Lancaster) over his first (Edward I). In support of this contention, the story was put about that the ancestral Edmund (whose taking of the Cross had earned for him the name of Crouchback) was in fact the elder of the two brothers, but that, having been born a cripple, he had been set aside in favour of the more prepossessing Edward. Whatever Henry's own views as to the merits of this extraordinary and highly improbable fiction, he took the precaution of placing the fifth Earl of March under restraint, though his young rival was permitted to inherit his estates.

The King also concerned himself with securing the succession, for though a widower,[1] he was happily not without viable issue. Some twenty years earlier, he had wed Mary de Bohun, who had borne him two daughters and four sons—Henry (his heir); Thomas (Duke of Clarence); John (Duke of Bedford); and Humphrey (Duke of Gloucester). Henry now proposed that his eldest son should be collectively created Prince of Wales, Duke of Cornwall, and Earl of Chester. He also requested that the new recipient of the Black Prince's titles should be formally acknowledged by Parliament as standing first in line for the throne.

Another move aimed at strengthening his position was the giving of active support to the Church in its struggle against the followers of Wycliffe, notwithstanding that his father (also for reasons of his own) had seen fit to take the other side. In 1401, the statute *De Haeretico Carburendo*, the first legislation of its kind in England, authorized the burning of Lollards and other heretics who refused to recant, or who, having confessed the error of their ways, showed any inclination to return to them.

By this time there had already been an indication of troubles to come. A group of dissident nobles had stormed and seized Windsor Castle, in the belief that the King was in residence. This attempt to make Henry a prisoner and reinstate his predecessor might well have succeeded, had not the intended victim received a last-minute warning which enabled his sons and himself to leave the castle a few hours before the assault

[1] He remarried early in 1403, his bride on this occasion being Joanna, daughter of Charles II of Navarre and the widow of John IV, Duke of Brittany. There were no offspring.

upon it was launched—a hurried and undignified departure which was speedily followed by the arrest and execution of the conspirators. No doubt it was this escapade which sealed the fate of the imprisoned Richard II, rumours concerning the decease of whom were soon afterwards confirmed when his lifeless body was brought to London and there exhibited, though this did not prevent Henry's enemies from subsequently spreading the tale that the dead monarch had contrived to escape from Pontefract and was intent upon regaining his throne.

The death of the former King also promised to have serious international repercussions. At the time of Richard's (second) marriage to Isabella of France in 1396, the union had been celebrated by the declaration of a twenty-year truce between the two countries. But now, with the deposition and decease of his son-in-law and the humiliation of his daughter, it was hardly to be expected that Charles VI would continue to respect the agreement, nor was it long before evidence of widespread French intrigues with Henry's disaffected Celtic subjects was forthcoming.

In Wales, sundry minor discontents flared into a major revolt when a leader appeared in the person of Owen Glendower (Owain Glyn Dwr), a local chieftain who could claim descent from Llewelyn. This Glendower had fought on the side of the English against the Scots at Berwick in 1385, and, as lord of Glyndfyrdwy and Cynllaith, he and his wife lived in style with their family ("a goodly nestful of young Princes") at Sycharth. But this peaceful existence was soon to end. In 1400, Glendower quarrelled with Lord Reginald de Grey, a powerful neighbour who was a member of the King's Council. So bitter did the dispute become, and so outraged was the Welshman's sense of justice, that he rebelled against authority, and with a band of supporters began attacking and burning nearby English settlements—those of Ruthin, Denbigh, Rhuddlan, and Flint among them.

This initial outbreak was quickly checked. But the culprit remained at large and in little more than a year made himself master of most of North Wales. After abortive attempts (in November 1401) to come to terms with the representatives of the King, Glendower took steps to spread the revolt by communicating with Irish and Scottish leaders. At the same time hostilities in Wales were intensified, with the result that in the following April he had the considerable satisfaction of besting his arch enemy, Reginald de Grey, whom he captured in the vicinity of his castle at Ruthin. Two months later, during a skirmish in Radnorshire, another distinguished prisoner was taken. This latest captive was Sir Edmund de Mortimer, uncle of the fifth Earl of March, and his falling into Welsh hands was to have far-reaching consequences, as will in due course be seen.

Glendower's activities had by this time served as an inspiration to other malcontents, notable amongst whom were two cousins of his, Gwilm and Rhys ap Tudor, members of a prominent landowning family which held the vill of Trecastle, in Anglesey. They were the sons of Tudor Vychan ap Gronw, whose eldest offspring, Gronw Vychan, had found favour with the Black Prince, and whose youngest boy, Meredydd ap Tudor, had taken to the wilds of Snowdonia after killing a man and, while a fugitive, became the father of Owen ap Meredydd, more familiarly known as Owen Tudor (of whom more anon). Early in 1401, meanwhile, the brothers Gwilm and Rhys ap Tudor, who had served Richard II as captains of archers, set off from Anglesey at the head of a body of supporters. Their destination was Conway.

At this time responsibility for the maintenance of law and order in the region devolved upon Sir Henry Percy, popularly known as Harry Hotspur, son of the first Earl of Northumberland. In his capacity of Justice of Chester and North Wales, Hotspur was at Denbigh when the almost incredible tidings reached him that the supposedly impregnable Conway Castle had fallen into rebel hands! Nor did the accompanying account of how the mighty Edwardian stronghold had been taken make the news any easier to bear.

It appeared that when the Tudor tribesmen were brought to a halt by the castle walls, the defenders had shouted derisive references to the evident hopelessness of the contemplated assault—as well they might, for the would-be attackers were ill-armed and possessed of nothing in the way of siege engines. But what was clearly beyond their strength to take by force, the insurgents nevertheless contrived to achieve by stealth. On the Friday of Passion Week, at a time when most of the members of the garrison were piously attending church, forty of the invaders rushed the castle gate (which one of their number had earlier wedged, thus ensuring that it could not be properly closed) and captured the stronghold without a drop of blood being shed!

Not long after this incident (which ended, tamely enough, with a conditional vacating of the stolen fortress), Henry Percy transferred himself to his northern homeland, where he assumed the duties of keeper of Berwick Castle and warden of the East

March. In this area Scottish raids were a constant threat, and in 1402 the Percies, father and son, intercepted and defeated an invading army at Homildon Hill. In company with more than a score of French knights, the English took many important prisoners, including the Earl of Douglas. But, before handing over this particular captive to the King, Henry Percy asked for an assurance concerning the ransoming of his brother-in-law Edmund Mortimer, negotiations for whose release from Glendower's clutches, unlike those in respect of Reginald de Grey, had been unduly prolonged.

Royal reluctance to arrange for the freeing of Mortimer (who, as a close relative of the Earl of March, was evidently regarded as safer in captivity than out of it) was thus brought into the open, and the outcome of the disclosure was twofold. On his side, Glendower was now able to convince his hitherto unwilling guest of the indifference of the King to his fate, with the result that Mortimer, on the understanding that his nephew was to have the English throne, elected to join the rebels, an alliance which was sealed, in November 1402, by his marriage to one of Glendower's daughters. And for their part, the growing dissatisfaction of the Percies, with whose indispensable aid Henry Bolingbroke had gained his Crown, at length decided them to withdraw their hitherto unswerving allegiance.

It was in July 1403 that the King received word that Henry Percy, accompanied by his uncle Thomas, Earl of Worcester, was in Shropshire, mustering supporters with the intention of joining Glendower and Mortimer in Wales. This was a union which it was plainly in the royal interest to prevent at all costs and, by moving with the utmost speed, Henry and a hastily gathered army reached Shrewsbury ahead of the insurgents, and so blocked their line of advance.

The clash of arms, which was not long delayed, took place on the outskirts of the town. It lasted until nightfall and, when it ended, it found the King victorious, the young Percy among the slain, and the Earl of Worcester a prisoner and a candidate for an early beheading. The Earl of Northumberland, on learning of the loss of his son and the execution of his brother, made formal submission after being given an assurance that his own death was neither contemplated nor desired by the King. But although the Earl was spared his life, he was left with little else, for he lost control of most of his castles and suffered the sequestration of his vast estates.

Glendower remained undeterred by the set-back, for he was in the midst of negotiations with Charles VI. Already a French fleet, under the command of Jean d'Espagne, had threatened

Caernarvon, and there was the promise of more men and ships to aid in making attacks upon coastal towns and strongholds. The policy of the insurgents, meanwhile, was to avoid pitched battles and to strike at all the English-held castles within their reach. These guerilla tactics were eminently successful. By the middle of 1404, both Aberystwyth and Harlech had been captured, and, within another six months, the rebel leader was in control of the whole of West Wales and had extended his authority eastwards towards Glamorgan.

At this juncture, the arrival of a French fleet at Milford Haven, and the landing of more than 12,000 troops, was heralded by the signing of a tripartite agreement on behalf of Glendower, Mortimer, and the Earl of Northumberland. According to the terms of this compact, the three men were to divide Henry's kingdom between them, the Earl and Mortimer sharing England, Glendower acquiring Wales, more explicitly defined as the region bounded by a line extending along

> . . . the Severn to the North Gate of the city of Worcester, thence to the ash trees on the main road from Bridgnorth to Kinver: thence by the high way, called the ancient way, to the source of the Trent, then to the source of the Mersey, and so along that river to the sea.

But this proposed division of the spoils was somewhat premature, despite initial successes of the combined French and Welsh forces which led to the downfall of not a few enemy strongholds, among them the powerful fortress of Caerphilly. For in 1406, disappointed by their failure to invade England by way of Wales (Woodbury Hill, near Worcester, was the furthest point reached), the French decided to return home, and, with their going, the tide of events at last began to move in Henry's favour.

The royal vengeance first reached out to the Earl of Northumberland who, after vainly seeking further aid in France, made his way to Scotland with the intention of promoting an uprising there, only to be intercepted and slain near Tadcaster early in 1408. And later this same year, Prince Henry, acting on his father's behalf, began a determined attempt to regain some of the Welsh strongholds which had been lost, and succeeded in taking Aberystwyth. Harlech Castle was also closely invested—with the rebel leader and members of his family trapped inside! A long siege followed, in the course of which Edmund Mortimer was killed. But when at last the fortress fell, Glendower himself managed to escape, though he spent the remainder of his life a hunted man and died in obscurity.

Harlech was recaptured early in 1409, and, from then on, Henry's reign remained comparatively peaceful. The troublesome Scots had been effectively quietened by the capture of James Stuart, the heir to the Scottish throne,[1] while the French were scarcely in a position to make further mischief, thanks to an outbreak of civil strife which had attended the growing insanity of Charles VI and the struggle for power which had developed between members of the royal family.

But, although Henry could now regard himself as firmly established upon his throne, his last years were marred by persistent ill-health and by the evident ambition of his son to rule in his ailing stead. Nevertheless, and despite periods of severe incapacity, the King obstinately declined to abdicate, and he retained control until almost the day of his death in March 1413.

II

At the age of twenty-five, Henry V came to the throne imbued with the romantic notion that he had a divine mission to perform, that it was his bounden duty to conquer France as a prelude to mounting yet another Crusade against the infidels, who continued to defile the Holy Land by their presence. In so far as the first part of this programme was concerned, circumstances undoubtedly favoured the contemplated aggression. In the kingdom of the unfortunate Charles VI, whose sick mind alternated between periods of insanity and lucidity, a deadly struggle for power had developed between the brother and the uncle of the stricken monarch, in the persons of Louis d'Orleans and John the Fearless of Burgundy. In 1407, this internecine rivalry had led to the assassination of the Duke of Orleans in the streets of Paris by the followers of the Duke, since when the murdered man's son Charles and his supporters had acknowledged the leadership of Count Bernard VII of Armagnac. The country was thus torn by civil war, as Burgundians and Armagnacs each sought to gain the upper hand, while a vacillating Queen Isabel supported first one side, and then the other.

Conditions nearer home were also propitious for Henry. In Wales, Owen Glendower remained in hiding, his revolt

[1] The boy had been seized at sea by the piratical Sir John Prendergast and handed over to the English authorities, so that, instead of arriving at the French Court, his intended destination, his journey ended at the Tower of London, where he remained for the next eighteen years.

virtually at an end, while the continued presence of James Stuart in the Tower ensured the docility of the Scots. And in England itself, apart from an unsuccessful attempt to place a reluctant Earl of March upon the throne, perhaps the most serious challenge to the established authority came from the Lollards, against whom the King acted with such severity that the movement was driven underground, there to await the coming of the Reformation.

Even so, it was evident that Wycliffe's contention about dominion (and hence ownership) being founded upon grace, and his questioning of the Church's title to wealth and power, had made a greater impression upon the populace than had other of his doctrines, if only because it lent colour to the facile belief that the confiscation of ecclesiastical properties would lead to the abolition of taxation. It was to help divert the attention of the faithful from this illusory prospect, it has been suggested, which prompted Archbishop Chichele to assure the King of the undoubted validity of his claim to the French Crown, thus confirming him in his decision to bring about a renewal of fighting in the Hundred Years War.

By virtue of his descent from Edward III, Henry claimed the restoration of the entire Angevin heritage, and in 1415, in order to emphasize the reasonableness of this just demand, he landed at the mouth of the Seine with an expeditionary force of 9,000 men, more than two-thirds of whom were archers. His plan for the conquest of Normandy called for the capture of the port of Harfleur, but, despite the use of cannon, the town proved to be so strongly fortified, and so well defended, that it was able to hold out for six weeks, by the end of which time fever had so depleted the ranks of the invaders that the King's military advisers advocated an immediate return to England.

Instead, Harfleur was garrisoned, while Henry, accompanied by less than half his original force, elected to strike across Normandy to Calais, confident of his ability to win his way through. It was intended to remain in the vicinity of the coast and, when the marchers reached a point some four miles inland from Dieppe, they came to the castle of Arques, whose defenders fired upon them from the battlements. These shots, however, soon ceased when the English threatened to burn down the town, and food and wine were proffered by way of dissuasion.

From Arques the trail led into Ponthieu and so to the estuary of the Somme, where reports were received that strong enemy forces were in the neighbourhood. Henry decided to seek an undisputed passage higher up the river, and this was duly found after making a detour of sixty miles or so. The journey to Calais then continued without incident until, at the village of Agincourt, not much more than a day's march from their destination, the intruders found their way barred by an army of some 50,000 men.

Although greatly outnumbered, the English were assisted by the weather (which was exceedingly wet, making the ground unsuitable for the French cavalry) and by the fact that the road ahead of them was screened on either side by woodland, which gave protection to their flanks. Their opponents, it seemed, counted on overwhelming them by the sheer weight of their attack, but, unfortunately for this intention, the narrowness of the battle-front deprived them of their numerical advantage, and, time after time, expert archery sufficed to stem the rush. In a matter of hours, the issue was decided as French losses continued to mount, their dead totalling at least 1,500 knights and more than 4,000 men-at-arms.

After this resounding victory (in the achieving of which, no more than 300 of his soldiers died), Henry returned, via Calais, to England, more than ever convinced that his purpose in France found favour in Heaven. Nor was he alone in this comforting belief, for the highest ecclesiastics in the land were of the same opinion. Agincourt, Bishop Beaufort hastened to assure Parliament, was one of a "trinity of divine judgements" indicative of the righteousness of Henry's cause, while, according to Archbishop Chichele, not only St. George (whose aid the King had invoked on the field) but also the revered St. John of Beverley had been instrumental in influencing the outcome, the last-named having so over-exerted himself on the day of the battle that a gush of holy oil was seen to trickle from his tomb.

While preparations were being made to complete the conquest of Normandy, Harfleur was left to defend itself against repeated attacks by Orleanist forces under Count Bernard. But the bridgehead held, and in 1417, at the beginning of August, Henry landed in the neighbourhood with 12,000 men. He also had the promise of assistance from the Burgundians, with whose leader he had come to a secret understanding, the arrangement being that, while the English forces assailed the Armagnacs from the sea, John the Fearless would move against Paris.

Both sides made good progress. By the spring of 1418, Henry was in control of lower Normandy and was about to lay siege to its capital city of Rouen, which he entered (after starving its inhabitants into submission) early in the new year. The Burgundians, meanwhile, had entered Paris and massacred several thousand of the Armagnacs, Count Bernard among them. The Duke of Burgundy thus found himself in power, thanks to the assistance of an ally whose services he now no longer needed, and whose presence in Normandy could not be regarded as other than a serious threat to French sovereignty. He accordingly tried to form a united front against the English by approaching the Orleanist faction, the leadership of which had passed to the Dauphin,[1] Charles, Count of Ponthieu. But Charles had other plans—he was himself endeavouring to come to a private understanding with Henry on behalf of the Orleanists. Nevertheless, he readily agreed to a meeting between John the Fearless and himself, which it was arranged should take place on the bridge at Montereau. And here, on 10 September 1419, the unsuspecting Duke of Burgundy walked to the death which his enemies had seemingly planned for him.

This treachery sealed the fate of France, for it ended all immediate hope of co-operation between the two rival factions. The murdered man's son and successor, Duke Philip, lost no time in coming to terms with the English invader, terms duly set forth in the Treaty of Troyes. Among other items, it was here stipulated that Charles VI was to retain his throne during his lifetime, but that, on his death, the French Crown was to pass, not to his son Charles, but to King Henry of England, who in the meantime undertook to wed the French monarch's daughter Catherine of Valois, a marriage which duly took place at Troyes on 2 June 1420.

But if it was Heaven's intention that Henry should accomplish the conquest of France, it was no part of the divine plan that he should reign over that troubled land, as future happenings were soon to show. Those who framed the Treaty of Troyes did so on the assumption that the comparatively young Henry V would outlive the ailing Charles VI, thus enabling the new dynasty to become firmly established before the death of its founder, and that in the meantime, the disinherited Dauphin, even if he did not accept the situation, would be unable to offer effective resistance from those Armagnac territories which still acknowledged his leadership. In the event, both these assumptions were to prove to be ill-founded.

[1] The name given to the heir of the King of France. The Dauphin was at this time the future Charles VII, the fifth son of Charles VI. His four elder brothers were all deceased, two of them having died (believed poisoned) as recently as 1415 (Louis, Duke of Guienne) and 1417 (John, Duke of Touraine).

III

With the ratification of the Treaty of Troyes, Henry V became Regent of France and the nominal master of the country. But in fact, his undisputed jurisdiction, apart from the isolated territory of Guienne, extended no further south than the Loire, beyond which river the Dauphin and his supporters exercised control and steadfastly declined to relinquish it. Such defiance could not go unanswered, and, two days after his wedding, the royal groom led an army against the Armagnac strongholds of Montereau (the taking of which enabled Duke Philip to recover the body of his murdered father) and Melun.

After the fall of Melun, Henry took time off to visit Paris. Then, accompanied by his bride, he journeyed by way of Normandy to London, where Catherine was duly crowned. Precisely one month later, Thomas, Duke of Clarence, was defeated and slain in an encounter with enemy forces in the county of Anjou. This disaster, coupled with the death of his brother, hastened the King's return to France, where he spent the remainder of the year in pursuit of the Dauphin (who continued to elude him) and in attacking his northern outposts. And it was while directing a siege against the town of Meaux, in the course of which operation dysentery among the English troops became rife, that Henry himself contracted the disease. He succumbed to it, after months of illness, on the last day of August 1422—six weeks before the demented Charles VI followed him to the grave on 11 October.

But although death thus robbed Henry of his father-in-law's Crown, his wife Catherine, at the time of his decease, had recently provided him with a son. And this infant, a mere nine months old, who was at once acknowledged as King Henry VI of England, subsequently attained the French throne, at any rate for a time.[1] The royal interests, meanwhile, were looked after by his two uncles—John, Duke of Bedford, who assumed control in France, and Humphrey, Duke of Gloucester, who (under the guidance of the Council) attended to affairs at home.

With the death of Charles VI, the Dauphin proclaimed himself King of France and, as Charles VII, established his Court at Bourges. It thus fell to the Dukes of Bedford and Burgundy to take up arms against the pretender. Their combined forces were victorious at an opening encounter at Cravant, in 1423,

[1] He was crowned in Paris in 1431, two years after attending a similar ceremony in London.

in the course of which it was observed that the Scots were still actively engaged in aiding their French friends. With a view to bringing this military assistance to an end, James Stuart was promised his release from the Tower in return for the payment of the customary ransom, and on condition that all his countrymen were recalled from abroad. To a young man who had spent the greater part of his life in captivity, there could be but one response to so tempting an offer, and in a very short time *le roi de Bourges* (as Charles VII was disparagingly referred to by his enemies) found himself fighting his battles alone.

His forces suffered another defeat at Verneuil in August 1424, but later in the year a rift developed between the allied leaders, thanks to an ill-considered adventure on the part of the Duke of Gloucester. The highly impressionable Humphrey had become enamoured of Jacqueline of Hainault, the refugee wife of John, Duke of Brabant, whom he proceeded to marry on the strength of a divorce of somewhat dubious validity obtained from the obliging Anti-Pope Benedict XIII. But worse was to follow. Not content with acquiring the spouse of a member of the House of Burgundy, Humphrey of Gloucester, urged on by his wife, then undertook to relieve the ex-husband of certain of his territorial possessions, and invaded Hainault with an army of 5,000 men. But after making good progress, he at length found himself opposed by the troops of Philip of Burgundy, to whom his kinsman had appealed for help. Things then began to go badly for the invader, and early in 1425 he judged it expedient to abandon the enterprise, though the Countess Jacqueline was not to be dissuaded from conducting a defence of Mons in person, a decision which led to her capture. As for the Duke of Gloucester, he returned safely to England, having in the meantime transferred his affections to Eleanor Cobham, his wife's lady-in-waiting!

This unedifying episode put a severe strain on Anglo-Burgundian relations, nor was the allied cause assisted by the course of subsequent events in France itself. In 1428, it was decided to invest the city of Orleans, an important gateway to the south. The town was strongly defended, the siege protracted, and, in the midst of it all, Charles was prevailed upon to send a relief force in response to the impassioned urgings of a peasant girl by the name of Jeanne Darc (afterwards called D'Arc). She claimed that St. Michael had come to her in a vision, and had tendered his personal assurance that the French King was destined to triumph over his enemies.

The successful relief of Orleans and the crowning of Charles at Rheims were, however, followed by an inexplicable failure on the part of the nationalist forces to reach and enter Paris. Nevertheless, in so far as the English were concerned, the eventual outcome of the D'Arc intervention was a disastrous sequence of events which led to their expulsion from France. The visionary who helped to bring this about, meanwhile, was apparently soon deserted by her ghostly guardians. In May 1430, at all events, she was captured by Burgundian forces while assisting in the defence of Compiègne, and Duke Philip was only too happy to hand over the prisoner to his allies in return for the sum of 10,000 gold crowns (some £80,000). Her subsequent trial, prejudiced by the superstitions of Holy Church and disgraced by grave judicial irregularities, ended in her being denounced as a witch and condemned to the stake. But her real crime, as is now conceded, was that she roused the fighting spirit of her countrymen and showed them the way to victory.

That victory was brought appreciably nearer when Philip of Burgundy and Charles VII composed their differences (Treaty of Arras, 1435). And to add to the misfortunes of the English, within a few days of this agreement having been concluded, the Duke of Bedford died. The loss of this able commander led to divided counsels at home, where the Duke of Gloucester wanted to intensify the war and the Bishop of Winchester (Henry Beaufort) to bring it to an end. This indecision on the part of his enemies, not to mention the added assistance of the Burgundians, enabled Charles to make a triumphal entry into Paris, and thereafter to extend his authority over extensive areas of the country.

After losing most of Gascony in 1442, the hard-pressed English at last decided to seek what terms they could, and in 1444 William de la Pole, the Earl (later Duke) of Suffolk, was able to arrange a preliminary two-year truce which allowed for the marriage of Henry VI, now twenty-three years of age, to Margaret, the fourteen-year-old daughter of Réné, Duke of Anjou. The wedding was celebrated in April of the following year, and, three months after the ceremony, French envoys arrived in Westminster, intent upon obtaining the surrender of Maine as one of the conditions of a permanent settlement.

After much vacillation (and suspected equivocation) on the part of his opponents, the impatient Charles renewed the war, which was now so vigorously pursued that in the course of the next five years he acquired Maine and completed the occupation of Normandy. The last remnants of Henry V's French conquests were thus lost, and with the subsequent overrunning of Guienne, all that remained in English hands was the port of

Calais and the Channel Islands.[1] In this inglorious fashion, the Hundred Years War was at last brought to an end.

In England, the closing years of the struggle were marked by serious internal disorders. The weakness of the government encouraged (or compelled) members of the nobility to take the law into their own hands, and in this they were assisted by the presence of large numbers of disbanded troops, recently returned from France. These men were taken on as armed retainers, ready at their employer's bidding to plunder the district or attack a neighbour. And although the problem presented by the existence of these private armies was no novelty (Richard II had earlier found it necessary to forbid such "livery and maintenance"), the difficulty was that the law prohibiting them had fallen into abeyance and the central authority was powerless to reimpose it.

Nor was the widespread occurrence of "murders and Ryottes agaynst the peace" the only trouble. There was also much scheming and plotting in high places, as the Duke of Gloucester was to learn to his cost. In 1447, when he arrived at Bury to attend Parliament, he was arrested on a trumped-up charge and cast into prison, where he was soon afterwards discovered dead in his bed, presumably murdered. The removal of one so close to the King left Richard, Duke of York, in a particularly exposed position. Not only was he now next in line for the throne, but his claim to it was, if anything, superior to that of the present occupant, in that, through his father, the Earl of Cambridge, and his mother, Anne Mortimer, he could claim descent from the second and fourth sons of Edward III, whereas the Lancaster line was confined to the third of that monarch's offspring.

Ominously enough, the Earl of Cambridge had earlier been implicated in a plot against the life of Henry V, and had been executed for high treason. Though Richard's own loyalty to the House of Lancaster was not seriously in question, with the death of the Duke of Gloucester it was considered advisable to consign him to the political backwater of Ireland, there to occupy the post of the King's Lieutenant. The appointment, as it happened, was to the recipient's advantage, for, although he had earlier served as Regent in France, the responsibility for the more recent turn of events in that country was clearly not his.

Both people and Parliament were in search of a scapegoat,

[1] Calais continued to serve as a military outpost until 1558, when it was relinquished. But the English hold on the Channel Islands (a part of the original Duchy of Normandy, where French remains the official language) is still maintained.

and the brunt of popular discontent for the continuing English defeats abroad was borne by the Duke of Sussex. In January 1450, he was charged in the Commons with treason, it being alleged, among other wildly improbable things, that he was guilty of conspiring with the French to bring about an invasion of his own country, and that he had fortified Wallingford Castle on the enemy's behalf. Fearing for the safety of his counsellor in the face of these accusations, the King intervened and banished him for a period of five years, and, by thus exercising the royal prerogative, contrived to save his life. The Duke sailed for France at the end of April, only to be intercepted and killed by his enemies at sea. His headless body was flung upon the beach at Dover, where it remained until Henry could arrange for its burial.

News of the loss of Normandy was then received, and the increasing public disquiet manifested itself in a series of local uprisings, one at least of which attained mammoth proportions. This was the rebellion led by Jack Cade, an Irishman who called himself John Mortimer. He claimed to be a cousin of the Duke of York, on whose behalf he marched to London at the head of some 30,000 discontented citizens, voicing demands for governmental reforms and the re-instatement of his supposed kinsman to a position of authority.

The King, however, preferred to retain the services of Edmund Beaufort, second Duke of Somerset, notwithstanding the loss of Normandy, which had occurred during his Lieutenantship, and whom he now promoted to Constable of England. Duke Richard, meanwhile, judging that the time for intervention was approaching, deserted his post in Ireland and made his way to London, intent upon taking a more active part in the affairs of the nation.

Though he had been declared of age in 1437, the fact was that the King had proved to be unfit to rule. By all accounts he was a gentle and compliant person, tamely submissive to his much more forceful wife, and dependent for advice upon a group of favoured ministers (prominent among whom were members of the Beaufort family) whose policies and ideas were pleasing to the Queen and himself. In the event, the result had been altogether disastrous. The war with France was drawing to its inevitable and humiliating close, there was widespread lawlessness and public unrest at home, and the government of the country was completely discredited in all eyes save its own.

Richard's opportunity came in 1453, when on 10 August Henry displayed the first symptoms (complete lack of memory and infantile behaviour) of the insanity which he had inherited from his maternal grandfather. After the royal illness had been discussed at an assembly of all the barons, and despite demands on the part of Queen Margaret that she should be appointed Regent, the Duke of York was nominated by the lords spiritual and temporal to be "chief of the Kynges Counsaill" during the emergency. This was in March 1454. But the year which brought Richard to power also saw his prospects of succeeding to the throne diminished, when in October the Queen was safely delivered of a son. And as if this were not disappointment enough, the Duke's return to a position of authority was not long maintained. A feature of the royal malady was its periodic nature, and at Christmas the King suddenly and unexpectedly became normal again. For the first time in months he was able to recognize the familiar faces of his household. When shown his infant son, of whose existence he had been completely unaware, he inquired as to the boy's name, and learned that it was Edward.

Early in the New Year, Henry (dominated, as always, by the Queen) set about re-grouping his advisers. The Duke of Somerset was released from the Tower (where he had been kept without trial, a circumstance to which he in all probability owed his life) and restored to favour. Various Yorkist ministers were deprived of office (Richard Neville, Earl of Salisbury, ceased to be Chancellor; John Tiptoft, Earl of Worcester, was removed from the Treasurership), while Richard found himself excluded from the deliberations of the Council. For him and his followers, the moment of decision had evidently come.

The Duke conferred with the Earls of Salisbury and Warwick, and the conclusion reached was that their only recourse was to arms. Thus was taken the fateful decision which precipitated the thirty years of conflict which, because the Yorkist emblem was a white rose and the Lancastrians (in retrospect) adopted a red rose, came to be called after that flower. But essentially, the so-called Wars of the Roses were a series of encounters in a struggle between the private armies of rival royal interests, with a seat on the throne as the prize.

At the outset, the two sides were fairly evenly divided between representatives of the English nobility. The Yorkists, led by the Duke (who, in 1438, had married Cecily Neville, daughter of the first Earl of Westmorland) and his two eldest sons, Edward (Earl of March) and Edmund (Earl of Rutland)[1] had

[1] In all, his wife bore him eight sons and four daughters. Of his sons, four died in childhood, the survivors being Edward and Richard (each of whom attained the throne); George (who was created Duke of Clarence); and Edmund (who was killed in battle).

the support of the aforementioned Earl of Salisbury and his son Richard (Earl of Warwick), together with that of Richard Neville (Earl of Westmorland), John Mowbray (Duke of Norfolk), and the Lords Abergavenny, Cobham, Fauconberg, and Bouchier. The leading Lancastrians, with the Queen at their head, consisted of the second Duke of Somerset and other members of the Beaufort family, the Duke of Exeter (Henry Holland), the Earls of Pembroke (Jasper Tudor), Wiltshire (James Butler), Shrewsbury (John Talbot), Rivers (Richard Wyndeville), and Lords Clifford, Beaumont, and Egremont. There were also a few notables who had occasion to transfer their allegiance from one side to the other in the course of the struggle.

The conflict was long-drawn-out and intermittent, its battles, for the most part, small scale affairs. In the first encounter, which took place at St. Albans in May 1455, some 3,000 men were engaged on either side. The fighting was over in less than an hour, and ended in a victory for the Yorkists, thanks to a flank attack led by the young Earl of Warwick. King Henry sustained no more than an arrow wound in the neck, but the Duke of Somerset was among the dead. He thus made way for the Duke of York, who assumed his title of Constable of England.

The King was apparently willing to overlook what had happened, and to accept the new administration with good grace. But Queen Margaret had no such intention, and in 1458 an affray which almost cost the Earl of Warwick his life warned the Yorkists that they must continue to be on their guard. After this, both they and their opponents began to muster their supporters, and in September of the following year an armed clash occurred at Bloreheath, in Yorkshire. The Lancastrians, though numerically superior, were compelled to give way, thus allowing the Earl of Salisbury to link up with the Duke of York at Ludlow, where the two leaders were joined by Warwick.

Their combined forces amounted to no more than 6,000 men. But against them Henry brought up an army which was at least five times as large—and let it be known that a pardon awaited those of his enemies who cared to ask for it. Many defections took place, whereupon the Yorkists acknowledged the hopelessness of their situation by quietly withdrawing under the cover of darkness. The Duke, accompanied by his son Edmund, sought safety in Ireland, while his other son, Edward, fled to Calais with Salisbury and Warwick.

But the Lancastrian triumph, though seemingly complete,

was shortlived. Within less than a year, the three Earls had returned from Calais with an army of 3,000 men. They were welcomed in London, where only the Tower held out against them, and, while his father attended to its capture, Warwick, accompanied by the Earl of March, went out to meet and overwhelm the royal forces at Northampton, with the result that the King once again found himself a prisoner. The Duke of York (who at this crucial moment was still in Ireland) shortly arrived on the scene and formally demanded the throne on hereditary grounds. His claim, presented in the form of a genealogical table, was given due consideration by the Lords, who decided against the deposition of Henry, but agreed that, on his death, Richard should succeed him.

Queen Margaret, it need hardly be said, was not prepared to accept this exclusion of her son. At the time of her husband's capture, she and the young Prince Edward were in Staffordshire, from where they fled to Wales, to find refuge with Jasper Tudor, the Earl of Pembroke. Other of their supporters who had not been present at the Battle of Northampton also made offers of help, and in a matter of months a large army was assembled in the north. By the end of the year, when the Duke of York at last set out from London at the head of 6,000 troops to deal with the threat, he was outnumbered by more than two to one, and suffered a resounding defeat at Wakefield. Indeed, the encounter cost him his life, for he died on the field of battle, as did his son Edmund.

At this time, Richard's other son, Edward, was stationed at Shrewsbury, guarding the Welsh March. When he heard the news, his first thought was to join up with Warwick, but, on learning that the Earl of Pembroke was on the move, he turned to meet and rout his forces at Mortimer's Cross, midway between Ludlow and Hereford. In the meantime, after their success at Wakefield, the Lancastrians, under Henry Beaufort, third Duke of Somerset, accompanied by the Queen and her son, began to march south with the intention of occupying London. On the way, they clashed with Warwick in the vicinity of St. Albans, dispersing the Yorkists. And to make their victory complete, in the confusion of battle, King Henry managed to give his guards the slip and make his way through the lines to join his family!

It was the hope of the Queen that the King and herself would be allowed to enter London unhindered, despite the Yorkist sympathies of its citizens. But while negotiations to this end were in progress, the Earls of March and Warwick joined forces and forestalled the Lancastrian intention by entering the city themselves. The inconvenient fact that, having lost possession of the King, they could no longer profess to be acting on his behalf, the Yorkist leaders sought to overcome by the bold expedient of denouncing the Lancastrian claims to the throne. The deposition of Henry in favour of Edward of March was then announced, to the acclamations of the populace (4 March 1461). But whatever the Londoners might decree, it was clear that this was an issue which could only be decided on the field of battle.

IV

The decisive encounter, which was to induce Parliament to accept and confirm the kingship of Edward IV, took place less than a month later at Towton, in Yorkshire. Here, the opposing forces, some 40,000 men in all, engaged in what has been described as the bloodiest battle ever fought on English soil. No quarter was expected or given. After ten hours of bitter fighting in a blinding snowstorm, the Lancastrian lines broke, and, at the end of a relentless pursuit, their dead were to be counted in thousands. The Earl of Northumberland and many other leading supporters were among the slain, but Henry and the Queen, in company with the Dukes of Exeter and Somerset, managed to escape. The royal entourage made its way northwards, there to plot and plan anew with Scottish and French help.

Thus far, castles had played little part in the struggle, but now several of the Northumberland border fortresses came into prominence, if only briefly and as a haven for some of the refugees. Lancastrian sympathizers had still to be cleared from the area, and, after Warwick and his brother John Neville (the new Lord Montague) had frustrated enemy attempts to seize Carlisle and Durham, the fighting centred round the three strongholds of Alnwick (the site of a Norman castle, acquired in 1309 by Sir Henry Percy and largely rebuilt by him); Dunstanburgh (the handiwork, in part, of John of Gaunt, and notable for its massive gatehouse); and Bamburgh (with its rectangular stone keep dating from about the middle of the twelfth century).

Of these structures, the last-named, magnificently sited on the brink of the North Sea, had been surrendered to Edward after the Battle of Towton, and entrusted by him to the care of Sir William Tunstall. But not long afterwards, in anticipation of coming events, Sir William's brother Richard, who was a firm Lancastrian supporter, took over the castle and held it for Henry and the Queen. The events in question (a proposed invasion of England) were heralded by the arrival in Northumberland of a mixed force of Lancastrian supporters, who also occupied the castles of Dunstanburgh and (after a brief struggle) Alnwick.

From his headquarters in Warkworth Castle, Warwick set out to retrieve the lost strongholds. According to a paper preserved among the Cottonian Charters, the position at this time (December 1462) was that Bamburgh (from which the Queen had earlier departed for Berwick) was held by the Duke of Somerset, Lord Roos, and Sir Ralph Percy; that Dunstanburgh was in the possession of Sir Richard Tunstall, Sir Philip Wentworth, and Dr. Moreton; and that Alnwick was occupied by Lord Hungerford, Sir Thomas Fyndern, Sir Robert Whitingham, and a number of "frensshmen".

The Yorkists regained all three places after a siege of less than a month, and the inmates were treated with considerable leniency. Not merely were the Duke of Somerset and Sir Ralph Percy spared their lives, but, on their swearing allegiance to Edward, they were allowed to retain their estates—Sir Percy was even given charge of Bamburgh and Dunstanburgh, a trust which he soon afterwards betrayed. Thanks to his treachery, and that of Sir Ralph Grey, a dissatisfied Yorkist, by the middle of 1463 both Bamburgh and Alnwick castles were once again in Lancastrian hands. From Alnwick, moreover, a raiding party set out and was successful in capturing the castle of Skipton, in Yorkshire, while the strong border fortress of Norham was also taken.

About this time, Queen Margaret sailed for Flanders with the idea of trying to enlist more active support, while Edward, for his part, was planning to bring Lancastrian resistance to an end by reaching an understanding with the Scots. Lord Montague was sent to meet their representatives, and to escort them back to York for a discussion. On his outward journey, in the vicinity of Hedgely Moor, he found his way blocked by a Lancastrian force, which he attacked and scattered. This was in April 1464, and in the following month, having fulfilled his Scottish mission, he was able to surprise the enemy at Hexham, an encounter which led to the capture and execution of the Duke of Somerset (who, like Sir Ralph Percy, had soon defected) and many other notables, among whom were Lord Roos, Lord Hungerford, and Sir Edmund Fitzhugh.

This and other punitive measures, in conjunction with the fifteen years peace recently concluded with the Scots, soon brought effective Lancastrian resistance in the north to an end. Skipton had surrendered immediately after the Battle of Hexham, and other castles occupied by the enemy were soon regained. Warwick and Northumberland first gave their attention to Alnwick, whose garrison yielded on the condition that their lives would be spared. Thereafter, admission to Dunstanburgh was gained on similar terms, though Bamburgh, where the traitorous Sir Ralph Grey knew he could expect no mercy, was not so easily taken.

The besiegers were well armed with artillery which had been shipped to Newcastle and from there hauled overland to the scene of operations. They were, however, anxious not to do irreparable damage to a royal fortress if this could be avoided. Warwick accordingly gave notice to the defenders that the siege would continue for seven years, if need be, and that, for every gunshot that caused damage to the castle masonry, a Lancastrian head would fall.

Still the defenders declined to surrender, whereupon the great guns (bearing such names as "London", "Newcastle", and "Edward") were brought to bear. After much damage had been done to the castle walls, a cannon ball chanced to crash its way into Sir Ralph Grey's private quarters, leaving him unconscious beneath a heap of debris. At this, the garrison made haste to capitulate, so that when their unsuspecting commander came to his senses, it was to find himself a prisoner and booked for early execution.

Lancastrian resistance was now almost at an end. Henry, though still at large, was a fugitive. No longer able to find safety in Scotland, he managed to elude his pursuers until June 1465, when he was caught and taken to the Tower. Elsewhere, only one castle remained in enemy hands—the grim, mountain-top fortress of Harlech, which continued to hold out for another three years.[1]

By this time, Edward was firmly established upon the throne, thanks in large measure to the assistance he had received from the three Neville brothers—Richard (Earl of Warwick), John (Earl of Northumberland), and George (Archbishop of Canterbury). In return, this trio, especially the power-hungry

[1] David Abenon, its Captain, capitulated on 24 August 1468 after a siege which had gone on, intermittently, for seven years. The surrender was brought about by the failure of a last desperate attempt on the part of Jasper Tudor, the attainted Earl of Pembroke, to relieve the fortress. Its garrison was found to consist of precisely half a hundred men, and among those captured was the Earl's twelve-year-old nephew, the future Henry VII.

Earl of Warwick, clearly expected that they would be rewarded by being called upon to advise and guide the King in the years ahead. But an early indication that, irrespective of their wishes, Edward intended to go his own way, was provided by the matter of his marriage.

Sensibly enough, Warwick envisaged a political match, designed to strengthen the Yorkist position abroad. Edward, who in his early twenties was already displaying a marked partiality for the opposite sex, was probably not thinking in terms of anything so binding as marriage at all—until he chanced to meet a widow whose irresistible charms were increased rather than diminished by her insistence that if she was to share his bed, it could only be as his wife.

The name of this paragon of feminine virtue was Elizabeth Woodville. She was a daughter of Sir Richard Woodville and Jacquetta of Luxemburg (widow of the great John, Duke of Bedford) who in 1452 or thereabouts had married Sir John Grey. Subsequently, her husband (a Lancastrian!) had been killed at the second Battle of St. Albans, leaving her with two sons to provide for.

Edward and his not so sprightly widow (she was five years his senior) were secretly wed early in 1464, though news of the ceremony was discreetly withheld until the end of September. On hearing of it, Warwick was much put out, nor were he and other members of the Yorkist nobility at all pleased by the spectacle of members of the Woodville family being raised to positions of great wealth and influence at their expense. Elizabeth's father was created Earl Rivers and awarded the treasurership of the kingdom; her five sisters were found eminently suitable mates, ranging from the Duke of Buckingham to the sons and heirs of the Earls of Kent and Essex; Thomas, her eldest son, achieved fame and fortune by marrying the Lady Anne, heiress of the Duke of Exeter; and her young brother John was likewise provided with a wealthy and aristocratic wife, in the person of the Dowager Duchess of Norfolk. For a man of no fortune who was barely out of his teens, the Duchess was no doubt to be regarded as the catch of the season—always providing the groom could reconcile himself to the fact that his bride had been thrice married before, that she was eighty years of age, and that she was a grandmother in her own right!

The Earl of Warwick's hopes of arranging a useful foreign alliance through the marriage of a member of the English royal family now rested on Edward's sister Margaret. The Earl favoured a link with France, whose Charles VII had recently been succeeded by his son, Louis XI, and apparently the King did nothing to discourage him from pursuing the matter. Warwick approached the French monarch in person, and was gratified to learn that Louis favoured the proposal, and was prepared to send ambassadors to England for a detailed discussion. When Warwick returned, however, it was to find that, during his absence, Edward had been busy making other arrangements, which called for the marriage of his sister to Louis's rival, Duke Charles of Burgundy!

From this time on, the disillusioned Warwick seems to have enlisted the support of the one person who might conceivably succeed to the throne if the King failed (as was the case at this time) to produce a male heir: Edward's brother Clarence. A marriage between Clarence and Warwick's daughter Isabella was accordingly arranged and duly celebrated in Calais on 11 July 1469, from where the two conspirators then issued a proclamation, in content highly critical of Edward's rule, and declaring the authors' intention of providing him with more capable counsellors, i.e. themselves. They then left Calais for London, gathering supporters on their way.

The King, meanwhile, found himself faced by a series of uprisings, and, after suffering a reverse at the Battle of Edgecot, he was in no position to oppose Warwick and Clarence when they and their followers arrived on the scene. After being offered professions of loyalty, Edward was placed in Middleham Castle for safe-keeping, until a threatened Lancastrian outbreak persuaded his captors of the wisdom of allowing him his freedom. This set-back to Warwick's plan to keep the King under his personal control led to further intrigues, which ended in his being forced to flee the country.

As a fugitive, it now seemed to Warwick that his only prospect of success lay in removing Edward and restoring Henry, whose Queen had recently turned for help from the Duke of Burgundy to Louis of France. That astute monarch saw in Warwick's proposal possibilities for making mischief against England, and, after much persuasion, Queen Margaret was prevailed upon to overcome her hatred and distrust of the one man who, above all others, had brought humiliation and imprisonment to her husband. Warwick, for his part, and as a token of good faith, offered his young daughter Anne in marriage to Prince Edward, and, agreement having been reached, there were set in motion the events which were to earn for the renegade Earl his title of "Kingmaker".

Despite urgent messages from the Duke of Burgundy, warning him of what was afoot, the King did not concern himself unduly about the threatened invasion. And when, in September 1478, Warwick landed at Dartmouth to dispute Edward's right to the throne, the King was in Yorkshire, attending to an uprising which had conveniently drawn him thither. Too late, he realized the danger of his position when he learned of a conspiracy on the part of the invader's brother to make him a prisoner—the disgruntled Montague, though now a marquis, had recently been relieved of the earldom of Northumberland. Thus outmanœuvred, Edward prudently fled to the coast, where he obtained passage on a ship sailing for France, and so found safety with his Burgundian brother-in-law.

Within a month of his arrival in England, Warwick was able to enter London, where his first act was to release Henry from the Tower and proclaim him King. Queen Margaret and her son elected to remain abroad for the time being, perhaps in anticipation of possible trouble. But the country accepted the change calmly enough, and the government continued under a new administration with Warwick at its head.

Edward, however, was not content to lose his kingdom without a fight on anything approaching equal terms, and in March 1471, accompanied by his brother Richard, Duke of Gloucester, he landed at the mouth of the Humber with an army of 1,200 men. He then began to march south, gaining support as he went, including that of his estranged brother Clarence, who brought him an additional 4,000 men. Warwick, meanwhile, moved into the Midlands, there to menace the intruder with a force nearly twice as large, though for the time being he avoided battle.

Leaving this threat in his rear, Edward took the calculated risk of making for London, relying on the traditional Yorkist outlook of its citizens to allow him to enter unopposed. In this he judged aright, with the result that the luckless Henry once more found himself a prisoner. But by this time Warwick had been strongly reinforced and was bearing down upon the capital. The clash came at Barnet, from which Edward emerged the victor, with the Earl and his brother among the dead.

The Battle of Barnet was fought on 14 April—the very day on which Queen Margaret and her son landed at Weymouth with the nucleus of an army intended to assist Warwick in his struggle against Edward. In view of the disastrous tidings with which she was greeted shortly after her arrival, it was decided to join up with Jasper Tudor in Wales, where support for the Lancastrian cause was strong. But Edward, anticipating such a move, brought the Queen to battle at Tewkesbury, where once again the outcome was a decisive Yorkist victory. When the fighting and the subsequent executions were over, the Queen was a prisoner, her son, the young Prince Edward, was dead, and not a male member of the once powerful House of Beaufort remained alive. The demise of one more leading Lancastrian had yet to follow. On 21 May, when Edward entered London in triumph, his return to the city was the signal for the immediate murder of Henry VI, with whose death the last representative of the legitimate Lancastrian line perished.

Even so, there were still some leading Lancastrians who refused to acknowledge defeat, notable amongst whom was John de Vere, thirteenth Earl of Oxford. After surviving the disaster at Barnet, he managed to make his way to France, where he and his brothers George and Thomas began gathering supporters and making plans to continue the fight. After fitting out a small squadron at Dieppe, they set sail for the Cornish coast towards the end of September 1473, accompanied by eighty or more (according to one account, 397) men, intent upon seizing and holding St. Michael's Mount.

This conical shaped island of granite was ideally suited to their desperate purpose, situated as it was some 500 yards from the mainland, to which it was connected by a natural causeway passable only at low tide. Indeed, the value of the place as an isolated retreat had been recognized in Saxon times, when it served, first as an abode of hermits and then as the site of a Benedictine monastery of which Edward the Confessor was the founder. According to the subsequent Domesday Survey, the establishment was at this time under the jurisdiction of one Brismar the priest, its demesne (the manor of Truthwell) consisting of two hides of land which had never paid geld.

After the Conquest, the Mount came into the possession of Robert of Mortain, the new Earl of Cornwall, who made a present of it in 1088 to the Norman abbey of Mont St. Michel, an association which continued until the dissolution of alien religious houses under Henry V. Long before this, however, the strategic possibilities of the island had also claimed attention. In 1193, when Richard I found himself a prisoner of the Emperor, it was seized and fortified by Henry de la Pomeroy, acting on behalf of that would-be usurper of the English throne, the King's brother John. The release of Richard from captivity, and the unexpectedness of his arrival home, so unnerved the Mount's new occupant that he anticipated his just deserts by dying of fright, after which the expelled monks were able to return to their hill-top abode. And more than two and a half centuries later, their successors were still ensconced in what had continued to serve as a combined fortress and shrine when John de Vere and his followers appeared on the scene disguised as pilgrims, a subterfuge which gained them possession of the island and its stronghold.

The victor of Barnet and Tewkesbury was quick to accept this reckless challenge to his newly established authority, and on 27 October Edward issued a commission, calling upon local knights and other leading citizens to array the King's liege of the county, that John, late Earl of Oxford, might be brought to subjection. In response to this summons, an army of 6,000 fighting men was assembled in the vicinity of the Mount, which was also assailed from the sea by a trio of vessels whose captains were ordered "to be about the basement of St. Michael's Mount" until such time as "the said place be gotten or yelden to the King's obedience".

The contemporary chronicler John Warkworth recounts how, after the citadel had been under attack for several months, during which period it had become evident that the defenders occupied a near-impregnable position, another and more effective method of gaining entry was tried. During a lull occasioned by one of the truces which the combatants observed after particularly heavy bouts of fighting,

> The King and his Council sent unto divers that were with the Earl of Oxford privily their pardons, and promised to them great gifts and lands and goods, by the which divers of them were turned to the King against the Earl; and so in conclusion the Earl had not passing eight or nine men that would hold with him; the which was the undoing of the Earl. For there is a proverb and a saying that "A castle that speaketh and a woman that will hear, they will be gotten both"; for men that being in a castle of war that will speak and entreat with their enemies, the conclusion thereof (is) the losing of the castle; and a woman that will hear folly spoken unto her, if she assent not at one time, she will at another.

Thus members of the garrison were prevailed upon to desert their commander, so compelling him to surrender, though access to the fortress, in which there was found "victual enough till Midsummer after" was not gained until 15 February, nearly half a year after its occupation by the King's enemies. The redoubtable John de Vere, still as defiant as ever, was incarcerated in Hamme Castle, near Calais, where he perforce lingered until he succeeded in making his escape in time to assist the ultimate triumph of the Lancastrian cause a decade or so later.

In the meantime, apart from a half-hearted invasion of France in 1475 (which ended by Louis XI buying the invader off, notwithstanding the indignant protests of Edward's Burgundian ally) and such incidents as the execution of his brother Clarence for treason three years later, the King was able to spend much of the remainder of his reign in the comparative quiet of the embrace of his many mistresses. So great was their number that no contemporary chronicler troubled to keep count of them, let alone record their names, from which it is clear that the ladies concerned were devoid of political aspirations. Most of the royal lovers were recruited from among the daughters and wives of the good citizens of London, with whom, nevertheless, the King contrived to remain on excellent terms.

He was also mindful of his obligations to his wife. Elizabeth, after presenting him with a succession of daughters,[1] at last managed to provide him with an heir. His first son, Edward, was born at Westminster in 1470, and his second, Richard of Shrewsbury, in 1473 (a third, George, Duke of Bedford, died in infancy). Thus, when death overtook the fast-living monarch at the age of forty, it found him alone in bed for once, utterly worn out by his boudoir exertions, but happy in the knowledge that the continuation of his line was seemingly assured.

V

As it turned out, the purely nominal reign of the twelve-year-old Edward V proved to be the shortest occupation of the throne in English history—from April 1483 until June of the same year. From the outset, the boy's uncle Richard, Duke of Gloucester, was determined to wrest from the Woodville family by force the protectorship which he regarded as his by right. His first move was to seize his young nephew and lodge him in the Tower, where he was soon joined by his young brother. To allay mounting suspicions, the boy King's coronation was announced for June. But, on the 26th of that month, it was Richard of Gloucester who was enthroned, a circumstance preceded by widespread executions and imprisonments among the Woodvilles and their friends, though the Queen herself found safety in sanctuary.

The usurper sought to justify his actions by maintaining

[1] Their names were: Elizabeth (of whom more anon); Mary; Cecily; Margaret; Anne; Katherine; and Bridget, all of York.

that, because the late King had been promised to the Lady Eleanor Butler before his marriage to Elizabeth, therefore his offspring by her were illegitimate, thus making him the rightful heir to the throne. With nothing more than this weak and implausible argument to support his claim, the disposal of his two young nephews inevitably followed. Although it has long been popularly supposed that the boys were smothered while they slept, in fact the manner of their death is not known. But that they were murdered at their uncle's command, there can be little doubt.[1]

There remained, however, another young claimant to the throne who was safely out of Richard's reach. He was Henry Tudor, a grandson of that Owen Tudor whose miscreant father, Meredydd ap Tudor, had fled to the wilds of Snowdonia. Sir Owen Tudor (as he in due course became) was a squire at the Court of the infant Henry VI, where his strikingly handsome appearance caught the appreciative eye of the Queen Mother. Although there is no evidence to show that the widowed Catherine and he ever married, some indication of the closeness of their association is provided by their five sons, two of whom gained prominence—Edmund, Earl of Richmond, and Jasper, Earl of Pembroke.

Towards the end of 1456, shortly before his wife Margaret (daughter and heiress of John Beaufort, first Duke of Somerset) gave birth to their son Henry, Edmund Tudor died. The fatherless boy was brought up by his uncle Jasper until, with the surrender of Harlech Castle in 1468, Henry fell into Yorkist hands. Edward IV placed his young prisoner under the guardianship of William Herbert, successor to the disinherited Jasper as Earl of Pembroke. But during Henry VI's brief return to power in 1470–1, the boy had been restored to the care of his uncle, by whom he was taken to Brittany after the downfall of Lancastrian hopes at the Battle of Tewkesbury. With the wholesale extermination of the male members of the House of

[1] In 1674, during repairs undertaken in the reign of Charles II, a wooden chest was unearthed at the foot of a stone stairway outside the White Tower. Inside the box were found the skeletons of two children. That the bones were those of the young Princes seems more than likely, but although a subsequent examination, conducted as recently as 1933, established that the remains were those of infants aged about ten and thirteen, it was not possible to determine the year of their death with precision. C. R. Markham, meanwhile, had advanced the argument that the boys had been kept alive throughout Richard's reign, and that it was his Lancastrian successor who was responsible for their deaths. There is no reliable evidence to suggest, however, that the victims were seen alive after the autumn of 1483.

Lancaster which that encounter entailed, Henry Tudor became John of Gaunt's heir.

VI

After his formal coronation, which took place on 6 July 1483, Richard III set out on a tour of his realm, a journey which took him to York, by way of Reading and Oxford. During his absence from London, one of his chief supporters, Henry Stafford, second Duke of Buckingham (whose wife was a Woodville and who, though he was a Yorkist by choice, was a Lancastrian by birth) joined in a conspiracy which aimed at securing the Crown for Henry Tudor. In October, the young aspirant to the throne attempted to make a landing at Poole, but his reception convinced him that the time was not opportune, and he perforce retired, leaving Buckingham to face capture and execution.

Richard continued to regard the Lancastrian threat seriously, and, not knowing where his opponent might choose to land next, he established himself at Nottingham Castle, strategically placed in the centre of his kingdom. Here, he remained in residence throughout most of 1484, and in the following year, he took the precaution of having "Henry Tydder" and his supporters attainted by parliamentary decree, dismissing his rival's claims to the throne as the impudent presumption of a misbegotten upstart whose paternal grandfather was a bastard and whose mother was descended from an illegitimate offspring of John of Gaunt. And as an additional safeguard against invasion, a fleet of ships was stationed at Southampton, while castles were alerted throughout West Wales—at Pembroke, Tenby, Haverfordwest, and elsewhere in the area.

Nevertheless, it was a time of uncertainty and nervous expectation, nor was the prevailing tension lessened by the fact that dissatisfied members of the nobility and lesser gentry were known to be quietly slipping out of the country to join Henry Tudor, as an alternative to remaining in a realm where it could be said that

> The catte, the ratte, and Lovell our dogge
> Rulyth all Englande under a hogge.

The state of royal irritability may be judged from the fact that the circulating of this thinly veiled reference to the King (whose cognizance was a white boar) and his favourites Sir

William Catesby, Sir Richard Ratcliffe, and Lord Francis Lovell, cost a certain William Collingbourne his life.

On 7 August 1485, accompanied by his uncle Jasper and 2,000 men, Henry Tudor landed at Milford Haven, a region where he might expect to find friends and gain support for his cause. A fortnight later, his augmented army faced that of Richard in the neighbourhood of Market Bosworth. A third force was also in the vicinity, gathered by Thomas, Lord Stanley (afterwards Earl of Derby) and his brother, Sir William Stanley. Lord Stanley was in the difficult position of being called upon to assist the King (who held his son George, Lord Strange, as a hostage) when his inclination was to side with Henry Tudor, whose twice widowed mother was now his wife.[1] In the event, the Stanleys at first remained aloof, but once the issue had been joined, Sir William's intervention in support of Henry proved decisive, and, when the battle ended, Richard III lay dead upon the field.

[1] Three years after the death of Edmund Tudor in 1456, Margaret Beaufort married Henry Stafford, a younger son of the Duke of Buckingham. In 1482, once more left a widow, she found a new husband (though only after he had agreed to respect her chastity) in Thomas, Lord Stanley. Lord Strange was the eldest of his six sons by a former wife, Eleanor Neville, sister of the "Kingmaker".

CALAIS IN THE SIXTEENTH CENTURY

Chapter Five

The House of Tudor

I

EVEN THOUGH THE years of civil strife had eliminated great numbers of the old nobility (few members of the English peerage now living can trace their titles beyond 1485), from an hereditary standpoint, the twenty-eight-year-old Henry Tudor's rightful place in line for the throne was at the end of an embarrassingly lengthy queue of claimants, which included his own mother.[1] Accordingly, one of his first acts was to summon Parliament, that the Lords and Commons might be invited to accept the verdict of Bosworth Field and confirm the Crown to the victor and his issue. Once this formality had received

[1] Whose title, however, was overshadowed by the baton sinister, notwithstanding the Act legitimizing the Beauforts which had been instigated by the obliging Richard II. In 1407, his successor had confirmed this ruling by letters patent, and at the same time inserted a clause excluding the Beauforts from the right of succession to the throne. But even though, legally, this provision was invalid (since Henry IV's afterthought could not override an Act of Parliament), the taint of bastardy tended to remain.

attention, he then set about consolidating his position in other ways.

It so happened that Richard's death had been preceded by that of his wife Anne and his only son Edward. With the loss of his heir, the former King's search for a successor had led him to the offspring of his brother George (Duke of Clarence) and his sister Elizabeth (wife of John de la Pole, Duke of Suffolk, respectively his nephews Edward, Earl of Warwick and (his final choice) John de la Pole, Earl of Lincoln. But on the subsequent death of his wife, it was rumoured that he planned to marry his niece Elizabeth, eldest daughter of Edward IV. The suggestion was probably unfounded, for it disregarded the question of consanguinity and ignored the fact that Richard had already had occasion to dismiss his brother's children by Elizabeth Woodville as illegitimate. It may well be that the story arose in answer to a declaration earlier made by Richard's Lancastrian opponent (who sought to gain the support of disaffected Yorkists thereby) to the effect that he himself proposed to marry the lady.

This undertaking Henry Tudor now carried out, in part to bolster his somewhat dubious claim to the throne, but also, by uniting the Houses of Lancaster and York, to remove the cause of dynastic strife and so bring the Wars of the Roses to an end. Due regard, of course, had still to be paid to the ambitions of other possible rivals, the most serious threat, potentially at any rate, being that offered by the existence of the ten-year-old Earl of Warwick. Since the execution of his father in 1478, the boy had been kept under house arrest at the castle of Sheriff-Hutton, in Yorkshire, an arrangement which it would clearly be imprudent to allow to continue, and henceforth he was lodged in the Tower for greater security. As for the Earl of Lincoln, the merits of his claim to the throne were not to be compared with those of his cousin, and his professions of allegiance to Henry were accepted for what they were worth.

But elsewhere, both at home and overseas, there lurked intransigent Yorkists who were far from ready to give up the struggle. Abroad, Edward IV's sister Margaret, the Dowager Duchess of Burgundy, remained an implacable enemy of the Tudor régime. Hostility towards the King was also widespread in Scotland and Ireland, while, in England itself, at least one notable survivor of Bosworth Field was still at large. This was Lord Lovell, who soon became the centre of a group of conspirators which included the traitorous Earl of Lincoln.

Their plan was to foment a rebellion in the name of the Earl of Warwick, and, apparently in the cynical expectation that the royal prisoner had already been quietly disposed of, a substitute was provided in the person of Lambert Simnel, the son of an Oxford joiner. In preparation for the rôle he was to be called upon to play, young Simnel was taken to Ireland by a priest named Symonds, and coached for the part. Lovell and Lincoln, meanwhile, made their separate ways to the Court of Margaret of Burgundy, there to collect 2,000 German mercenaries. Accompanied by this force, the two leaders then sailed to join Simnel in Dublin, where the credulous Irish had already acclaimed him. King Henry's response to this was to parade the real Earl of Warwick through the streets of London, though he made no move against Ireland. Instead, like Richard before him, he stationed himself at Nottingham, content to await developments.

The enemy landing took place on the Lancashire coast, as a prelude to a march across country to Yorkshire. On 16 June 1487, the King faced his opponents at Stoke, near Newark, and effectively demonstrated the superiority of the English bow over the German pike and the Irish spear. Many of the invaders perished in the encounter, among them the Earl of Lincoln, though the body of his fellow conspirator was not to be found.[1] As for Lambert Simnel, he was taken prisoner, and lived to find honourable employment as a royal scullion.

Henry now summoned his second Parliament, that attainders might be passed upon Yorkist sympathizers who had been concerned in his attempted overthrow, thus giving him the disposal of their titles and estates. At the same time he called for the setting up of a special tribunal, designed, by virtue of the supreme powers vested in it, to deal effectively with sundry misdemeanours, outstanding among which was the still prevailing practice of livery and maintenance.[2] As a result, recalcitrant nobles, who had hitherto done much as they pleased, suddenly

[1] Francis Lovell vanished without trace, and it was assumed that, after escaping from the field of battle, he managed to make his way abroad. But, in the eighteenth century, the discovery of human remains in a secret chamber in one of his manor houses gave rise to the conjecture that the fugitive, after reaching this place of refuge, may have inadvertently been left to starve to death there.

[2] As constituted by Parliament in 1487, the Court consisted of judges who were also members of the Privy Council. Because the room they occupied at the Palace of Westminster had stars painted on its ceiling, the tribunal came to be known as the Court of the Star Chamber, and its extensive and arbitrary powers enabled it to reverse the decisions of corrupt or intimidated lower courts. Under the Tudors the Star Chamber was an instrument of reform which served the ends of justice reasonably well. In later times, however, the Stuarts so abused its wide powers that the Long Parliament (1641) insisted upon its abolition.

found themselves deprived of their private armies and compelled to heed those laws of the land which it had for so long been their custom to ignore or defy.

On the Continent and elsewhere, meanwhile, Henry's enemies continued to plan his downfall, and it was not long before a new pretender appeared. He professed to be the Duke of York, the younger of the two murdered Princes in the Tower, who had succeeded (so he claimed) in escaping from his uncle Richard's clutches. In reality, he was a Flemish youth whose name was Peter Osbeck, better known as Perkin Warbeck. He appears to have been persuaded to take part in the deception while on a trading voyage to Ireland, from which country he went to France (where King Charles VIII welcomed him for a time), then to Flanders (to be acclaimed by Margaret of Burgundy) and eventually to Scotland (whose James IV recognized him as the prospective King of England, and provided him with a near relative of his, the Lady Catherine Gordon, for a wife).

These moves were forced upon the pretender by Henry's diplomatic activities. After making a show of going to war with Charles VIII over Brittany, the English King allowed himself to be bought off for the staggering sum of £149,000. The payment was made in accordance with the terms of the Peace of Étaples, which also stipulated that Perkin Warbeck was to be expelled from France. Next, the impostor's continued presence in Flanders was made unwelcome by the application of economic pressure when, in 1493, the sale of unfinished English cloth to Flemish craftsmen was forbidden. This ruinous prohibition led to the signing of the *Intercursus magnus*, a commercial treaty with political implications: neither of the governments concerned was to harbour rebels against the other.

Encouraged by Margaret of Burgundy, Warbeck had earlier attempted a seaborne invasion of Kent, an ill-fated venture which had ended with the capture and hanging of more than 150 of his supporters. Thereafter, he found refuge in Scotland, from where, in 1496, another descent upon England also failed to arouse the expected response. A third—and last—expedition was directed against Cornwall, where Tudor taxation had recently given rise to much unrest. The spurious Duke arrived at Penzance by way of Ireland, and though accompanied by no more than 120 men, took possession of the (seemingly unguarded) fortress on the summit of St. Michael's Mount without opposition. Leaving his wife Catherine within the safety of its walls, he then went to Bodmin, and in less than a week gained a following of several thousand malcontents.

An attempt to capture Exeter was abandoned when word was received of the approach of royal troops. But the impending battle was avoided by Warbeck losing his nerve and deserting his followers. He was caught trying to reach the coast, confessed himself a fraud, and was placed under restraint. That his confinement was far from rigorous is shown by the fact that he afterwards attempted to make off again, mounted on a horse which had been provided for his daily exercise. He was pursued, recaptured, and placed in the Tower. Here, he planned a second escape, this time in the company of the Earl of Warwick, and when, on top of this yet another impersonator appeared in the guise of Ralf Wulford, the exasperated Henry ordered their execution forthwith.

Yet one more troublesome claimant to the throne remained to be dealt with—Edmund de la Pole, Earl of Suffolk. After John de la Pole had been killed at Stoke while in revolt against the King, his brother Edmund had agreed to forego his father's ducal title in exchange for the return of the family property which had been sequestrated. But in 1501, discontented with his lot and (as a son of Edward IV's sister Elizabeth) nursing a claim to Henry's throne, he fled to the Continent, where his aspirations received the support of the Emperor Maximilian I, an earlier sponsor of Perkin Warbeck.

But, in the course of the next five years, a series of misadventures led to the fugitive's undoing. The Emperor had installed his protégé in residence at Aix-la-Chapelle, from the safety of which town he was unwise enough to wander. He thus fell into unfriendly hands, and eventually came into the possession of the Archduke Philip, Maximilian's son. Here, he was safe enough—until, in 1505, the Archduke and his wife Joanna, while on their way to Spain, were driven by a storm to take shelter in Weymouth harbour. An alert Henry insisted upon taking charge of his uninvited guests, and at Windsor, where they were lavishly entertained, they perforce lingered until the King had extracted a promise that his missing Earl would be returned to him.

In addition to this determined and relentless pursuit of his enemies, the King also sought to safeguard his position by means of foreign alliances, and during the later years of his reign he was assiduous in his endeavours to arrange politically advantageous marriages for his children and (after the death of his wife) for himself. Before she died in 1503, Elizabeth bore him seven children, only three of which, however, reached an adult age—the future Henry VIII, and Margaret and Mary Tudor. In the furtherance, meanwhile, of Anglo-Spanish understanding (designed to check the territorial ambitions of France), Henry had betrothed Arthur, his ten-year-old son and heir, to Catherine, a daughter of Ferdinand, King of Aragon, and his wife Isabella, Queen of Castile. But although the young couple were duly married and made their home at Ludlow Castle, in the year following that of her wedding, Catherine of Aragon was left a widow.

For some time prior to this tragic event, Henry, in an attempt to placate the Scots, had been dangling the prospect of marriage with his daughter Margaret before the eyes of a not very enthusiastic James IV, and by his persistence eventually promoted an exchange of vows whereby James (a notorious libertine) and Margaret (a bride of fifteen) were joined together in holy matrimony. It was not destined to be a particularly happy association, still less an enduring one, but it was a union, nevertheless, which a century later was to place a Stuart upon the English throne.

Margaret was thus disposed of in 1500, and, with the sudden death of his son Arthur two years later, soon followed by that of his wife, Henry made the somewhat startling proposal that he should become the husband of his own daughter-in-law, thereby ensuring the retention of her dowry. But Queen Isabella preferred an alternative and matrimonially more attractive arrangement for her daughter, and it was finally decided that Catherine should find a new consort in the King's only surviving son. This having been agreed, the royal widower, still intent upon securing another wife for himself, then took the opportunity (conveniently provided by the enforced stay of Catherine's sister Joanna and her husband at Windsor) to obtain the promise of the hand of Archduke Philip's sister Margaret. But when, six months later, the Archduke died, the lady concerned hastened to repudiate the agreement, whereupon her unabashed suitor lost no time in approaching the bereaved Joanna, undeterred by the knowledge that she was bordering on the insane. Even so, his ardour cooled somewhat when he learned that, everywhere his prospective bride went, so did the embalmed corpse of the defunct Archduke!

Henry was (for those days) an elderly forty-six when Queen Elizabeth died and, in his declining years, he undoubtedly made something of a spectacle of himself in his attempts to find a replacement. But prior to this his monarchical achievements were impressive enough. By firm rule and a policy of conciliation, he restored order to a land suffering from anarchy and chaos, in the process successfully overcoming the determined opposition of not a few intractable opponents who wanted the civil war to continue. Inevitably, the methods he employed were highly autocratic (throughout his reign, an acquiescent Parliament met on only seven occasions), but he was possessed of an innate sense of justice, and the short shrift he meted out to the over-mighty among the nobility endeared him to the great majority of his subjects, though many of them were less enthusiastic about his inordinate fondness for money—i.e. their money. Certainly, by no means the least of his accomplishments concerned finance. When he came to the throne in 1485, he found trade disrupted and the treasury empty. On

FIGURE 13
Warkworth Castle, Northumberland. A view of the cruciform keep, built on the top of a Norman motte (from a photograph).

the day of his death, nearly a quarter of a century later, commerce was flourishing and the state coffers were full to overflowing.

II

Within a few weeks of his accession, in the interests of Anglo-Spanish understanding, and armed with a special dispensation which had been granted (with some slight show of hesitation) by Pope Julius II in 1503, Henry VIII married his brother's widow Catherine. Almost from the outset, he thus involved himself in the political intrigues of the day, which centred round an Italy made up of a number of independent realms, notably those of Venice, Milan, Florence, and Naples, together with the Papal States.

The situation, as Henry found it, was that the rich duchy of Milan had recently been forcibly acquired by France, whose King Louis XII was then joined by Julius II and others in making a concerted attack upon the Venetian Republic, certain of whose territories bordered on the Papal domain and Milan. But, having assisted in the despoliation of an inoffensive neighbour, the Pope grew increasingly apprehensive about the future intentions of some of his confederates, and this led to a sudden change of policy. Assisted by the aggrieved Venetians and France's former Spanish ally, he now sought to call a halt to the aspirations of Louis by reconstituting an earlier so-called Holy League, which Henry of England, as Ferdinand's son-in-law, was called upon to join. And in agreeing to do so the King was influenced by Thomas Wolsey, a newly appointed member of his Council, whose outstanding organizing and negotiating ability had brought him to the royal notice.

The arrangement was that the main attack of the combined English and Spanish forces should be directed against Guienne, but, when Henry sent his promised troops to the border province of Guipuscoa, their Spanish allies failed to join them. Instead, the presence of the English army was used by the artful Ferdinand to screen him from French attack while he took over the independent kingdom of Navarre. And, after having achieved his aim, he then made a truce with Louis which acknowledged his possession of the newly acquired territory!

Henry's painful introduction to the wiles and duplicity of continental diplomacy taught him a sharp lesson. In the following year, he crossed to Calais in person, from where he besieged and captured the towns of Thérouanne and Tournai. While he thus busied himself, James IV of Scotland took the opportunity to lead an army across the English border in support of France, only to be defeated and killed in an encounter with Thomas Howard I, Earl of Surrey (afterwards Duke of Norfolk) at the Battle of Flodden Field.

Henry himself now came to an understanding with Louis, sealing it with a marriage alliance. Since 1508, his sister Mary had been betrothed to Charles who, as the son of Joanna and the Archduke Philip, was the grandson of both Ferdinand of Aragon and the Emperor Maximilian. The nuptials had been fixed for not later than the middle of May 1514, by which time it had become evident that the absent wooer did not intend to fulfil his obligations. The King accordingly offered Mary to his erstwhile French antagonist, whose wife Anne of Brittany had recently died.

At this time, Louis XII was fifty-two years of age, worn out and decrepit, and nearly three times as old as his proffered bride. She, a spirited young girl of eighteen, in acceding to the demands of her brother, made it clear that, as soon as she was free to do so, she intended to marry the man of her choice—Charles Brandon, Duke of Suffolk. Her opportunity, as it happened, came soon enough, for within three months her enfeebled husband was dead.

Louis was succeeded as King of France by his son-in-law Francis I, who at once confirmed the English alliance and no less promptly stirred up trouble for Henry in Scotland. The time was not far distant, however, when Francis would be seeking Henry's help, for, in the course of the next few years, both Ferdinand and Maximilian followed Louis to the grave, leaving a vast heritage to their grandson Charles. The recipient had already succeeded to territories in the Netherlands and elsewhere on the death of his father in 1506, and, with his election as the Holy Roman Emperor Charles V, not to mention his accession as King Charles I of Spain, he held sway over lands greater in extent than those of Henry and Francis combined.

This altered situation meant that the English King held the balance of power between his two continental rivals, each of whom now sought to enlist his aid in the impending struggle against the other. Despite an amicable and ostentatious meeting between Henry and Francis in 1520 (on the famous Field of the Cloth of Gold), it was Charles who ultimately gained the promise of England's support, a bargain ratified (despite his earlier cavalier treatment of Henry's sister) by his betrothal to that trustful monarch's four-year-old daughter Mary.

Charles now advanced claims to Milan and Burgundy, and the first phase of his war against France ended in his favour with the defeat and capture of Francis at the Battle of Pavia, in 1525. The English, having served their purpose, were now denied any share of the spoils, while the Emperor's undertaking to marry Henry's daughter was abandoned in favour of a contemplated (and more politically advantageous) union with the Infanta of Portugal. As for the captive Francis, he was taken to Madrid and there compelled to sign a treaty which involved the making of extensive territorial concessions to his enemy.

This agreement, it need hardly be said, he at once repudiated as soon as he had been set at liberty, and, in an attempt to restore the *status quo* of 1522, he formed a coalition against Charles, in which he was supported by Pope Clement VII[1] and the leaders of other Italian States, notably Venice, Milan, and Florence. The outcome, however, was disastrous for the most influential of his allies, for the Holy See's association with France provoked an attack upon Rome, in the course of which an undisciplined force of German and Spanish mercenaries sacked the city and made the Pope their prisoner. Charles professed to be horrified by this turn of events, but, although he disclaimed all responsibility for the behaviour of his troops, he had no scruples about taking advantage of the situation as he now found it.

For England and the papacy, the consequences of the Emperor's possession of Clement VII were to be far-reaching and profound. The prestige of the Church of Rome had already been severely shaken by the multiplicity of rival Popes which had arisen during the Great Schism, while the authority of its teaching was beginning to be questioned by scholars who had recently gained a sight of the (to them) new and thought-provoking knowledge contained in the writings of the ancient Greeks.

At this period of mounting crisis in its affairs, the Church might have been saved from dismemberment had it been able to produce leaders worthy of its apostolic mission. Instead, it was served by self-seeking nepotists such as Calixtus III and Sixtus IV, dedicated to the aggrandizement of their families. Even the kindly Innocent VIII (who at least had the grace openly to acknowledge his illegitimate offspring) freely engaged in the dubious practice of creating new offices, that they might be sold to the highest bidder, while, under the administration of the sinister and far more corrupt Alexander VI,[2] the fortunes of the Holy See, at any rate morally, reached their lowest ebb.

The inevitable reaction came during the incumbency of Leo X, whose grandiose plans for the beautification of Rome prompted him to seek the necessary funds by the sale of indulgences on an unprecedented scale. Growing opposition

[1] Pope Julius II died in 1513. He was followed by Leo X (1513–21) and Adrian VI (1522–3), who was succeeded in turn by Clement VII (1523–34) and Paul III (1534–49).

[2] As Cardinal Rodrigo Borgia, he formed an association with Vanozza Catanei, a Roman lady of easy virtue who bore four of his children (Juan, Cesere, Lucretia, and Jofre), two of whom subsequently achieved a notoriety matched only by that of their dissolute father.

to this wholesale offer of salvation by purchase found expression in the fulminations of the Saxon monk Martin Luther, who, in October 1517, publicly denounced the practice in a challenge which he nailed to the door of a church in Wittenberg. His excommunication inevitably followed, but this and other of the rebel's outbursts had won him many adherents and gained him powerful friends. Thanks to their protection, he escaped martyrdom, and so lived to see the rapid spread of German Protestantism.

The movement received no official encouragement in England. On the contrary, to his credit (or discredit, according to the point of view), Henry's response was to pen a vindication of the seven sacraments in refutation of Luther's heretical ideas, in return for which theological broadside a grateful Leo X promulgated a Bull conferring upon the royal author the coveted title, *Fidei Defensor*.

This was in 1521, and when, some years later, Henry decided to seek ecclesiastical sanction to set aside his wife, it probably never occurred to him, as an ardent and acknowledged Defender of the Faith, that, by so doing, he was in any way endangering the authority of Rome. He was acquainted, of course, with the fact that the Church did not, and could not, openly countenance divorce. But he was also well aware of papal susceptibility to the glint of gold, and he knew that persons of privilege and position, such as himself, could always expect some way round such a difficulty to be found.

Despite his long association with Catherine of Aragon, she had failed to provide him with an heir (at least four of her sons had been stillborn, or had died soon after delivery). In 1519, the would-be father had even undertaken to lead a Crusade against the Turk, should his long-awaited son arrive, but an indifferent Heaven, it seemed, was content to leave the infidel undisturbed. And by 1525, when his wife attained the age of forty, Henry (himself a virile thirty-four) had to face the fact that the only issue he was likely to have by his Queen was their daughter Mary, now a child of nine.

But if a female succeeded to the throne, serious matrimonial and dynastic complications were likely to arise in the event of her marriage, while, if she remained unwed, that would merely prolong, but would not solve, the problem of the missing heir. Such was the King's dilemma, which had already been noted and commented upon by Sebastian Guistinian, the Venetian ambassador, when he sent home a despatch listing those who were beginning to entertain hopes of the Crown. High up on the list was the name of Edward Stafford, third Duke of

Buckingham, who was afterwards incautious enough to make reference to his descent from Edward III, a hint not lost upon Henry, who deprived him of his prospects by finding an excuse for lopping off his head.

In his desperation, the King turned to a royal bastard whose existence, prior to 1525, seems to have been effectively concealed. This child of chance had been born six years earlier, the product of a passing fancy which Henry had entertained for the boy's mother, Elizabeth Blount, a sister of the fourth Baron Mountjoy. The presence of this unsuspected offspring was now brought to public notice by his being created Duke of Richmond and Somerset, and serious consideration was given to the proposal that his claim to the throne should be strengthened by marriage to his half-sister, an incestuous union which the Pope was prepared to condone if the King would undertake to abandon any intention of ridding himself of his Queen.

But, by the beginning of 1527, Henry had become enamoured of Anne Boleyn, a younger daughter of Sir Thomas Boleyn, newly created Viscount Rochford and Earl of Wiltshire. Her sister Mary had been the King's mistress for some little time (a fact to which her father owed his ennoblement), but Anne was not so readily persuaded to stray from the path of virtue, and her repeated refusals to enter the royal bedchamber as a lover merely increased the frustrated Henry's determination that she should do so as a wife.

For his part, Pope Clement VII was by no means insensible to the needs of a monarch who lacked a suitable successor. The problem, moreover, was far from new, and there were precedents enough to guide him, however dubious the authority of some of these might be considered.[1] It so happened that, a century earlier, a certain Dona Blanca had proved incapable of providing her husband with an heir, whereupon the deprived Henry IV of Castile had been granted a dispensation which enabled him to take a second wife. And in September 1530, with this case in mind, the Pope secretly suggested to the King that here was a way out of his difficulty.

But Henry had no Solomonic inclinations and he did not relish acquiring a plurality of wives, even on the authority of the Old Testament. Neither, at this time, did he view with favour another of Clement's suggestions, which was that the King should take the matter into his own hands, grant himself

[1] In return for royal assistance in promoting the private interests of the Borgia family, Pope Alexander VI had seen fit to allow Louis XII of France to repudiate his wife Joanna for the good and sufficient reason that the King wanted to acquire Brittany by marrying its Duchess.

Harlech Castle, Merionethshire, its site a rugged headland, some 200 feet above sea level. (*Photo:* Aerofilms and Aero Pictorial Ltd.)

Caernarvon Castle and its associated town defences, from an engraving by J. Boydell, first published in 1750. (*Photo:* Crown Copyright)

Royal Windsor, Berkshire. A castle of many periods and the principal residence of the monarchs of England since the days of William the Conqueror. In this aerial view the original motte (upon which now stands the famous round tower) and the outlines of its twin bailey system are clearly to be seen. (*Photo:* Aerofilms and Aero Pictorial Ltd.)

St. Michael's Mount, Cornwall. (*Photo:* Aerofilms and Aero Pictorial Ltd.)

a divorce in an English court, and so present the papacy with a *fait accompli* which could be argued about afterwards. In seeking to put the responsibility for the decision where he considered it rightly belonged, Henry preferred to express grave (if recently discovered) doubts as to the validity of the dispensation which had permitted his levirate marriage in the first place, in support of which contention he piously quoted Leviticus xx, 21:

> The man who takes his brother's wife in marriage does a forbidden thing, bringing shame on his own brother; children they shall have never.

This was a ruling more in keeping with the royal requirements than the antithetical injunction to be found in Deuteronomy xxv, 5:

> When two brethren share the same house, and one dies childless, his widow must not take a husband elsewhere; the survivor must wed her, and beget her children in his dead brother's name.

Resting his case on the third rather than the last of the five books of the Pentateuch, what Henry now desired from Clement was an *ex officio* pronouncement to the effect that he was not, and at no time had been, bound to Catherine of Aragon in holy wedlock at all. But the Pope, alas, was hardly in a position to provide him with anything of the kind, if only because, after the sack of Rome in 1527, he had remained a virtual prisoner of the Emperor Charles—and the unwanted Catherine was his captor's aunt! However, in a last attempt to reach an amicable settlement, Cardinal Lorenzo Campeggio was sent to London, charged with the impossible task of restraining the King or, this failing, of persuading the Queen to follow meekly in the steps of Louis XII's discarded wife Joanna, by consenting to enter a nunnery. But even as a personal favour to the Pope (who undoubtedly found himself in a most invidious position), Catherine was not prepared to imperil her immortal soul by admitting that she had been living in sin for the past twenty years, still less to concede that her daughter by Henry had been born out of wedlock, and the mission accomplished nothing.

Cardinal Wolsey, the King's chief minister (whose foreign policy had also collapsed in ruins about him) now retired in disgrace. He was replaced as Chancellor by Sir Thomas More, whose religious scruples were likewise to lead to his resignation, and later to his death. In the meantime, at the suggestion of a Cambridge don named Thomas Cranmer, the question of whether a man might lawfully marry the widow of his deceased brother was submitted to English and European universities for consideration. Not surprisingly, the learned opinions thus obtained proved to be as contradictory as the edicts of the Holy Writ which had inspired them, though the fact that not only Oxford and Cambridge favoured Leviticus, but also Paris and Toulouse, Bourges and Ferrara, Pavia and Padua, so gratified the English monarch that he rewarded the instigator of the inquiry with the Archbishopric of Canterbury.

Henry also discovered another source of strength and inspiration in Thomas Cromwell, a man of humble birth who had earlier been in Wolsey's service, and who afterwards became Earl of Essex. It was he who initiated a series of Parliamentary enactments (relating to Annates, Appeals, Dispensations, *et al*) which culminated, in 1534, in the decisive Act of Supremacy that signalled the final break with Rome. In recognizing the King's Majesty as the Supreme Head of the Church of England, it was laid down that

> . . . our said Sovereign Lord, his heirs and successors Kings of this realm, shall have full power and authority from time to time to visit, repress, redress, reform, order, correct, restrain, and amend all such errors, heresies, abuses, offences, contempts, and enormities, whatsoever they be . . . any usage, custom, foreign laws, foreign authority, prescription, or any other thing or things to the contrary hereof notwithstanding.

The need for drastic action had become apparent at the beginning of 1533, when Anne Boleyn, having surrendered at last to the importunities of the King, found herself with child. She and the masterful Henry were married without further delay, at a private ceremony conducted in such secrecy, however, that neither the place nor the date of it is known. An obliging Archbishop Cranmer, with the approval of Convocation, subsequently pronounced the King's marriage to Catherine null and void, and in June the new Queen was crowned in Westminster Abbey. The astrologers of the day, then, as now, occasionally unlucky in their guesswork, assured the expectant monarch that the child would be a boy. To their consternation and the royal father's acute disappointment, it proved necessary to christen the infant Elizabeth.

Two years or so later, when he was still without his hoped-for heir, a visit to Wolf Hall, the home of Sir John Seymour, provided Henry with a glimpse of his host's daughter Jane, a sight sufficient to convince him that what the succession really needed was another and more fertile Queen. His unwilling and overhasty second marriage, he now inclined to believe, had been accomplished by witchcraft, and for this reason alone was to be regarded as invalid. Not long thereafter, the unsuspecting Anne, because of friendships made, it may well be, in answer to the infidelities of her husband, found herself charged with having taken as many as five lovers, her own brother among them. Despite strenuous denials (the monotony of which was ultimately relieved by one solitary, torture-extracted confession of guilt), all five of the accused were condemned and executed, two days before Anne herself was led to the block.

Catherine of Aragon had providentially died a natural death earlier in the year, and with Anne Boleyn also out of the way, the only bar to Henry's marriage with Jane Seymour (a descendant, on her mother's side, of the ubiquitous Edward III) was her consanguinity to the King in the third and fourth degrees. This minor technicality was quickly and expertly brushed aside by Archbishop Cranmer, so enabling the marriage to be celebrated forthwith. On 8 June, Parliament was assembled, that it might attend to yet another formality—the passing of an Act of Succession which bastardized Elizabeth and settled the Crown on Henry's children, if any, by his third wife. Perhaps with his illegitimate son, the Duke of Richmond, in mind, an escape clause empowered the King to make other arrangements should he have no issue by Jane. But, although the young Duke died soon afterwards, later in the year the situation was saved by the Queen giving birth to a son on the eve of the feast of St. Edward. The boy was named accordingly, though the joy attendant upon his arrival was marred by the untimely death of his mother.

It was an essential part of Henry's foreign policy to keep alive the jealousies of his rivals, and, with this aim in view, fresh marriage negotiations were simultaneously pursued in both the French and Spanish Courts, the King representing to the Emperor Charles that he would not be averse to finding a new wife in Christiana, the Duchess of Milan. She had wed the Duke at the age of thirteen, and was now, at any rate by repute, a virgin widow of sixteen. Her alleged reply to Henry's proposal, however, was a somewhat disconcerting intimation that if only she were possessed of two heads, she would gladly place one of them at the King's disposal!

But the political considerations which had led to the offer were soon overshadowed by other events. After a preliminary suspension of hostilities towards the end of 1537, in the following June a ten-years' truce was agreed between Francis and

Charles at Nice, thanks to the mediation of the Holy See in the person of Paul III. Despite the threat offered by this association of King, Emperor, and Pope, however, Henry carried on with the dissolution, already begun, of the English monasteries (which were answerable only to Rome), together with the systematic destruction of relics and images, among them such pious frauds as the renowned Boxley Crucifix, revealed at last as no more than a contraption of wood and wire. Even the revered shrine of Thomas Becket did not escape the purge, the bones and relics of the Saint being consigned to the flames.

A Bull of excommunication had been prepared against Henry as long ago as 1535, though its execution had been suspended in the faint hope that the culprit might mend his ways. Its publication in France and elsewhere was now threatened, and the Emperor Charles was urged to make his peace with the Turk, that he might give his undivided attention to the infidel nearer home. France, too, was called upon to assist in the enterprise, and even Scotland received a visit from a papal envoy. It seemed that a triple invasion of England was imminent.

Henry reacted to the situation with vigour. Like his father, he was a firm believer in the doctrine that nothing contributes to stability of government so much as an absence of alternatives, as indeed his disposal of the Duke of Buckingham had already demonstrated. Conveniently enough, there were known papal sympathizers among such leading families as the Poles and the Courtenays, whose members could boast of the royal blood in their veins, and this monarchical affinity, coupled with the veriest suspicion of treason, was enough to condemn not a few of them.

The removal of potential traitors from within the kingdom was accompanied by active preparations to resist any would-be invaders from without, as the Kent historian William Lambarde (1536–1601) recounts:

> Onely of this I hold me well assured, that King Henrie the Eighte, having shaken off the intolerable yoke of the Popish tyrannie, and espying that the Emperour was offended for the divorce of Queen Katherine his wife and that the French King had coupled the Dolphine his sonne to the Pope's niece, and married his daughter to the King of Scots, so that he might more justly suspect them all, than safely trust any one, determined (by the aide of God) to stand upon his owne gardes and defences: and therefore with all speede, and without sparing any cost, he builded Castles, Platfourmes and Blockhouses, in all needful places of the Realme.

The threatened danger disclosed to what extent domestic and military architecture had gone their separate ways. Thanks to the abolition of livery and maintenance, the private stronghold, via the defended manor house (chronologically represented by Stokesay (1291) and fourteenth- and fifteenth-century examples bearing such names as Maxstoke, Nunney, Old Wardour, Raglan, Tattershall, Wingfield Manor, and Kirby Muxloe) had made way for the Tudor mansion, sometimes of stone or half-timber construction, but more often built of red brick, and replete with windows of glass, oak-panelled walls, and elaborate staircases. As for the castles of an earlier age, even in

FIGURE 14
Stokesay Castle, Shropshire. An early example (1291) of a defended manor house, viewed from the north-west (from a photograph).

Tudor times many of these structures were already in a ruined state, abandoned by owners who preferred a less Spartan way of life, as the peregrinations of John Leyland, the royal antiquarian, served to show.

The main burden of coastal defence thus devolved upon a network of newly built strongholds which stretched all the way from Hull to Milford Haven, the more vulnerable southern and south-eastern parts of the country being the first to be strengthened in this manner. Five of these forts (none of which now remains) were built on the Thames at Tilbury and

Gravesend, while others were located in the vicinity of Deal, Dover, Walmer, and elsewhere. Although there was considerable variation in plan and detail, the buildings were invariably compact and so designed that they could be defended in all directions by artillery mounted on squat platforms, arranged in one or more tiers about a central tower (referred to as the keep).

One of the largest and the most important of the series was that erected at Deal, where it is still to be seen. Essentially, it consists of a round tower, three stories high, from the circumference of which there protrude a dozen semi-circular bastions, arranged in two tiers of six. In all, these components and their parapet walls provide, in the shape of gunports or musket embrasures, no less than 145 openings for use with firearms, in addition to which the edifice is surrounded by a broad and deep moat.

The fortress entrance, approached by way of a drawbridge, was defended by a portcullis, while an associated passageway was provided with holes in its roof through which assailants could be fired on from overhead. And as an extra precaution, the inner door of the entrance hall (which occupied some two-thirds of one of the lower bastions) was made to open inwards, i.e. towards the central keep, an arrangement intended to prevent an attacker who had succeeded in gaining admittance from converting the castle lobby into an isolated stronghold.

Within the central keep, the basement served as a storeroom (for food, ammunition, and other necessities; it also contained a well), the ground floor was evidently the kitchen and appears to have accommodated the garrison of twenty-four men in addition, while on the first floor were located the Captain's quarters. Internal passages and stairways connect the various floors and also lead to the tower roof, which is topped by a lantern. A feature of the basement is an internal gallery which extends continuously round the perimeter walls of the lower bastions, which at this level are pierced by more than half a hundred gunports, commanding the encircling moat, access to which could be gained by the defenders through a postern gate.

Deal and its associated fortresses, with their massive walls and rounded surfaces, designed to deflect enemy shot, were reinforced by a flotilla of mobile batteries. To this end, the Royal Navy, which owed its beginnings to the previous reign (with the building of the *Regent* and the *Sovereign*, both vessels of some 700 tons) was greatly expanded, and the fleet soon numbered 150 galleys and ships, ready to sail at short notice. And as yet another precaution, Thomas Cromwell urged upon the King the advisability of fostering friendship with the anti-papal Princes of Germany. This, he suggested, could best be achieved by the marriage of His Majesty to Anne, the elder sister of Duke William of Cleves. Henry was dubious about the proposal, for, notwithstanding his bitter quarrel with Rome, he was no Protestant, and, when he finally consented to the match, he did so with reluctance, purely on the grounds of national necessity.

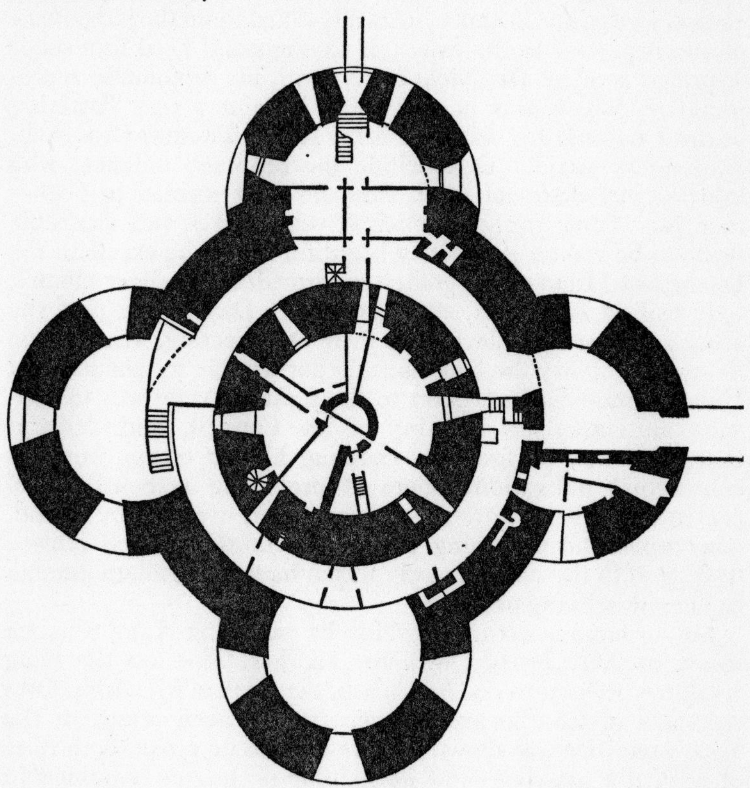

FIGURE 15

Walmer Castle, Kent. Plan of one of Henry VIII's coastal forts, showing first-floor level (based on a drawing in B. H. St. J. O'Neil's *Castles*).

Some while earlier, the King had confided to the French ambassador, Charles de Marillac, that, in his view, the selection of a wife was far too delicate a matter to be entrusted to a deputy, and that the only satisfactory course was the making of a personal inspection. From this, it is difficult to escape the conclusion, either that Henry's standards of feminine beauty were peculiarly his own, or that he was more easily pleased than most. Certainly his wives display such unvarying and downright plainness that William Stubbs (who, as a nineteenth-century Bishop, was surely no advocate of disespousal) was moved to concede that it provided "if not a justification, at least a colourable reason for understanding the readiness with which he put them away".

But as it happened, Anne of Cleves was not Henry's personal choice. In this one instance, he rashly relied upon the judgement of another, even to the extent of paying small heed to a sober appraisal sent by Dr. Nicholas Wotton, his diplomatic representative, which was accompanied by a not very flattering portrait painted by Hans Holbein. It was Thomas Cromwell, desperately anxious to conclude the proposed alliance, who told the expectant monarch what he most wanted to hear—that his young (only thirty-four years old!) and desirable bride-to-be was so exquisitely beautiful that "she excelleth the Duchess of Milan as the golden sun excelleth the silver moon".

It was at Rochester, on New Year's Day, 1540, that the King and Anne of Cleves had their first meeting. What Anne thought of Henry the historians do not trouble to recount. But Henry's immediate reaction to the sight of Anne was to convoke an emergency meeting of his Council, and demand that some way be found of enabling him to escape from his contractual obligation. Short of provoking war instead of cementing peace, however, no way out was to be found, whereupon the protesting Henry reluctantly allowed himself to be wed to the unlovely lady whom he was ungallant enough to liken to a Flanders mare.

But to honour his undertaking by marrying Anne was one thing, to share his bed with her another. This last the King resolutely refused to do. And when, the mask of friendship from the faces of Charles and Francis having been removed, the King's sacrifice was shown to have been to no purpose, the fate of both the marriage and its sponsor no longer remained in doubt. On 10 June, the luckless Cromwell was arrested and lodged in the Tower, prior to his execution at Tyburn. On 9 July, the union itself was annulled by the combined efforts of the Convocations of Canterbury and York, on the dual grounds of pre-contract (it was held that Anne had earlier been promised to a son of the Duke of Lorraine) and an excusable lack of marital enthusiasm on the part of the disenchanted groom. As for the bride, she very sensibly accepted both the ruling and the consolation prize of £4,000 per annum which went with it.

These events had been set in motion by Thomas Howard II, third Duke of Norfolk, and other of Cromwell's enemies, who had deliberately sought to bring about his downfall by providing the despondent King with a distraction in the shape of Catherine Howard, Norfolk's niece. Her preliminary encounter with the monarch, contrived with the assistance of the owner of the premises, was at the house of Stephen Gardiner, Bishop of Winchester, and in a matter of months Henry had disposed of his fourth wife and acquired a fifth. The plan, it seemed, had worked to perfection.

But what the unsuspecting monarch did not know was that the morals of Catherine Howard were not very much better than his own, and soon irrefutable evidence reached the Privy Council that, not content with having compromised herself with more than one man before her marriage, the Queen's conduct had in no way changed after it. To hide such knowledge from the King was unthinkable, to reveal it a hazardous and highly unpleasant duty. Archbishop Cranmer was charged with the task of disillusioning Henry, whose genuine fondness for his latest bride at first disinclined him to believe his ears. But the charges, alas, were no fabrication, and, as they involved more than a pre-nuptial lapse, the conduct of the accused amounted to high treason.

In January 1542, a sympathetic and understanding Parliament relieved the King of responsibility in so painful a matter, and passed an Act of Attainder. This Bill sent the Queen to the block. It also stipulated that, in future, any unchaste woman who married the King committed a capital offence—a mirth-provoking provision which caused Eustace Chapuys, the realistic ambassador of Charles V, to remark that "few, if any, ladies now at Court would henceforth aspire to such an honour".

Nevertheless, yet another wife was found to meet the royal needs in the person of thirty-one-year-old Catherine Parr. According to Chapuys, she was not nearly so beautiful as Anne of Cleves, so presumably the lady was possessed of other qualities. She had at any rate been twice married before, and on the death of John, Lord Latimer, her second spouse, her hand had at once been sought by Sir Thomas Seymour, the King's brother-in-law. Fate, however, decreed that he was to be her fourth, not her third, husband, and in the meantime, "overruled by a higher power" she became Henry's Queen, and so contrived to remain until his death in 1547.

III

Although Parliament had obediently barred both of Henry's daughters from the succession and declared them illegitimate, on the occasion of his marriage to Jane Seymour, the King had been given the right to dispose of the Crown as he saw fit, and in the event he ultimately nominated his three children Edward, Mary, and Elizabeth—in that order. Should none of the three have issue, it was directed that their successor should be sought among the descendants of Mary, Duchess of Suffolk. The Scottish marriage of his other sister Margaret was ignored.[1]

Edward VI was nine years old when he came to the throne, and had yet to attain his sixteenth birthday when he died, with the inevitable result that throughout his brief reign he was dominated by others. At the onset, the boy King's uncle, Edward Seymour, Earl of Hertford (afterwards Duke of Somerset), assumed the title of Lord Protector, and for a while succeeded in maintaining his position as the most powerful noble in the kingdom.

One of his first moves was to make an attempt to resolve the Scottish problem which had been inherited from the previous reign. But his despatch of an army against Edinburgh, and the slaughter of 10,000 native defenders of that city, did not endear the Scots to the invaders, or persuade them that Edward, King of England, was a desirable match for Mary, Queen of Scots. On the contrary, it led to the young lady being sent to France, where she was wed to a grandson of Francis I, who soon after the marriage succeeded his father (Henry II) as King Francis II.

The failure of this and other of Somerset's policies brought about his downfall, and his place was taken by the unscrupulous Duke of Northumberland (alias John Dudley, Earl of Warwick).

[1] No doubt because of the continued pro-French inclinations of his northern neighbours—for which the King himself was largely to blame. In 1542, when Francis I and Charles V renewed their squabbling, and so put an end to the threat of a combined assault against England, Henry seized the opportunity to claim suzerainty over Scotland. Its ruler, his nephew King James V, not unnaturally declined to discuss the matter, and, in the course of the hostilities which ensued, the Scottish forces suffered a humiliating defeat at Solway Moss, whereupon James died of a broken heart, leaving his kingdom to his daughter Mary, who was barely a week old.

Under duress, the Scots then agreed to the betrothal of their infant Queen to Henry's son Edward. But the English King's claim to the Scottish throne, in which he still persisted, was another matter, and when Francis I intervened to the extent of sending men, money, and ships, the marriage contract was repudiated in favour of a proposed French alliance.

About this time, the consumptive Edward's health gave much cause for concern, and Northumberland, an extreme Protestant in religious matters, began to view with alarm the prospect of so devoted a Catholic as Mary attaining the throne. He accordingly prevailed upon the King to make a will excluding both of his sisters from the succession, recognizing in their stead a granddaughter of Mary, Countess of Suffolk, in the person of Lady Jane Grey—upon whom the scheming Northumberland forced the hand of Lord Guildford Dudley, one of his sons, in marriage.

By one means and another, the assent of the Privy Council to the arrangement was obtained on 21 June 1553, a fortnight before the King died. News of his passing was then withheld to enable Northumberland to make the Princess Mary his prisoner, but she, warned of his intentions, fled to East Anglia. On 10 July, Jane was proclaimed Queen, but the people responded by calling for Mary, and ten days later Northumberland acknowledged the extent of his miscalculation by adding his own voice to the popular clamour. But it availed him nothing, for no sooner had Mary entered London in triumph a fortnight later than he found himself a prisoner in the Tower.

IV

Mary I of England was a spinster of thirty-seven when she came to the throne, understandably embittered by the events which had brought so much unhappiness to her mother and herself. At one time and another, not a few marriages had been proposed for her—to the Emperor Charles V, to King Francis I, to his second son, Duke Henry of Orleans, even to the Duke of Richmond, her own bastard half-brother—but always she had been a pawn in the devious political manœuvrings of her father, whose eventual repudiation of her mother had brought doubt upon the legitimacy of his offspring by her.

These humiliations, including the forcible renunciation of her faith, had been borne with great fortitude and courage and now, as England's Queen, she was intent upon the restoration of Catholicism, accompanied and assisted by her marriage to Archduke Philip of the Netherlands who, as the son of the Emperor Charles, was destined to be the future King Philip II of Spain.

These policies aroused strong opposition among a section of her subjects, the proposed Spanish alliance provoking a widespread uprising led by Sir Thomas Wyatt, who had the support of the Duke of Suffolk. The outbreak was suppressed with some difficulty, and not only were its leaders and some 200 of their followers executed, but as a precautionary measure Suffolk's daughter, the Lady Jane Grey, and her husband were also put permanently out of the way. Even the Princess Elizabeth narrowly escaped being implicated, on the grounds that she had earlier been in correspondence with Wyatt.

Mary and Philip were then married at Winchester in July 1554, after a wary Parliament had ordained that, although the bridegroom might bear the courtesy title of King of England, he was to take no part in the government of the realm, and could not succeed his wife in the event of her predeceasing him. A return to Catholicism, however, which was not ruled out, was signalled by an acknowledgement of the authority of Rome in matters theological and the formal repeal of the anti-papal legislation of Henry VIII, whereafter the scent of frying Archbishops and lesser mortals spread throughout the land as some 300 recusant Protestants, Thomas Cranmer among them, found death at the stake.

While these Christian activities were in progress, Mary's frustrated husband decided to return to his own domain, and, soon afterwards, having assumed the kingship of Spain, he found himself at war with Henry II of France, whose help Rome had secretly enlisted to end Spanish occupation of southern Italy. King Philip responded by launching an attack against the Papal States, and called upon his wife to assist him in his struggle against France. The Pope retaliated by making use of the spiritual weapons at his command, with the ironic result that the devout Mary found herself ranged against Paul IV at the side of her excommunicated husband. For her country it proved to be a pointless and costly enterprise which, early in 1558, resulted in the loss of Calais, England's last possession on the French mainland. But by this time a much needed change of management was on the way, for what the Queen had on more than one occasion hopefully imagined to be indications of pregnancy proved to be symptoms of dropsy, to which complaint she succumbed towards the end of the year.

V

In accordance with the terms of their father's will, Mary was succeeded by her half-sister Elizabeth I, who came to the throne of a realm torn by religious strife, heavily in debt, and embroiled in a profitless war with France at the behest of a foreign power. Certainly it was an unpromising start to a reign of nearly half a century which, however, posterity was to acclaim as one of the greatest periods in the country's history. For in the course of it England was transformed into a commercially sound and united nation, backed by a navy which, thanks to the leadership and exploits of such men as Walter Raleigh, Martin Frobisher, and Francis Drake, was second to none. And, to add to the glories of the reign, it also proved to be an age of unparalleled literary achievement, as the writings of William Shakespeare, Edmund Spenser, Francis Bacon, Richard Hooker, and many another bear witness.

And yet, at the onset, the new Queen's own position was far from secure, even though Parliament, reversing an earlier pronouncement, had acknowledged her legitimacy in 1554. Even so, according to the Church of Rome, at the time of Elizabeth's birth her mother had been unmarried, in consequence of which the Pope not only formally denied her right to the Crown, but went so far as to maintain that it was his to dispose of as he saw fit, on the grounds that England remained a fief of the Holy See! And an eminently suitable candidate, it appeared, was available in the person of Mary Stuart, Queen of Scots, who, as a granddaughter of Henry VIII's elder sister Margaret, had an undeniably strong Tudor claim to the throne.

But that another Mary and another Catholic should rule over them was something which the majority of Englishmen were far from ready to accept, and the papal pretensions merely had the effect of identifying Protestantism with patriotism, thereby strengthening Elizabeth's position. She, of course, was regarded as an anti-papalist, since it had been made abundantly clear that she could not be both Queen of England and a faithful adherent of Rome. Her supposed partisanship, however, derived from the circumstances of her birth, not from her religious convictions, and there is little evidence to show that she entertained any particular preference, one way or the other.

Prudence dictated that she move with caution, and in the early days of her reign she was careful not to give unnecessary offence to the susceptibilities of the more orthodox among her people. Thus, on her first public document, the Queen's customary titles were followed by an innocuous "and so forth" instead of by the contentious phrase "Supreme Head of the Church", as used by Henry VIII and Edward VI. In general, she endeavoured to avoid both the Protestant excesses which had characterized the reign of her brother, and the Catholic extremes which had accompanied the accession of her sister. The path she followed, in short, was essentially a compromise, intended to please as many of her subjects as possible. To this end, one of her first acts was to decree a return to Anglicanism (Acts of Supremacy and Uniformity, 1559).

At this juncture Pope Paul IV was replaced by Pius IV, during whose pontificate relations with England were finally broken off in 1561, though it remained for his successor, Pius V, to take the extreme step of issuing the Bull *Regnans in Excelsis*, deposing and excommunicating Elizabeth. But this belated edict, issued during February 1570, came more than ten years too late to achieve its purpose, for, during the whole of a critical decade, English Catholics had been left without any clear indication of Rome's intentions or desires.

Elizabeth, at all events, was by this time much more firmly established on the throne and in the affection of her people. At the age of twenty-five she had accepted the Crown in open defiance of the Pope, imbued with her father's concept of strong rule, tempered by an appreciation of the fact that autocracy, to be effective, must have a considerable measure of popular support. Her subsequent success was largely due to personal shrewdness, not least in the selection of able ministers who served her faithfully and well. Outstanding among these indispensable aides were Sir William Cecil (afterwards Lord Burghley), who became the Queen's principal secretary within a few days of her accession, and who remained in her service for forty years, and Sir Francis Walsingham, who came to the fore in 1573.

England's foreign policy was intended to avoid open war, at any rate until the nation was unified and strong. In 1559, the Treaty of Cateau-Cambrésis ended existing hostilities with France, at the cost of what was to prove to be the permanent loss of Calais (the port, which at first it was agreed should be ceded to England after a period of eight years, was later relinquished by her in return for the sum of 222,000 crowns) and in 1560 the Treaty of Edinburgh, designed to assist the anti-papal cause in Scotland, ensured the withdrawal of French troops from that country.

In the years which followed, Elizabethan diplomacy was remarkable as much for its deviousness and its double-dealing as for the results it achieved in maintaining a precarious balance of power by the deceptions practised upon one enemy after another. A much-used bait was the possibility of marriage with the Queen, a prospect which caused more than one foreign Prince to refrain from attempting to seize by force a kingdom he hoped to obtain by way of the altar. Her suitors were many and varied (more than a dozen came forward in the first two years of her reign!) and ranged from Ivan the Terrible of Russia and Henry III of France to the Archduke Charles of Austria and the half-witted Eric XIV of Sweden. Even Philip II of Spain made haste to seek the hand of his sister-in-law, and Elizabeth, by making a show of understandable hesitation in the face of so many flattering offers, contrived to keep alive the ardour of at least one of her admirers until she reached the age of fifty!

The publication of Pius V's excommunicatory Bull, meanwhile, was a move which, at any rate in theory, not only absolved the Queen's subjects from their allegiance, but invited foreign intervention, and in the years ahead it provided an official excuse, not to say encouragement, for a series of attempted Romanist revivals, characterized by plots which were directed, not merely against Elizabeth's authority, but against her life. Inevitably, many of these conspiracies centred round Mary Stuart, who had fled from her native Scotland to find safety in a not too onerous captivity in England.[1] She was a dangerous, unwelcome, and self-invited guest of whom the Queen was constantly being urged to rid herself, advice which she steadfastly declined to accept for nearly twenty years. However, when Mary was shown to have been involved (with Anthony Babington and others) in yet another plan to murder her royal host, she at last brought upon herself the retribution she had escaped for so long.

It was by this time apparent that it was Philip of Spain who offered the greatest threat to English sovereignty. Nor was His Hispanic Majesty without some cause for complaint. Quite apart from Elizabeth's polite rejection of his earlier marriage overtures, he had since been greatly provoked in other ways.

[1] After the accidental death of her French husband, King Francis II, in 1560, followed by the loss of her mother a year later, Mary returned to Scotland as ruler of that kingdom. She was then a young widow of eighteen, and in 1565 she chose to marry her cousin Henry Stuart, otherwise Lord Darnley, a worthless drunkard whom she soon came to despise and loathe. By way of solace, she unwisely made a companion of David Rizzio, her Italian secretary, whom the jealous Darnley and some of his companions murdered before her eyes.

Three months after this episode, the Queen gave birth to Darnley's son, who was christened James. Undeterred by the fate of Rizzio, Mary then formed an association with James Hepburn, fourth Earl of Bothwell, a scoundrelly ruffian who was afterwards suspected of complicity in the killing of Darnley. The subsequent marriage of Mary and Bothwell caused a revolt among the Scottish nobles, led by the Earl of Moray, the Queen's bastard half-brother. Mary was placed under restraint in Lochleven Castle, and forced to abdicate in favour of her infant son. But in May 1568 she escaped, and, after making an unsuccessful attempt to regain the throne, sought refuge in England.

Thanks to the foresight of his predecessors Ferdinand and Isabella in sponsoring the exploratory voyaging of Christopher Columbus, he had found himself the ruler of vast territories in the Americas, from which there was now pouring a most gratifying and seemingly endless supply of gold and silver.

The presence of this treasure on the high seas while in transit from the New World to the Old proved too great a temptation to Spain's enemies, and when the French began attacking and plundering the plate ships, the English were not slow to follow suit. Philip's ambassadors had protested often and in vain, and Elizabeth's expressions of insincere regret were not made any more palatable by the knowledge that, while the Queen publicly deplored the piratical activities of her nationals, privately she encouraged them in their depredations by supplying them with ships and money.

The Spanish monarch had more than once considered sending a retaliatory expedition against England, and, when the news was received of the execution of Mary Stuart, in deference to whose safety he had previously stayed his hand, he hesitated no more. And after months of preparation, his grand invasion fleet (132 vessels, mounting 3,165 cannon)[1] set sail in the early summer of 1588. But the much vaunted Invincible Armada failed to live up to its name. Walsingham's spies kept him informed of the enemy's movements, and with Charles Howard of Effingham, Lord High Admiral, in command of the ships of the Royal Navy, Hawkins, Drake, and their fellow officers attacked and drove off the galleons, many of which subsequently foundered in a storm, so that less than half of the Spanish fleet found its way home.

War with Spain was not the only outcome of the death of Mary Stuart, the Queen's ostensible heir. It also served to emphasize the problem of the succession, as aggravated by Elizabeth's failure to take a husband—Parliament was by now reconciled to the fact that the Queen had no real intention of ever marrying.

As always, there were a number of claimants, among them descendants of Henry VIII's two sisters, in the persons of Arabella Stuart and Catherine Grey. But at once the obvious and the most acceptable candidate was the Protestant offspring of a Catholic mother—Mary Stuart's son, James VI of Scotland,

[1] The English, who commanded no more than 21 warships of 200 tons or over, assisted by some armed merchant ships and ancillary vessels, were certainly outnumbered, though by no means as heavily as the figures might suggest. Of the 132 Spanish vessels, rather less than 40 were equipped for serious fighting, the rest being transport ships and attendant craft.

Nunney Castle, Somerset. A defended manor house of the late fourteenth century, protected by what is reputed to be the deepest moat in England. (*Photo :* Crown Copyright)

Deal Castle, Kent, one of the coastal fortresses built by Henry VIII. (*Photo :* Aerofilms and Aero Pictorial Ltd.)

The end of an era. Examples of the systematic slighting of Royalist strongholds by Cromwell's forces is to be seen (*above*) in the ruins of the once powerful Goodrich Castle, Herefordshire, and (*below*) in the remains of the fifteenth century defended manor house at Ashby-de-la-Zouch, Leicestershire, "the last great English fortress of the Middle Ages". (*Photos:* Aerofilms and Aero Pictorial Ltd.)

a choice which carried with it the hope that it would lead to the unification of the two kingdoms. And so it came about that, with the death of Elizabeth early in the morning of 24 March 1603, she was succeeded by a member of the House of Stuart who derived his claim to the throne from Margaret Tudor.

Chapter Six

Kingship at the Crossroads

I

WHEN IN 1567 Scotland's Queen Mary was compelled to abdicate in favour of her son, who thus became James VI, the boy was barely a year old, so that during the next decade the affairs of the northern kingdom remained in the hands of a succession of Regents, notably the Earls of Moray (James Stuart), Lennox (Matthew Stuart) and Morton (James Douglas). After the downfall and execution of Morton in 1581, the young King was dominated for a while by his kinsman Esmé Stuart, who had arrived from France two years earlier, secretly intent upon winning Scotland back for Mary, or at any rate for Rome. But the Protestant lords anticipated these designs by forcibly breaking-up the association and driving the royal favourite into exile.

One of the monarch's tutors during his boyhood had been George Buchanan, a noted scholar and theologian who was both an unrelenting taskmaster and a stern disciplinarian. His despotism unintentionally instilled in his pupil a lasting distaste for Presbyterianism and the Scottish Kirk, and, as soon as he was old enough to do so, the King set about freeing himself from the grip of his elders, that he might pursue a policy of his own choosing. In the course of a prolonged struggle he was able to make himself independent of the rival politico-religious groups which sought to dominate him, with such success that, by the end of the century, he was firmly in control of some four-fifths of his turbulent kingdom.

This he achieved by skilfully playing one faction against another, even to the extent of communicating with the Pope, who was hopefully led to believe that, notwithstanding his correspondent's Protestant upbringing, a lasting revival of Catholicism in Scotland was not entirely beyond the bounds of Divine intention. But by this time James's primary concern was how to ensure his eventual succession to the throne of England, and his next move was to conclude an alliance with Queen Elizabeth, in the expectation that, by so doing, he would have more to gain (and certainly less to lose) than by attempting to enlist the support of her enemies. In the event, the strength of the new Anglo-Scottish understanding was severely tested a year or so later, when the King received word of the trial and impending execution of Mary Stuart. Acutely aware that too vehement a protest on his part might well endanger his territorial ambitions, his letters of deprecation contained nothing that could be construed as a threatening attitude. After all, and mother or no mother, it was not as though he had ever known the deposed Queen whose Crown had been thrust upon his infant head.

The beheading of Mary took place at Fotheringay Castle on 9 February 1587. As a result of the decapitation, James had to deal with much restiveness at home, but he managed to control the hotheads who wanted to go to war with England. He did write to Elizabeth, however, suggesting that the hurt she had been compelled to inflict upon the honour of her faithful ally could best be salved by the making of some material recompense—such as his formal recognition as the lawful and nearest successor to the English throne. But the Queen was not to be beguiled into naming James as her heir, and she would add nothing to an earlier undertaking that any right or title he might have in the matter would receive consideration when the time arrived—always providing that he continued to conduct himself in a friendly manner towards the realm over which he aspired to rule.

None of this brought much comfort to James, the uncertainty of whose position was increased when Robert Parsons, a well-known English Jesuit, mischievously ventured to publish a discourse on the subject of Elizabeth's successor. He gave it as his considered opinion that the religious views of a claimant were of far greater weight and importance than mere hereditary rights, and, having thus dismissed all the Protestant candidates, James in particular among them, he nominated in their place two descendants of John of Gaunt, in the persons of His Catholic Majesty King Philip II of Spain, and his daughter, the Infanta Isabelle Clara Eugenia!

But there was, of course, not the slightest prospect of either of these nominees attaining Elizabeth's throne, nor did an acceptable alternative exist to the needlessly apprehensive James. And although the Queen continued to decline to make provision for her passing, her leading minister took it upon himself to approach and reach a secret understanding with the Scottish monarch. In acting thus, Sir Robert Cecil (first Earl of Salisbury and son of Lord Burleigh) made it clear that he intended no disloyalty to his mistress, whose resolute refusal to contemplate her own demise compelled him, as a responsible statesman, to anticipate the event by quietly making the necessary preparations behind her royal back. As a result of this foresight, James VI of Scotland was proclaimed James I of England in London within eight hours of Elizabeth's death, though it was several days of hard riding later that the tidings were received by the new monarch himself.

At first, James was highly gratified by the attentions of the enthusiastic crowds which gathered to greet him as he journeyed south. But once his destination had been reached, the adulation of the public, and his being made an object of curiosity whenever he appeared out of doors, soon lost its charm. On his being told that nothing pleased the people more than an opportunity to see their King at close quarters, his eventual reaction was to offer to pull down his breeches, that the onlookers might be vouchsafed the added pleasure of a sight of the royal anatomy not normally exposed to view. But if James was quick enough to tire of the attentions of his subjects, it was not long before he, in turn, succeeded in making an adverse impression on some of them.

It was not merely that his personal appearance bordered on the grotesque (he had a shambling gait, a tongue that was too large for his mouth, and a tendency to dribble as he spoke) or that to the more sophisticated Londoners he seemed uncouth and sadly lacking in the polished manners of the English Court. The real trouble, it soon transpired, was that James was both the most learned and the most pedantic monarch who had ever been crowned at Westminster. Such were his powers of erudition, indeed, that, numbered among his literary outpourings, were two books on the subject of kingship—*The True Law of Free Monarchies* (published anonymously in 1598) and *Basilikon Doron* (which followed in 1599)—wherein he expounded his exalted ideas about the God-given nature of royal authority. The author of these works, it appeared, was conscious, not only of his own infallibility, but of a divinely inspired mission to rule.

Having regard to his success in imposing his will upon his unruly Scottish subjects, there was some excuse, perhaps, for the high esteem in which he held his own capabilities. As for his new responsibilities in England, his attitude towards these was that he had come to the throne, not as a novice Prince stepping into the shoes of his father, but as a practised ruler who had been a King for thirty-eight of his thirty-nine years. In short, as he loftily informed the assembled members of Parliament, he was an old and experienced monarch, who could justly claim to be an acknowledged expert in the art of government. But what he completely failed to appreciate was that there was small comparison between the state of affairs as he had found them in Scotland and those which he now had to face in England.

At least one familiar aspect, however, was provided by contending religious groups whose members the Elizabethan compromise had failed to satisfy, and who now looked to the new monarch for satisfaction. On the one hand were extreme or erstwhile Catholics who were opposed to the break with Rome, or who at any rate considered that it had gone too far, while on the other were implacable anti-papalists who claimed that the process had not yet gone far enough. For their part, these advocates of further purification (hence the term Puritan) were quickly disillusioned. On their petitioning the King, a conference was held at Hampton Court, at which an incautious reference to Presbyterianism so antagonized James that, with the declaration "No Bishop, no King", he warned the malcontents among his audience that, unless they conformed to the usages of the Established Church, he would harry them out of the kingdom.

The Catholics were equally disappointed in their expectations, even though there was a temporary lifting of the recusancy fines they had been required to pay. As it was, the outcome of this concession soon led to its withdrawal. So many adherents of Rome who had hitherto concealed their allegiance now disclosed it, that James took alarm, ordered all priests out of the country and gave instructions that the collecting of fines should be resumed. In the face of what were considered to be these unduly oppressive measures, a group of Catholic gentry—

Robert Catesby, Thomas Winter, Thomas Percy, Guy Fawkes, and others—decided to rid themselves of the King and his ministers by blowing up the Houses of Parliament, though not before an attempt was made to save the life of a brother-in-law of one of the conspirators by sending him a cryptic message, warning him not to attend the opening ceremony which was due to take place on 5 November:

> Think not slightly of this advertisement but retire yourself into the country, where you may expect the event in safety, for though there be no appearance of any stir, yet I say they shall receive a terrible blow this Parliament, and they shall not see who hurts them.

It was by way of this note that the Government learned of its peril, and, thus put on its guard, was able to foil what inevitably came to be dubbed the Gunpowder Plot.[1]

Puritan hostility towards James was equally implacable, if somewhat less bloodthirsty. After the rebuff he administered at Hampton Court, the King had to face the reformers in the Commons, where they were to be found in large numbers. And as James was soon to discover, a noticeable decline in the influence of the Upper House during the preceding century had coincided with a steady increase in the power and prestige of the Commons.[2]

It had long been recognized that government was the prerogative of the King, who could consult Parliament if he were so disposed, but whose usual reason for summoning that body was, not to ask the advice of its members, but to seek additional supplies of money. Thanks to this recurrent royal need, down through the years one privilege after another had been gained by the assembly in return for the provision of financial aid until,

[1] In more recent times, the Jesuit John Gerard, in his *What Was Gunpowder Plot?* (Osgood McIlvaine & Co., London, 1897) developed the theory that in fact there had been no such conspiracy, and dismissed the affair as a governmental invention designed to discredit the Catholics. It is perhaps unnecessary to add that this is a thesis which does not bear examination. No sooner did it appear than it was refuted by Samuel R. Gardiner in his *What Gunpowder Plot Was* (Longmans, Green & Co., London, 1897).

[2] Thanks to the dissolution of the monasteries, the Upper House had been deprived of abbatial representation, one effect of which was to give rise to an assembly in which the Lords Spiritual found themselves outnumbered by the Lords Temporal, a situation which prevails to this day. Thus, the first Parliament of Henry VII could boast two Archbishops, nineteen Bishops, and twenty-eight Abbots, but only twenty-nine lay peers. By contrast, that of James I contained eighty-two lay peers and a mere twenty-six head of Bishop. Membership of the House of Commons at this time approached the five hundred mark.

with the advent of Henry VII, Parliamentary recognition of his claim to the throne had taken precedence over hereditary right.

If at this time members of the Commons were consciously striving for a more direct say in the affairs of the nation, it was an ambition which received little encouragement in the reigns which immediately followed. And yet the Tudors, despite their autocratic ways, had been sensible enough to use their theoretically despotic powers with discretion, to cajole rather than to threaten when resistance was encountered, and even to give way on occasion in the face of determined Parliamentary opposition.

James Stuart had other ideas. Imbued as he was with the

FIGURE 16
Chepstow Castle, Monmouthshire. A view of the east front (from a photograph).

notion of the divine right of Kings, he regarded himself as the chosen instrument of Heaven, as a terrestrial agent of the Almighty whose slightest wish was not to be questioned, but instantly obeyed. In such challenging circumstances, a serious clash with the Commons was sooner or later inevitable.

The first Parliament of the reign, which met on 19 March, 1604, was dissolved on 9 February 1611, and it was in the course of its five sessions (the second of which was to have been greeted by the explosion of thirty-six barrels of gunpowder) that a series of preliminary skirmishes occurred over procedural and other matters. During these discussions, the King, in return for the surrender of certain of his feudal privileges, had been offered an assured income, sufficient for all his needs. James, however, declined to be bribed into relinquishing any of his God-given rights, and the proposed Great Contract fell through.

This offer to place the royal revenue on a sound and realistic basis had been a tacit acknowledgement of the fact that not all the King's troubles were of his own making. In England, the previous century had been an era of mounting inflation, in part the result of Henry VIII's lavish spending on military preparations. The great wealth this monarch had inherited from his father soon vanished, whereupon Thomas Wolsey began to enrich the depleted treasury by reducing the silver content of the coinage. Further debasements followed, to be matched by an inevitable rise in commodity prices, a dual process which continued until, in 1560, Elizabeth's Secretary of State was compelled to call in the devalued currency and issue sound money in its place. But this reform, long overdue, coincided with an unprecedented influx of precious metals into the European economy from Spanish possessions overseas, so that no lasting benefit was achieved.[1]

By the time James arrived on the London scene, eager to exchange the poverty of Scotland for the comparative affluence of England, it was to find that Elizabeth had bequeathed to him a debt of £400,000, a totally inadequate income, and a legislature whose members were not prepared to advance him the additional sums he needed except at a price he was reluctant to pay. And when in 1614 the King called his second (the so-called Addled) Parliament, it was dissolved after a few weeks of quarrelling over money matters without a single enactment having been made. Moreover, so acrimonious had the debate become that, at the end of the proceedings, four members of the Commons were confined in the Tower.

For the next seven years James struggled along as best he could, aided and abetted by his favourites Robert Carr (promoted Lord Rochester and Duke of Somerset) and, after the downfall of this upstart following his involvement in a murder, the equally notorious George Villiers who, in the course of a phenomenal rise in the royal esteem, successively became Master of the Horse, Knight of the Garter, Baron, Viscount,

[1] It has been estimated that, in the year 1500, the total amount of gold in Europe amounted to less than 200 tons. By the end of the century, the figure had more than trebled, virtually the whole of the increase having come from the Americas. The supply of silver obtained from this source was equally prodigious—£1,500,000,000 worth of the metal having been received from Peru alone!

Earl, Marquis, Lord High Admiral, and finally, Duke of Buckingham.

Until the end of 1620, James somehow managed to live on the proceeds of forced loans, the sale of titles, and other dubious money-raising devices.[1] Then, faced with the prospect of financing an armed intervention in Bohemia, he had no option but to summon Parliament, which met on 20 January. But when at length the Commons sought to concern itself with the foreign policies it was being called upon to finance by petitioning the King, James greeted the twelve members of the deputation with a derisive "Bring stools for these ambassadors!" and intimated that such matters were none of Parliament's business.

The reply of the Commons was to make the famous Protestation of 18 December 1621, asserting that:

> The liberties, franchises, privileges, and jurisdictions of Parliament are the ancient and undoubted birthright and inheritance of the subjects of England, and that the arduous and urgent affairs concerning the King, State, and defence of the Realm, and of the Church of England, and the maintenance and making of laws, the redress of mischiefs and grievances which daily happen within this Realm, are proper subjects and matter of counsel and debate in Parliament.

What James thought of this far-reaching claim was quickly made evident. With his own hands he tore out the page on which it had been inscribed in the Journal of the House, and then dismissed the Assembly. But this was by no means the end of the affair, even though a little over three years and one more Parliament later, such mundane matters had ceased to concern the monarch. For his successor, a momentous issue had been raised concerning the government of the country: Was the will of the King, or that of Parliament, ultimately to prevail?

II

In his early twenties King James had married Anne of Denmark, by whom he had Henry (who died at the age of

[1] A peerage and a seat in the House of Lords was to be had for £10,000, while for the lesser fry among the socially minded, the hereditary title of baronet, retailing at a tenth of that sum, was specially created. Although the sale of honours still continues, such transactions are now performed less openly (under the guise, say, of a contribution to party funds) albeit on occasion even this procedure can get out of hand, as witness the scandals allegedly associated with the David Lloyd George administration of 1922.

nineteen), a second son (his successor, Charles I), and a daughter, Elizabeth, whose marriage to Frederick V, the Elector Palatine, involved her father in Bohemian affairs. In 1622, partly with a view to finding an ally for his son-in-law, who was in the midst of fighting a losing battle against the Catholic Emperor Maximilian of Bavaria, James gave his blessing to a proposed marriage between his surviving son and the Spanish Infanta. But when, in the following year, Prince Charles and the Duke of Buckingham journeyed to Madrid to make arrangements for the match, the negotiations had broken down because of insurmountable religious difficulties, accompanied by a belated realization that the wily Spaniards (who had not the slightest intention of assisting the cause of the Protestant Elector Palatine) were merely playing for time.

This duplicity so incensed the Prince and his companion that they returned home intent upon war, and with little difficulty gained royal support for a new foreign policy. This entailed the formation of an alliance against Spain, to be promoted by the betrothal of Charles to the French Princess Henrietta Maria, sister of King Louis XIII, regardless of the fact that this was a union which also promised to involve the making of extensive concessions to Roman Catholicism. The marriage treaty was nevertheless signed and ratified towards the end of 1624, and, with the death of James in the following March, it was as King of England that Charles wed his fifteen-years-old bride by proxy in Paris. Six weeks later his wife arrived at Dover, accompanied by more than 400 attendants, not to mention twenty-nine priests and a Bishop. This retinue, as embarrassing for its content as it was for its size, soon found its way back to France at the insistence of the groom, who had in mind the interests of domestic peace at the Palace as much as the susceptibilities of his Queen's Protestant subjects throughout the Realm.

At the onset of his reign Charles had to face a hostile Commons at home and a series of expensive foreign commitments abroad. Being desperately in need of money from the one with which to finance the other, he summoned his first Parliament forthwith (June 1625), but so antagonized his audience by loftily declining to discuss foreign affairs that he was voted but a fraction of the sum demanded. Members then went on to discuss tunnage (on wine and beer) and poundage (on dry goods), the traditional grant of customs duties which, since the days of Edward III, it had been customary to bestow upon a new monarch for the duration of his reign. The unco-operative Charles received the donation for one year only, nor was his temper improved when a second session, held at Oxford at the beginning of August, was equally unproductive. On his encountering a storm of protest over Buckingham's gross mismanagement of the war against Spain, the King declared Parliament dissolved.

Still in need of supplies, Charles called a second Parliament in February of the following year, though not before he had taken the precaution of ensuring that several of his most troublesome critics would not be present, by arranging for their appointment as sheriffs, i.e. to an office which would preclude their attendance at Westminster. This subterfuge availed its author little. The Commons obstinately declined to discuss the King's wants before airing its many grievances, including the manifest shortcomings of Buckingham. The King would have none of this, and sharply reminded the gathered members that

> Parliaments are altogether in my power for the calling, sitting, and dissolution; therefore as I find the fruits of them good or evil, they are to continue or not to be.

The Lord High Admiral was nevertheless impeached, and, to save the Duke, Parliament was dismissed, still without there having been any grant of supply. Charles now tried to augment his income by collecting tunnage and poundage in the absence of formal sanction, coupled with attempts to obtain from the counties what were euphemistically described as Free Gifts, and when this expedient failed, by the undisguised compulsion of a Forced Loan. The summoning of a third Parliament became unavoidable, however, when England, through the combined folly of Buckingham and the King, drifted into war with France, whose Cardinal Richelieu was not the man to accept treatment, even from a supposed ally, which included flagrant violations of a marriage treaty, the stopping and searching of French merchantmen on the high seas (on the grounds that they might be carrying Spanish goods), and the encouraging of the Protestant Huguenots to revolt against their King.

As on previous occasions, the Commons insisted upon considering grievances before supplies, though eventually the King was offered the considerable sum of five subsidies (worth some £350,000), subject to his accepting a Petition of Right. This called, among other things, for an end to compulsory gifts, loans, benevolences or taxes without the consent of Parliament, and to the arbitrary imprisonment of those who refused to meet such unlawful demands. But no sooner had Charles given his reluctant consent to the Petition than he was assailed for violating its provisions by his unauthorized collecting of tunnage and poundage! This was an interpretation which the outraged monarch absolutely refused to accept, and Parliament was prorogued.

In the interval between the ending of this session and the start of the next, the Buckingham problem was resolved by the assassination of that gentleman by John Felton, an aggrieved army officer. But Buckingham's removal brought no peace to Westminster, for, no sooner did the second session begin (20 January 1629), than it led to an uproar which ended in an adjournment, though not before the Speaker, Sir John Finch, had been prevented from vacating the Chair (by two members who forcibly held him down) while a resolution was passed condemning innovations in religion and the unlawful collecting of tunnage and poundage. This act of defiance was answered by the arrest and imprisonment of nine of the ringleaders, and by Parliament's dissolution. It also left Charles convinced that the Commons was intent upon making the King's government impossible, and so decided him to rule alone.

This he contrived to do for more than a decade, thanks to a belated show of wisdom in bringing to an end the ruinously expensive wars against France and Spain. By the end of 1630 peace had been negotiated with both countries, thus allowing the English monarch a reasonable prospect of raising sufficient supplies to meet his normal expenditure from non-Parliamentary sources. Tunnage and poundage continued to be collected, while more novel expedients included the revival of a long-forgotten statute (dating back more than 350 years, to the time of Edward I!) in the shape of an enactment which required freeholders of land of an annual value of £20 either to accept the responsibilities of knighthood or pay a fine.

Considerable sums were also obtained by other questionable means. These, if not wholly illegal, were certainly not in keeping with the constitutional developments of the times—the imposition of ship-money throughout the land (a tax hitherto levied only on coastal towns); the threatened sequestration of family estates on the grounds that they belonged to the Crown (but which the owners were graciously allowed to retain by remitting a stipulated amount); the granting of monopolies, e.g. for the manufacture of soap (the law merely forbade the making of such exclusive arrangements with individuals; it was evaded by the formation of Companies); and the inflicting of heavy penalties upon those brought before the Star Chamber and its ecclesiastical counterpart, the Court of High Commission (which judicial committees, composed of subservient judges, became instruments of legalized robbery and extortion, not above resorting to torture and mutilation).

Prominent among these dispensers of injustice was William Laud, a stern disciplinarian and a cleric who had found high favour with Charles, by whom, after a series of rapid preferments, he was appointed Archbishop of Canterbury in 1633. His High Church views were anathema to the Puritans, while his attempt to introduce ceremonial uniformity of worship gave rise to serious disturbances in Scotland, where the Covenanters (members of the National League and Covenant) bound themselves to reject all such religious innovations. Feeling ran high throughout the northern kingdom, and in Glasgow a meeting of the dissenters voted for the abolition of episcopacy, while, by 1639, the inhabitants of Edinburgh had become sufficiently roused to seize the castle and raise an army.

Charles marched to meet the insurgents, with a force so inadequate that, on encountering them, he was compelled to agree to a truce. Thus outmanœuvred, but determined to obtain satisfaction, he turned in desperation to the English Parliament. But that obstructive body, after being ignored for eleven years, was less than ever inclined to assist the King until its long outstanding complaints were settled, and, as soon as this became apparent, it was dissolved (The Short Parliament, 13 April–5 May 1640).

Unfortunately for Charles, although the assembly had been dismissed, his troubles remained. In August, the impatient Scots once again set out to invade England and, encountering no effective resistance, quickly occupied most of Northumberland. The intruders not only insisted that the King redress their wrongs, but that he do so with the advice of the legislative body he had recently dissolved. And, to reinforce this demand, it was intimated that, until satisfaction was received, they proposed to stay where they were—at the King's expense!

The Fifth (and fateful Long) Parliament of the reign thus came into being on 3 November 1640, and it was destined to outlive its convener. The proceedings began with an onslaught on the King's chief advisers which that help-seeking monarch was powerless to prevent, and both Archbishop Laud and the Earl of Strafford were impeached and consigned to the Tower. As Thomas Wentworth, Strafford had earlier been prominent as a Parliamentary champion, but had sided with the King to show his disapproval of the Petition of Right. Charles had welcomed and ennobled this unexpected ally, and such was the feeling against him in the House that the impeachment was dropped and his conviction and execution ensured by the substitution of a Bill of Attainder, whereby the accused could be sentenced to death without the tiresome formality of a trial. So much for the Parliamentary liberties of the subject!

Emboldened by the weakness of the King's position, as shown by his readiness to sacrifice a faithful servant ("My Lord Strafford's condition," Charles is reported to have remarked as he signed the death warrant, "is more happy than mine"), his enemies went on to extract one concession after another, obtaining the royal assent to the Triennial Act (which required the summoning of Parliament every three years, with or without the approval of the Crown) and the abolition of the Courts of Star Chamber and High Commission. There was even a move to extirpate the episcopacy (the so-called Root-and-Branch Bill). This proposal, however, led to a protracted argument which was still unsettled when the session came to an end.

The Long Parliament had no sooner reopened (20 October 1641) than news was received of a serious uprising in Ireland, accompanied by the wholesale massacre of Protestants. To suppress the rebels would mean raising an army, and the Commons was reluctant to see such a force placed under royal command. A way round this difficulty was sought by the introduction of a motion requiring the King to employ ministers in whom the House had confidence, in effect a demand that officers of the Crown should be responsible to Parliament, not to the King. So revolutionary was this proposal considered by many members that it was passed by no more than forty-one votes, while in a subsequent debate concerning a Grand Remonstrance of Parliamentary grievances, the majority in favour dropped to eleven.

This evidence of mounting disagreement in the Lower House encouraged Charles to endeavour to reassert his authority. But, instead of adopting a conciliatory policy, which might well have brought many members to his side, he chose to order the impeachment of Lord Kimbolton and five members of the Commons, on the grounds that they had been in treasonable correspondence with the Scottish rebels. Jealous of its privileges, the House resisted an attempt by the Serjeant-at-Arms to arrest the accused, whereupon Charles, at the head of several hundred armed followers, himself tried to take the men by force, only to find that they had escaped down the Thames by boat.

In the face of such extreme provocation, armed conflict between King and Parliament now appeared imminent, in anticipation of which the monarch left London for the North, taking the Great Seal with him. He established his headquarters at York, where he was afterwards joined by his Parliamentary supporters—thirty-two peers and sixty-five members of the Commons. But it was not until Monday 22 August 1642, that the royal standard was raised at Nottingham Castle as a signal that the military phase of the struggle was about to begin.

The territory held by the opposing factions was about equal in area, the country being divided diagonally by a line extending from Hull to Gloucester, with the Royalist (Cavalier) forces in occupation of the northern part as far as the Scottish border, while the southern region was dominated by the Parliamentarians (Roundheads—a reference to the close-cut hair style favoured by the Puritans). The kingdom was also socially divided, in that the lesser gentry, the Anglican clergy, and the peasantry tended to side with the King, while the great nobles and members of the middle class, for the most part, supported Parliament.

Neither of the contending armies was very large, and their early movements took the form of raids and indecisive skirmishes in which the northern forces, under such dashing Cavaliers as Prince Rupert (the third son of Charles's sister Elizabeth) gained an initial advantage for the King, thanks in part to the incompetent generalship of their opponents. By the end of 1643, the Royalists controlled some three-quarters of England and Wales, a circumstance which led Parliament to enlist the aid of the Scots (with conversion to Presbyterianism as the price!), whereupon the King responded by calling upon the Catholic insurgents in Ireland for help, thereby alienating not a few of his English followers.

The Parliamentary cause was also assisted by the advent of new military leaders, outstanding among whom was a distant relative of Henry VIII's leading minister, one Oliver Cromwell. In a crucial encounter at Marston Moor (2 July 1644) Cromwell and his mounted Ironsides routed Prince Rupert, and thus gained control of York and Newcastle, though it was not until after the decisive Battle of Naseby, nearly a year later, that the King was forced to acknowledge defeat, which he did by surrendering to the Scots, by whom he was taken to Newcastle.

Charles was handed over to the Parliamentarians at the beginning of 1647, who confined him in Holmby House, Northamptonshire. But although a prisoner and at the mercy of his enemies, he still entertained hopes of exploiting religious differences between them—already there were signs of a breach between the Presbyterians in Parliament (who were clamouring for the demobilization of the militia) and the religious Independents of the Army (who were in no hurry to see themselves disbanded). Cromwell, who had so far remained aloof, decided to intervene in an attempt to control what he was not able to prevent. His first move was to acquire the person of the King, whereafter the Army moved into London and virtually took over the government of the country.

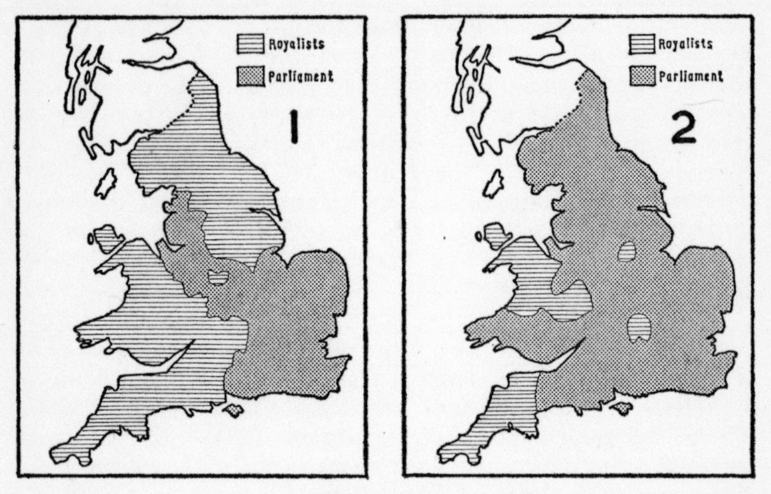

FIGURE 17

King *v*. Parliament. Map showing the areas held by Parliament (1) at the end of 1643; and (2) at the end of 1645. (Based on information from various sources.)

As for Charles, he eventually found himself held at Hampton Court, in a not too rigorous captivity from which, towards the end of the year, he was assisted in making an escape to the Isle of Wight. This destination was seemingly an afterthought, for a flight to Jersey had originally been intended, and as a result of a change of plan, the royal refugee once again ended up a prisoner.

His new place of confinement was Carisbrooke Castle, an ancient stronghold dating back to the Conquest, when William Fitz Osbern ordered the construction of a motte at the site, placing it at the junction of two baileys. Subsequently, the lordship of the island was granted to the Richard de Redvers whose son sided with the Empress Maud against Stephen, an error of judgement which led to the loss of his castle at Exeter in 1136. After this, the defeated Baldwin de Redvers unsuccessfully sought to continue his defiance from Carisbrooke, where (so the author of *Gesta Stephani* informs us) he was possessed of "a stately castle built of stone", a reference which points to the existence of a shell keep upon the mound at this period. In later years, a massive gatehouse and other features were added, including protective walls which in the reign of Elizabeth were enclosed by ramparts and bastions for artillery.

Carisbrooke thus emerged as a formidable and well protected fortress, which at the onset of the Civil War was seized and held by Parliamentary forces, its Royalist Governor being replaced by the Earl of Pembroke, who in September 1647 was succeeded by Colonel Robert Hammond. No doubt it was considered by those who had organized the escape from Hampton Court that the Colonel, who happened to be the brother of the King's Chaplain, would treat the fugitive with leniency and respect, and might even be prevailed upon to assist the royal party in making its way abroad. But the Governor, though not unsympathetic towards the King, was also mindful of his duty to the Army, so that Charles once again found himself under restraint, though at first he was allowed considerable freedom to move about, and was permitted to correspond with friends and enemies alike.

Characteristically, Charles repaid this last privilege, not only by entering into negotiations with Parliament, but also by making conflicting promises to the Scots, who were thereby induced to cross the border on his behalf, and who actually succeeded in reaching Preston before they were met and routed by Cromwell. At Carisbrooke, meanwhile, there had been several attempts to secure the release of the King, in one of which a certain Captain Barnabus Burley, after trying in vain to rouse the islanders on the captive's behalf, had answered for his failure to do so with his life.

Despite the serious limitations which were then placed upon his movements, the King found new would-be rescuers in Henry Firebrace (page of the royal bedchamber) and other of his loyal attendants, who were encouraged by the promise of assistance from a number of leading local inhabitants, one of whom undertook to provide horses, and another a boat. The arrangement was that during the night of 20 March, the King should let himself down from his bedroom window with the aid of a rope. Firebrace, waiting in the darkness below, would then escort his companion to the outer wall of the castle, over which he would be assisted and met by mounted guides on the far side.

But for one small miscalculation, the scheme might well have succeeded. The window of the royal bedchamber was barred, and Firebrace had earlier suggested a precautionary widening of the space between the metal uprights. The King, however, replied that he had already tested the existing opening with his head, and confidently asserted that where that would go, his body could undoubtedly follow. But in the event, this reasoning proved to be unsound, and on the night of the escape, the over-confident Charles found himself stuck so fast that it was only with the utmost difficulty that he was able to extricate himself and return disconsolately to his prison bed!

Plans (involving the use of aquafortis) were then made to deal with the "obstacle that hindered". But by this time, word of what was afoot was known to too many persons for it to remain hidden from the authorities, and when (on 28 May)

FIGURE 18

Carisbrooke Castle, I.O.W. A view of the Gatehouse (late fifteenth century). Other features are an eleventh-century motte with a twelfth-century shell keep on its summit. (From a photograph.)

the King made a second attempt to gain his freedom, it was to discover that the reception committee which awaited him was composed, not of his friends, but of his guards.

The Army Council now decided that the time had come to put an end to royal intrigues and escape attempts, and on 1 December the captive was taken from Carisbrooke to Hurst Castle, a small and isolated fortress located at the end of a long causeway on the other side of the Solent. In these cramped and uncomfortable quarters the King remained until 19 December, when he was moved to Windsor, from where, a fortnight earlier, an armed force had marched upon London.

Here, in anticipation of what was to follow, troops had been stationed at the entrance to the House of Commons, with instructions to deny admittance to all who were known to favour Presbyterianism or the monarchy, the fifty-three Independents who were allowed to take their seats constituting the derisively named Rump Parliament. On 1 January, at the behest of the Army, this body dutifully passed an ordinance to establish a special tribunal to try the King. The Lords, however, rejected the proposal, whereupon the Lower House resolved that henceforth "whatsoever is enacted, or declared for law by the Commons in Parliament assembled, hath the force of law". A High Court of Justice for the trial of the King was then set up, the proceedings beginning on 20 January. The outcome was hardly in doubt, and by the end of the month Charles had been condemned and beheaded.

There was another and scarcely less mournful outcome of the struggle, at the onset of which Prince Rupert had urged upon the King the desirability of manning all available strong-points, so as to compel their enemies to wear themselves out with siege warfare. Thanks to this obstructive policy, time and again in the course of the fighting, the Roundhead advance was impeded by the spirited defence of some moated mansion or ancient castle, which fortified structures thus came fleetingly into their own once again—many of them to sustain great and lasting damage as a result.

One of the first castles to be lost by the Cavaliers (with no great show of resistance on the part of its garrison, as it happened) was Farnham, in Surrey. But many others—Corfe, Donnington, Chepstow among them—proved to be much more tenaciously held, and each had to be closely besieged before the defenders could be starved into submission, or the walls behind which they sheltered breached by heavy siege guns, and the place taken by assault. To this last category belonged the Basingstoke residence of John Paulet, fifth Marquis of Winchester, which early in the conflict was marked down by Parliament as a hot-bed of Royalism and Romanism.

The Basing House of this period consisted not of one building, but of two. The Old House, known also as the Citadel, was a great circular structure standing on top of the earthen mound of a Norman motte and bailey, this last, presumably, the handiwork of Hugh de Port, to whom the district was granted after the Conquest. The Patent Rolls for the year 1349 make a reference to the Old Castle of Basing, and subsequently (by way of his wife Constance) this edifice came into the possession of a certain John Paulet. Three generations later, Sir William Paulet became the first Marquis of Winchester in 1551, and it was he who built the New House adjacent to the Old, choosing as a site an area of the bailey lying to the north-east of the Citadel.

Although, as a result of the many attacks made upon it nearly a century later, Basing House was finally razed to the ground, at least two drawings made at the time of the Civil War have survived, and happily these provide some indication of the appearance of the establishment. One of the sketches, an engraving by Wenceslaus Hollar (who was among those captured when the House fell) is taken from the south, and shows both Royalist and Roundhead defence works in the foreground. An archaeological investigation undertaken at the site some years ago, however, has revealed a number of discrepancies, e.g. no evidence of the existence of the octagonal turrets shown at the angles of the New House could be found, while a round tower which the artist labelled as "halfe battered donne" appears to have been rectangular—its base, at all events, was not circular. The other illustration (preserved in Warner's *Hampshire*), also dating from towards the end of the siege, relies even more upon the imagination, in that it shows the building as being protected by a non-existent wet moat.

Basing first came under attack in July 1643, when it was approached by a troop of Parliamentarians under Colonel Richard Norton. These intruders were soon driven off, however, by the musket fire of the six gentlemen and their servants who were then in residence, after which foretaste of trouble to come considerable effort was made to strengthen the existing fortifications, and to add outworks which enclosed an area of some fourteen acres.

The timeliness of these precautions was shown in the following November, when Sir William Waller arrived on the scene, armed with five guns of small bore and a demi-cannon capable of throwing a 24-lb. shot.[1] After attempts to demolish the gatehouse with the aid of this weapon had failed, Waller retired to nearby Basingstoke to regroup, and returned a few days later at the head of more than 6,000 infantry and five regiments of dragoons. He also brought back with him ten guns, ample ammunition, and scaling ladders.

Led by the Marquis, the defenders, now about 400 strong, nevertheless repelled the attack which followed, bravely assisted

[1] In his *Castles and Cannon*, B. H. St. J. O'Neil lists the following ranges as those attainable at the time of the Civil War. The distances given refer respectively to point-blank range and an elevation of ten degrees:

Falcon (2½-inch calibre): 320 and 1,920 yards;
Saker (3½-inch calibre): 360 and 2,170 yards;
Demi-culverin (4-inch calibre): 400 and 2,400 yards;
Culverin (5½-inch calibre): 460 and 2,650 yards.

by the ladies of the household, who busied themselves casting bullets from lead stripped from roof and turrets. The next day unexpectedly brought relief, for heavy and continuous rainfall so added to the discomfiture of the besiegers that the assault was called off.

Basing was again attacked in the following year, after it had become a rallying point for defeated Cavalier contingents from surrounding areas. On this occasion, a close siege was maintained for more than five months, and might well have brought about the eventual surrender of the fortress, had not outside help arrived in the person of Sir Henry Gage and his men.

By now supremely confident of his ability to withstand any attack, the Marquis boldly declared his intention of maintaining his position indefinitely. But he reckoned without the growing determination of his enemies, or the capabilities of the New Model Army, and the year 1645 found Oliver Cromwell engaged in a methodical reduction of those Royalist garrisons which were still holding out in Wiltshire and Hampshire. After taking Devizes and forcing the surrender of Winchester Castle (5 October), he turned his attention to Basing House, and so sealed its fate.

The place had already been invested for some weeks by Colonel Dalbier (Dol Beere) when Cromwell arrived, bringing with him a train of siege guns, including cannon and demi-cannon. On the garrison refusing to surrender, the fortress was subjected to a sustained bombardment and its walls breached. What was to prove to be the final assault was launched at 6 o'clock on the morning of 14 October, in the course of which the New House was stormed and taken. By 7.30 a.m. the Citadel had also been overwhelmed, the Marquis and some 200 of his followers being taken prisoner, among them the architect Inigo Jones, who at the age of seventy-two suffered the indignity of being bereft of his fine raiment and left with nothing more than a blanket to cover him.

According to one eyewitness, the ladies among the prisoners suffered likewise in the orgy of plundering which ensued, when "eight or nine gentlewomen of rank, running forth together, were entertained by the common soldiers somewhat coarsely", though it appears that the victims managed to escape from their persecutors with at least some clothes upon them. From these pleasurable activities, the attention of the troops then turned to the furniture and other contents, the total value of the loot thus obtained, much of it in the form of jewellery and plate, amounting to about a quarter of a million pounds.

To add to the prevailing terror and confusion, one of several fireballs used by the attackers continued to smoulder unnoticed throughout the day, until by nightfall the place was seen to be well alight. Too late, it was then discovered that many of the defenders had escaped immediate capture by taking to the cellars, from where their shrieks now reached the ears of an enemy who, though by no means indisposed to assist them, was powerless to help. Thereafter, faced by a blackened ruin which would have required many men to guard, Cromwell advocated its total destruction, and in the Parliamentary records for 15 October 1645, is to be found the entry:

> Resolved, that the house, garrison, and walls at Basing be forthwith slighted and demolished.

Even after the King at last acknowledged the inevitability of defeat by giving himself up to the Scots in the following May, not a few of the fortresses manned by his supporters continued to hold out, and it was only gradually that they were induced to end the hopeless struggle. The last of the purely English strongholds to remain in Royalist hands was Raglan, which surrendered on 19 August 1646. After this, the more remote castles of North Wales succumbed one by one—Flint on 24 August, Denbigh on 26 October, Conway on 18 December and in the following year, Holt on 19 January, Chirk on 28 February, Harlech on 13 March. Elsewhere, the fortified Scilly Isles, under the guardianship of Sir John Grenville, continued to offer defiance until 1651!

In view of the stubborn resistance offered by so many of these strongholds, Parliament decided that, with certain exceptions, the castles now under its control should be rendered incapable of further defence. And in accordance with this decision, there was begun a widespread programme of destruction, systematically undertaken, which left many a once fine and formidable structure no more than a useless, if picturesque, ruin.

III

Charles I was survived by half a dozen offspring—Charles and James (his eventual successors), Mary (Princess of Orange), Elizabeth, Henry (Duke of Gloucester), and Henrietta (Duchess of Orleans). But at the time of their father's execution, kingship was so discredited throughout the Realm that there was no immediate prospect of a return to monarchical rule. This became evident when the Rump Parliament formally abolished the title and office of King, together with the House of Lords, and further enacted that henceforth the people of England were to be ruled

> . . . as a Commonwealth and Free State by the supreme authority of this nation, the representatives of the people in Parliament.

The facts of the matter, however, suggested otherwise, for the Rump assembly was scarcely representative of the nation, nor did it exercise supreme authority, for it was dominated by the Army. What was in the process of being established, in effect, was not so much a democratic republic as a semi-religious, semi-military oligarchy.

Abroad, the new government was regarded askance by reason of its regicidal tendencies, and it soon found itself challenged on these grounds nearer home. In Ireland, the death of the King enabled the Marquis of Ormonde, who had been Lord Lieutenant under Charles, to unite Royalist and Catholic factions, a move which was countered by the arrival of Cromwell in Dublin with an army of 12,000 men. The rebels were crushed with a ruthless severity which was inspired by the, as yet, unavenged massacres of Protestants in 1641, and in less than a year the pacification of the island was complete.

By this time (June 1650) a more serious threat had arisen in Scotland, where the eldest son of England's executed monarch had landed (after a reluctant taking of the Covenant) and been acknowledged as King Charles II. His subsequent march southwards, however, came to an abrupt halt when Cromwell caught up with him at Worcester. Although Charles himself escaped capture, his cause was ruined, and after many romantic adventures, including a period of hiding spent among the branches of the Boscobel Oak, he succeeded in making his way to the Continent, there to linger in exile. Scotland, meanwhile, was subjected to the indignity of a Sassenach army of occupation whose Commander-in-Chief was a former Royalist officer, General George Monk.

In London, increasing friction between the Rump Parliament and the Army led to the emergence of Cromwell as the Lord Protector of England, Scotland, and Ireland towards the end of 1653. Thereafter, unsatisfactory attempts to combine authoritative rule with the existence of a legislative assembly were interrupted by the creation of military districts, each under the control of an officer with the rank of Major-General. However, the summoning of a third Cromwellian Parliament (made necessary for the usual reasons—the expense of a war, on this occasion against Spain) gave rise in the following year to the Humble Petition and Advice, in essence a plea for a return to a recognizable form of constitutional government with the Protector at its head performing the functions and bearing the title of King!

That the Army would never countenance such a proposal ensured that the country did not acquire an Oliver I and a Richard IV, though it was agreed that the eldest son of the Lord Protector should inherit his father's office, and that henceforth Parliament should once again consist of two Houses. But with Oliver Cromwell's death in 1658 the resignation of his successor soon followed, hastened by evidence of widespread public unrest. During a decade of the Puritanical dispensation, a host of time-honoured pastimes—cock-fighting and bear-baiting, horse racing and theatre going, swearing and ale drinking—had been discouraged or forbidden, and the less material delights of spiritual uplift offered in their stead. Thus the proposed return to a monarchical form of government had been a reflection of popular discontent with the present régime, sharpened by nostalgic memories of carefree days under Charles I, to which had since been added the possibility of a less Sabbatarian existence under Charles II.

A serious clash between the Army and the civil population was averted when General Monk marched his occupation troops from Scotland to London in support of the demand for an unfettered popular assembly. The outcome was the recall of the Long Parliament of 1648, for the dual purpose of appointing Monk as Commander-in-Chief and naming a date for the meeting of a freely elected gathering of the people. In accordance with an undertaking previously given, the brief session then ended in dissolution.

By this time Monk was persuaded that the restoration of the Stuarts was both feasible and desirable. An approach to Charles brought a promise that, not only would the events of the past be forgiven and forgotten, but that henceforth at least some regard would be paid to the wishes of the popular assembly. These assurances were conveyed to the new people's Convention when it met on 25 April 1660 (strictly, it was not a Parliament, since its members had not come together in answer to a royal summons). Both Houses were represented at this gathering, and, on the Lords voting that "according to the ancient and fundamental laws of this Kingdom, the government is and ought to be, by King, Lords, and Commons", the Lower House at once assented to the motion. On 8 May, Charles II was officially proclaimed King, and three weeks later his arrival in London on his thirtieth birthday, to the tumultuous applause of his subjects, gave notice to a wondering world that the bloodless restoration of the English monarchy was an accomplished fact.

IV

After his escape from the clutches of Cromwell at Worcester, Charles spent several poverty-stricken years in Paris before moving on to Cologne, Middelburg, and elsewhere. Finally, he settled in Holland, where, among a few devoted followers who administered to his daily wants and his nightly needs, was Lucy Walter, the ruined daughter of a ruined Royalist. In 1649, she gave birth to the future Duke of Monmouth, whose title she ensured by naming Charles as the putative father. He, being in no position to dispute the assertion, gallantly assumed responsibility for the child, whom he afterwards recognized to be of the royal blood, notwithstanding certain doubts which subsequently arose.[1]

If Charles's triumphant return to England in the guise of an unmarried father gave affront to the Puritans, his subsequent behaviour scandalized them even more, though the story that the amorous monarch celebrated his first night in London in the connubial embrace of the newly wed Barbara Villiers (whose husband, Roger Palmer, was rewarded with an earldom) may have had its origins in the over-exuberant reporting of an admiring chronicler. But the night of his arrival or not, in the course of the next decade the uninhibited Lady Barbara Castlemaine (afterwards Duchess of Cleveland) bore the King a succession of offspring, three of whom were sons, appropriately surnamed Fitzroy—Charles (Duke of Southampton), Henry (Duke of Grafton), and George (Duke of Northumberland).[2]

[1] Just as Charles did not confine his attentions to Lucy Walter, so she was not averse to the company of others. Among her paramours was Colonel Robert Sidney, to whom, it was noted in later years, the young Duke bore a striking and altogether remarkable resemblance.

[2] Although he acknowledged that either he or the Earl of Chesterfield was in all probability the father of her first child, Anne, in addition to which he accepted responsibility for Charles and George, the King was inclined to be somewhat dubious as to the paternity of Henry, which he at first attributed to one or other of Lady Barbara's non-monarchical admirers. These ranged from a professional strong man to the dramatist William Wycherley (whose first comedy, not inappropriately entitled *Love in a Wood*, was performed in 1671) and the handsome but impoverished John Churchill (whose boudoir services she rewarded with a douceur of £5,000 and an ensigncy in the Guards, thus setting him on the path to becoming the first Duke of Marlborough).

Charles decided to make Windsor his home, at any rate during the summer months, where the Castle, though it had ceased to be royal during the Civil War period, had earlier served as the principal residence of England's monarchs since the days of the Conquest, and which, as such, had undergone many alterations and improvements at the hands of successive tenants since the extensive renovations and additions ordered by Edward III. Thus Richard II (less than half a century later) had found it necessary to make emergency repairs to St. George's Chapel, which appeared to be in danger of imminent collapse. Henry VIII added a stone roof to this building, and elsewhere caused to be erected the great gateway which still bears his name, while his daughter Elizabeth also spent much money on the place.

With the outbreak of war between King and Parliament in August 1642, the Castle was at once occupied by Government forces under Colonel John Venn, it being recognized as being the "place of greatest strength in this part of the kingdom". Thereafter, apart from an unsuccessful attempt by Prince Rupert to recapture the stronghold later in the year, it ceased to play an active part in the struggle, serving merely as a prison for captive Royalists.

With the ending of hostilities, Parliament proposed to sell the Castle in order to raise much needed funds, and when this came to nothing, the premises were eventually taken over and used by Cromwell. But although there was evidently no intention of ordering the demolition of Windsor, neither was any attempt made to keep its buildings in a state of good repair, and when Charles II came to take possession of his ancestral home, he found it much dilapidated (St. George's Chapel was once again on the point of falling) and occupied by the homeless poor. After these unfortunates had been ejected, much needed repairs were carried out under the direction of Sir Christopher Wren who, as Master of the Works, redesigned the Castle interior, particular attention being paid to those rooms now known as the State Apartments. The work, which began early in 1661, continued for the next two years, and cost what was then the not inconsiderable sum of £2,743 15s. 5d.

In the political sphere, the accession of Charles was marked by the appointment of his brother James, Duke of York, as Lord High Admiral and Warden of the Cinque Ports, while George Monk (soon to be raised to the peerage as the Duke of Albemarle) was made Captain-General. For his Prime Minister and Lord Chancellor, the King relied upon the services of Sir Edward Hyde, his faithful companion and adviser during his years of exile, whom he created Lord Hyde towards the end of 1660, and in the following year raised to be the Earl of Clarendon.

The first (so-called Cavalier) Parliament of the reign, which assembled on 8 May 1661, proved to be overwhelmingly Royalist in sentiment, and in many ways so favourably disposed towards the monarchy that it was kept in being for the next eighteen years. From the onset, however, the new assembly proved to be as reactionary as it was Royalist, and certain of its measures designed to increase the authority of the Church of England were by no means pleasing to the King, whose religious sympathies inclined him towards Rome.

Between 1661 and 1665 a series of repressive measures were enacted—the Corporation Act (which, among other things, excluded all but members of the Established Church from the municipal corporations of the towns, a provision which incidentally affected the composition of the Commons, by way of borough elections); the Act of Uniformity (which required of clergy and teachers an unqualified acceptance of the Anglican Book of Common Prayer, and as a result of which more than 1,000 dissenting ministers relinquished their livings and their homes in protest); the Conventicle Act (which prohibited public meetings of more than five persons for purposes of worship not in accord with the established ritual); and the Five-Mile Act (which forbade nonconformist ministers to approach within five miles of any corporate town, or of any place where they had been preachers).

Although the King's chief minister was actually opposed to many of the stipulations contained in these harsh measures, the four Acts nevertheless came to be known as the Clarendon Code, and gained much unpopularity for their supposed sponsor. Again, the recent marriage of his daughter Anne to Charles's younger brother James (thus making him father-in-law to the heir to the throne) had provoked much jealousy in Court circles. And when, in the three years from 1665 onwards, London was successively threatened by another outbreak of the dreaded plague (in the course of which more than 50,000 people died), by a disastrous fire (whose flames swept through the heart of the city, destroying nearly 500 acres), and by the Dutch fleet (which sailed up the Thames and burned English warships which were laid-up in the Medway because of unpaid arrears in the seamen's wages), the obvious person to blame for these disasters was the luckless Earl of Clarendon.

His downfall was ensured by the fact that he had alienated Charles by his constant criticisms of that gay monarch's way of life, with particular reference to the royal preference for affairs of the heart to those of state, even though, in 1662, the King had obligingly done his part to ensure the succession by marrying the Princess Catherine of Braganza, daughter of John IV of Portugal. Naturally, this had in no way diminished his interest in other ladies of the Court, and when Frances Teresa Stuart had arrived to serve as Maid of Honour to the Queen, she did not long remain a maid, and in very short time retained little of her honour. So greatly was Charles taken up by his latest conquest, indeed, that Clarendon feared he planned to divorce the Queen in favour of "la belle Stuart". And to foil this intention (so Charles suspected), the young lady was encouraged to make a run-away marriage with the Duke of Richmond and Lennox. The King, however, proved himself equal to the occasion. Despite his great displeasure at her elopement, the Duchess was welcomed back to Court, the husband was posted overseas, and the old relationship was speedily resumed. Thus all ended happily—except, of course, for the neglected Queen, the exiled Duke, and the meddlesome Earl.

For the next seven years (1667–74), Clarendon's place was taken by the Cabal, a committee of five members of the Privy Council whose initials happened to make up the word (Clifford, Arlington, Buckingham, Ashley, Lauderdale). Two members of this influential group were Catholics—Thomas Clifford, the first Baron Chudleigh, and Henry Bennett, first Earl of Arlington. Lauderdale (later Earl of Guildford) was a Scottish peer with strong Anglican inclinations, who acted as governor of the northern kingdom and took little part in English affairs. Buckingham, the second Duke, was George Villiers, son of the earlier Stuart favourite, while Anthony Ashley-Cooper, first Earl of Shaftesbury, the most important of the councillors, was an astute politician who in the past had shown himself to be well versed in the art of changing sides when it became expedient to do so.

At the start of 1668, and despite the earlier differences which had led to the Medway incident, the Cabal reached an understanding with the maritime states of Holland and Sweden. This treaty between three Protestant peoples who shared a distaste for papalism was designed to counter the growing aspirations of Catholic France, already the strongest and most formidable nation in Europe, and it provided an obvious answer to the ambitions of Richelieu's able and unscrupulous successor, Cardinal Mazarin. It was, moreover, fully in keeping with England's traditional policy of seeking to maintain a continental balance of power.

Charles, however, tended to view the foreign situation in a somewhat different light, coloured as it was by his own domestic needs (in the form of ever-increasing supplies of money with which to keep his many mistresses reasonably happy and content) and the fact that he had close family ties with France, through his mother and his youngest sister Henrietta, who was married to the Duke of Orleans, brother of King Louis XIV. It was these circumstances which combined to wreck the Triple Alliance. For, although Charles blamed his perpetual shortage of funds on the inadequacy of his Parliamentary grant rather than on his own extravagance, he was wise enough not to seek to remedy the situation by resorting to the money-raising illegalities of his father. Instead, he chose to become a pensioner of Louis XIV, receiving from his scheming brother-in-law a payment of two million *livres* (some £200,000) and the promise of armed support, should this become necessary when it became known that the English monarch was in the pocket of France.

Nor was his abandonment of the Dutch the full extent of the English King's treachery, as set forth in the Treaty of Dover (1670). This infamous compact, arranged on behalf of Louis by Charles's favourite sister Henrietta, herself an ardent Catholic, was the outcome of a report from the French ambassador that the head of the House of Stuart wished for a reconciliation with Rome. It was accordingly written into the agreement that Charles and his brother would acknowledge the spiritual supremacy of the Pope and that England would be transformed, forcibly if necessary (hence the offer of French troops) into a Catholic absolutism.

That Charles well realized the dangerous nature of the game he was playing is indicated by the fact that two sets of Treaty documents were prepared, the Cabal as a whole signing a version which merely stipulated that, in return for cash, England would reverse her previous policy and aid France in attacking Holland. Only Clifford and Arlington, the King's two Catholic ministers, and Lord Arundel of Wardour, who was also of their faith, knew of the secret conversion clauses, to which they appended their signatures on 22 May. And that Louis fully appreciated the important part which feminine wiles had played in the achievement of this diplomatic triumph was shown, on the sudden death of Henrietta, by his despatch to London of a young and fetching intermediary in the person of Louise de Kérovalle. This ambassadress extraordinary promptly took to Charles's bed as though it were her own, became the Duchess of Portsmouth in very short time, made due contribution to the rapidly expanding ranks of the English nobility, and continued to exercise a powerful influence over the King until the day of his death.

The Treaty of Dover, meanwhile, resulted in neither the conversion of England nor the complete subjection of Holland. Although his brother James hastened to declare his allegiance to Rome, Charles deemed it prudent not to follow his example, at any rate for the time being. In the spring of 1672, however, he did embroil England in an unpopular war against the Dutch, who answered the duplicity and defection of their allies (Sweden, too, had been bought off by Louis) by entrusting their future to the youthful but capable Prince William of Orange. Despite grievous territorial losses, he successfully held the two remaining provinces of Holland and Zeeland against the combined assaults of the enemy, and, by what must have seemed to him the most pleasing of ironies, ultimately found himself occupying the throne of England as William III!

In so far as that island kingdom was concerned, meanwhile, Parliament brought hostilities against the Dutch to an end by refusing supplies, thus compelling Charles to make peace. The King was even less successful in an attempt to implement another of his undertakings to Louis when, in 1672, he endeavoured to lessen the penal restrictions imposed on Catholics by issuing a "Declaration of Indulgence for Tender Consciences". The Commons' reaction was to point out the illegality of the arbitrary suspending of an Act of Parliament, and to withhold much-needed funds. Nor were members satisfied merely to see the Indulgence quashed. They responded further by framing the Test Act, designed to remove all Roman Catholics holding office under the Crown by making a denial of the doctrine of transubstantiation a condition of employment.

The effects of this were far-reaching. The King's brother James, as a professed Catholic, was deprived of his post of Lord High Admiral. The measure also broke up the Cabal, since Thomas Clifford was forced to resign the Treasurership and someone, presumably Arlington, revealed to Shaftesbury how he and his two colleagues had been kept in ignorance of the true import of the Dover agreement. As a result of this disclosure, the hoodwinked minister began to vote against the King in Parliament, an act of disloyalty which inevitably led to his dismissal and, incidentally, brought into being the now familiar party-system of government.[1]

[1] In 1675, the disgruntled Earl and a number of other prominent members of both Houses founded the Green Ribbon Club, open to those of Round-

For the remainder of the reign, enlivened by Titus Oates and his imaginary Popish Plot, Shaftesbury and his opposition supporters strove desperately to prevent the accession of the Catholic James, who remained his brother's legal heir, thanks to the sterility of the Queen. A series of Exclusion Bills was introduced, which the King defeated by dissolving one short-lived Parliament after another, until his thwarted opponents resorted to conspiracies and intrigues, the betrayal of which led to their undoing. Thereafter, subsisting on French gold and leaving Parliament unsummoned, Charles ended his days in despotic contentment, secure in the knowledge that, on his death, his brother James would succeed him.

V

When, on 6 February 1685, Charles died, leaving his brother to attain the throne as James II (VII of Scotland), the position of the newcomer appeared secure enough, despite the determined attempts which had earlier been made to exclude him. With many of the Whig leaders in exile, the Parliament which the King summoned to meet on 19 May, immediately after his coronation, proved to be predominantly Tory and overwhelmingly Royalist, notwithstanding that the monarch was a professed adherent of Rome and his supporters in the House were almost solidly Anglican.

James had already said that he would support and defend the Church of England, and on this understanding Parliament and the people were content to accept him for what he was—a middle-aged Catholic King whose childless Queen shared his faith, but who was possessed by a previous marriage of two Protestant daughters, Mary and Anne, who were his ostensible heirs, and the elder of whom was the wife of William of Orange, the recognized champion of anti-papalism in Europe.[1] And to

head (subsequently labelled Whig, modern Liberal) sympathies who were opposed to the Cavalier (Tory, later Conservative) element in Parliament which supported the monarchy.

Originally, the terms Whig and Tory were derogatory nicknames, the one derived from Whiggamores (Presbyterian extremists given to the extermination of Bishops on the lonely Scottish moors), the other a name applied to a body of Catholic bandits in Ireland (who delighted in the total immersion of Saxon settlers in the local bogs).

[1] The marriage of the Earl of Clarendon's daughter Anne to James in 1660, after she had been his mistress for a number of years, was at the insistence of King Charles, when it was discovered that his chief minister of state was about to become a grandfather. Anne Hyde died in 1671, and two years later James took Maria d'Este of Modena as his second wife. The wedding of his daughter Mary to William of Orange was celebrated in 1677.

what extent James began his reign with the tacit approval of the majority of his subjects was demonstrated when there were attempted rebellions in Scotland and England, the one led by Archibald, ninth Earl of Argyle, the other by the Duke of Monmouth, the deceased Charles's eldest bastard, alleged and supposed. Both uprisings failed miserably, and ended with the capture and execution of their leaders.

Thus encouraged, James was emboldened to disclose something of his real intentions, which were nothing less than the reconversion of his kingdom to the Church of Rome. When Parliament, which had adjourned in July, reassembled in November, it was announced in the King's Speech that, in view of the recent unrest, the strength of the standing army had been increased and that it was to be officered by gentlemen of Catholic persuasion. The Commons, alarmed at the prospect thus unfolded, at once took strong exception to this arbitrary suspension of the Test Act, and refused to grant funds. The debate was accordingly adjourned, and Parliament prorogued. Nor did it meet again, though it was not formally dissolved until July 1687.

Heedless of the possibility that Tories and Whigs might unite against him in defence of the Anglican Church, James continued to pursue his Romanizing ambitions. In an effort to undermine Anglicanism and at the same time gain nonconformist support, he issued an Indulgence granting freedom of worship to all denominations, while a year later (27 April 1688), he followed this with a second declaration of liberty and conscience, and ordered that it be read in all places of worship. This called for an act of self-immolation which the Anglican episcopacy could hardly be expected to obey, and a hurried meeting at Lambeth Palace resulted in the sending of a petition to the King, signed by the Archbishop of Canterbury and six other Bishops, asking that the order be rescinded. James's answer was to arrest the Bishops and consign them to the Tower.

It was in the midst of this crisis, after fifteen years of marriage, that Mary of Modena at last gave birth to a son who showed every sign of surviving the experience. The nation was thunderstruck, and inclined to question the likelihood of the occurrence (the favourite Whig theory was that the infant was a foundling which had been smuggled into the royal bedchamber in a warming-pan). For, as it was at once realized, the new arrival opened up what was to the majority of Englishmen the intolerable prospect of a popish dynasty which might endure for centuries.

Reaction was prompt and ominously challenging. On 30 June, to the acclamation of the populace, the seven Anglican

Bishops were acquitted by a London jury, and, too late, James realized that in ordering their arrest, he had been guilty of a grave error of judgement. Precisely how grave was shown when, without further ado, a group of prominent citizens, Whigs and Tories both, sent a letter to William of Orange, inviting him to visit England at the head of an army, and assuring him of overwhelming popular support. Such a proposal obviously required careful thought on the part of the recipient, the venture itself considerable preparation, and it was not until the following October that the cautious Prince announced his decision to intervene in the affairs of his father-in-law's kingdom, that a free Parliament might be established and the Protestant succession preserved.

By now thoroughly frightened, James belatedly sought to make amends by reversing the tyrannical trend of the past three years. But the time for such reconsideration was over, even supposing it to be honestly intended. As the Dutch forces sailed along the English coast, the home fleet took care to avoid a successful interception, while on land the King's soldiers likewise declined to offer the invaders battle. Even the Princess Anne turned against her father, who at last perceived that all that remained for him was the ignominy of flight. This, too, was bungled. After hurling the Great Seal into the Thames, James set out on 11 December for Sheerness, only to find himself detained by some fishermen and brought back to London. At this crucial moment in the affairs of the nation, no person's presence in the capital could have been more unwelcome, and the unwanted captive was hurriedly returned to Rochester, from where he was encouraged to make a better job of escaping the country!

With the departure of the King, a number of intricate problems demanded attention. Strictly, the accession of a replacement required recognition by Parliament, which in turn could only assemble in response to a royal summons. The King, however, was no longer in office, and Parliament had been dissolved! This dilemma was resolved, as at the end of the Cromwellian interregnum, by way of a freely elected Convention, whose main function was to place a new occupant on the throne. Members of both Houses gathered on 22 January 1689, it being agreed:

1. That King James having withdrawn himself from the kingdom, the throne was vacant; and
2. That it was inconsistent with the safety and welfare of a Protestant kingdom for it to be governed by a popish Prince.

A further difficulty now presented itself. Although Prince William himself had a claim to the throne (he was a grandchild of Charles I), the rightful heir was his wife Mary, and after her, his wife's sister Anne. William, however, flatly declined to defer to his wife in the matter, and it was finally agreed that William and Mary should rule jointly, and the survivor for life; that the order of succession thereafter should be, first, the descendants of Mary; second, Anne and her descendants; and third, William's descendants.[1]

The formal offer of the Crown was accompanied by a Declaration (subsequently enacted as a Bill) of Rights. This, with stipulations which ranged from the making or suspending of laws and the exercising of the dispensing power to the levying of taxes and the maintenance of a standing army, all of which activities were declared to be illegal without the consent of Parliament, ensured the future dominance of that body. Other important constitutional changes followed, inaugurated by the Triennial Act of 1694 (designed to secure the permanence of Parliament) and this, together with subsequent legislation, effectively deprived the monarchy of any pretence to rule by divine right. Henceforth, the King of England was left in no doubt that he owed his title, not to High Heaven, but to the lawfully elected assembly of his subjects, and that it was incumbent upon him to behave accordingly.

[1] In the event, the childless Mary died before her husband, who did not take another wife. On his death in 1702, he was accordingly succeeded by Anne, who twenty years earlier had married Prince George of Denmark. Of their seventeen or so offspring, however, only one had survived infancy, and when in 1700 he also died, it was clear that further thought needed to be given to the problem of the succession, if James II and his descendants were to be excluded. Accordingly, in an Act of Settlement (1701), Anne's successor was declared to be her second cousin Sophia and "the heirs of her Body being Protestants". The Dowager Duchess Sophia, wife of the Elector of Hanover and a granddaughter of James I, was in her eighties when she predeceased Anne by a matter of four months, leaving the throne of England to be occupied by her son, who, as George I, established the House of Hanover.

Glossary

ADULTERINE: as applied to a castle, an unlicensed structure.

ANGEVIN: pertaining to Anjou.

ANGLO-SAXON CHRONICLE: the name given to a group of seven interrelated MSS. which constitute the primary source for the early history of England. They were compiled between the ninth and twelfth centuries.

ANNATES: first fruits—the entire revenue of one year, remitted to the Pope by Bishops and other ecclesiastics of the Roman Catholic Church on their appointment to a See or benefice.

ARBALAST: a powerful form of cross-bow.

ATHELING: originally, a member of a noble family. In later times, a term often restricted to a Prince of the blood royal, or to the heir apparent.

ATTAINDER: a Parliamentary Bill enabling an accused person to be deprived of civil rights without the formality of a judicial trial. It was first resorted to in 1459.

BAILEY: the ward or outer court of a feudal castle.

BALLISTA: a military engine in the form of an outsize cross-bow, able to discharge heavy arrows or stones.

BARBICAN: an outer fortification to a city or castle, often in the form of a gateway intended for the defence of a drawbridge.

BARON: in feudal times, one of a class of tenants holding lands by military service from the King. The term was afterwards restricted to those who were summoned by writ to the Great Council or (from the time of Henry III onwards) to Parliament. In modern usage, baron is the lowest rank in the hereditary peerage.

BARONET: the lowest hereditary English title, created by James I in 1611 as a means of raising money. It was on sale to all who were prepared to pay £1,000 into the Exchequer.

BATON-SINISTER: (improperly called bar-sinister), an heraldic indication of bastardy.

BATTLEMENT: a parapet on tower or wall, built with alternate open spaces and blocks of solid wall for purposes of defence.

BELFRY: a siege engine in the form of a moveable wooden tower, used both as an observation post and as a means of surmounting fortification walls.

BOLT: an arrow, especially that discharged from a cross-bow.

BORE: as used in medieval siege warfare, a heavy pole with a pointed, ironshod head.

BOROUGH: in early times, a fortified town, possessed of a municipal organization.

BURGESS: an inhabitant of a town (borough); strictly, a person possessed of full municipal rights.

BURH: an Anglo-Saxon strongpoint, fortified and manned for the protection of a district.

CABAL: a secret intrigue or political manœuvre. The name given in the reign of Charles II to a small committee of the Privy Council, the initials of whose five members happened to spell the word.

CAPETIAN: a member of the French dynasty founded in 987 by Hugh Capet, who was so called from the cloak he wore as Abbot of St. Martin de Tours.

CASTELLAN: the warden or constable of a castle.

CASTELLATE: to build or fortify in the manner of a castle.

CAT: a moveable penthouse, used by besiegers to protect themselves when operating in the vicinity of an enemy fortification.

CAVALIER: a Royalist in the great Civil War of 1642–9.

CEORL: (churl), a man of low degree; a peasant.

CHURL: same as ceorl.

CINQUE PORTS: a group of coastal towns (originally five in number, hence the name) in south-eastern England which enjoyed certain privileges on condition of providing warships. The original ports, to which others were later added, were Hastings, Romney, Hythe, Dover, and Sandwich. The Lord Warden of the Cinque Ports was also the Constable of Dover Castle.

COGNIZANCE: a distinctive badge or mark by which a person is known, e.g. a crest or a coat of arms.

CONSANGUINITY: in human relationships, descent from a common ancestor; of the same blood.

CONSTABLE: in ancient times, an officer of state of the highest rank; the warden of a castle.

CRENELLATE: to furnish with crenels—the gaps between the raised parts in the castellation on a battlement.

CROSS-BOW: a hand weapon, consisting of a bow fixed across a wooden stock, furnished with a groove or barrel for the missile and a mechanism for holding and releasing the string.

CURTAIN: the protective wall enclosing a castle courtyard.

DAUPHIN: from 1349–1830, the title of the eldest son of the King of France. It was derived from the Dauphiné and its lords, Counts of Vienne, in whose family it was a proper name.

DEMESNE: land possessed or occupied by the owner himself; hence royal demesne, the private property of the Crown.

DONJON: (whence dungeon), the central tower or keep in early castles, to which the defenders could retire when hard pressed.

DUKE: a leader or ruler; an hereditary title of nobility, ranking next below that of Prince, introduced into England by Edward III, when in 1337 he created the Prince of Wales Duke of Cornwall.

EALDORMAN: in Anglo-Saxon times, the governor of a shire. From the time of Canute, the term was superseded by Eorl.

EARL: Anglo-Saxon Eorl, regarded, after the Norman Conquest, as the equivalent of a French Count. In the peerage of today, a person ranking between a Marquis and a Viscount.

ELECTOR: one of the Princes of the ancient German or Holy Roman Empire entitled to take part in the election of the Emperor (911–1803).

ENCEINTE: an enclosure; the outer wall of a castle, including the flanking towers; the space so enclosed.

EORL: an Anglo-Saxon warrior; a nobleman next in dignity to the King. See Earl.

ESCALADE: the action of scaling a fortress wall by means of ladders.

ESCHEAT: under feudal law, the reversion of a fief to the King or other lord owing to failure of heirs, as when a tenant died without leaving a successor who was qualified to inherit under the terms of the original grant.

EXCHEQUER: under the Norman and Angevin Kings of England, the state administrative department controlling public revenue and finance. The name originally referred to the table covered with a cloth divided into squares, on which the accounts of the revenue were kept with the aid of counters.

FEUDALISM: the system prevailing in the Middle Ages over the greater part of Europe which determined the relationship between lord and vassal, the basis of which was the tenure of land in exchange for certain military services performed on behalf of the one for the other.

FIEF: (also feud, feoff), a fee; land held from a superior on consideration of service.

FRANK: one of the Germanic tribes from Franconia, who conquered Gaul in the fifth century and so founded France.

FREEMAN: one who is legally independent; a person who is not a slave, serf, or vassal.

FYRD: the Anglo-Saxon militia, composed of all males (thegns and freemen) capable of bearing arms in defence of the realm.

GARDEROBE: a latrine.

GELD: tribute; hence Danegeld, a tax (imposed in the tenth century) to buy off the Danes, or to defend the country against them.

GREAT COUNCIL: the King's Council of barons, bishops, and abbots.

HALL: the principal room of a medieval residence.

HAUBERK: medieval defensive armour, originally intended for the protection of the neck and shoulders, but which developed into a long coat of mail; a military tunic.

HIDAGE: a tax payable to the royal Exchequer, assessed on each hide of land.

HIDE: an area of land, varying from 60–120 acres, sufficient to support a family or household; the amount of land an eight-ox plough could keep under cultivation.

HOARD: (also hourd), a projecting wooden gallery, extending from the top of the external wall of a castle for the defence of its base.

HOLY ROMAN EMPIRE: a medieval dominion, formerly consisting of a part of the Roman Empire of the West, together with the territory of the Emperor Charlemagne.

HOUSECARL: among the Anglo-Saxons, a picked fighting man; a member of the royal bodyguard.

HUGUENOT: the name given in France to an adherent of the Reformation.

HUNDRED: ancient administrative division of a county or shire, notationally 100 hides; also formerly applied to the county itself, e.g. the Chiltern Hundreds.

IMPEACH: to bring a charge or accusation against.

INFANTA: a title bestowed upon any one of the legitimate daughters of the Kings of Spain and Portugal, except the heiress-apparent or the wife of an Infante.

INFANTE: a title given to the legitimate sons of the Kings of Spain and Portugal, other than the heir-apparent.

INTERDICT: an authoritative sentence excluding a particular place or person from religious functions.

JUSTICIAR: in Norman and early Plantagenet times, the chief political and judicial officer, who acted as Regent in the absence of the King.

KEEP: the inner and most strongly defended part of a castle; the donjon.

KNIGHT: in the Middle Ages, a military servant of the King or other person of rank; a feudal tenant holding land from a superior on condition of serving in the field as a mounted and well-armed man.

LEGATE: an ecclesiastical envoy; an official representative of the Pope.

LEVIRATE: an ancient custom among the Jews and some other races by which the brother or next of kin to a deceased man married his widow.

LIEGE: a superior an overlord entitled to feudal allegiance and service.

LIVRE: an ancient French monetary unit, about equivalent to a franc, which was divided into 20 sols or sous.

LOLLARD: an early Protestant; a heretic follower of Wycliffe.

LONGBOW: a bow drawn by hand, as distinct from a cross-bow; formerly made the same length as the height of its user.

LORD: a feudal superior; a person from whom an estate is held (lord of the manor); a baron; a peer of the realm.

MAGNA CARTA: the great charter which the barons obtained from King John in 1215; one of the charters upon which English personal and political liberty is based.

MANGONEL: a medieval military engine, used for hurling stones and other missiles.

MARCH: boundary, limit, frontier. Often used in the plural, as when making reference to the Welsh and Scottish Marches.

MARK: a medieval unit of weight applied to gold and silver, equal to about eight ounces. The basis of computation in England after the Norman Conquest was 20 sterling pennies to the ounce, so that the mark was equal to $20 \times 8 = 160$ pence = 13s. 4d.

MARQUIS: originally applied to the ruler of certain territories (frontier districts or marches). Subsequently, the title was indicative of a particular grade of noble rank, immediately below that of Duke and above that of Count. It was introduced into England at the end of the fourteenth century and used to designate a specific degree of the peerage, that between Duke and Earl.

MERCENARY: a fighting man hired by a foreign country.

MIDDLE AGES: the medieval period of European history, usually reckoned as extending from the downfall of the Roman Empire of the West in the fifth century to the beginning of the Renaissance (fifteenth century).

MOAT: a protective trench or ditch round a castle or fortified place, often, though not necessarily, filled with water.

MOTTE: an earthen castle mound.

MOUTON: a battering ram, used in siege warfare.

MURAL: of or pertaining to a wall; executed, fixed, or placed on a wall; hence the mural towers of castles and other fortifications.

NORMAN: an inhabitant of Normandy, one of the Scandinavian race of Northmen which occupied Neustria at the beginning of the tenth century, founded the Duchy of Normandy, and conquered England in 1066.

ORDINANCE: an authoritative direction, decree, or command. After 1649, the name "Act" was officially used, though, as all these "Acts" were expunged from the Statute-book at the Restoration, they are usually referred to as "Ordinances".

PALATINE: Count (English Earl) Palatine, a Count (or Earl) possessed of royal privileges and jurisdiction within his territory such as elsewhere belong to the King alone. Thus the Norman Hugh Wolfe was created Count Palatine of Chester by William the Conqueror.

PALISADE: a fence made of pales or stakes for purposes of defence.

PENTHOUSE: in castle warfare, a shed for the protection of besiegers.

PETRARY: a medieval military engine for discharging stones and other missiles.

PIPE ROLL: (Great Roll of the Pipe), annual record of accounts and matters relating to the Exchequer and royal expenditure, so-called because each document was rolled round a pipe and so assumed a tubular form.

PLANTAGENET: the name by which the House of Anjou is usually known, derived from *planta genista*, the broom plant, a sprig of which was invariably worn in his cap by Geoffrey of Anjou, father of Henry II.

POLL-TAX: a tax of so much per head, levied on every male inhabitant of a country.

PORTCULLIS: an iron-shod sliding door, suspended over the gateway of a castle or other fortified place, and lowered at the approach of an enemy.

POSTERN: a back door, especially a concealed gate or exit from the walls of a castle; a sally-port.

POUNDAGE: a subsidy of one shilling in the pound formerly granted by Parliament to the Crown on all imports and exports, with the exception of bullion and commodities paying tunnage.

PRINCE: a sovereign ruler of a state whose head has not the rank and title of King; the son of a sovereign, or other male member of the royal family; also a title given in official documents to English Dukes and Marquises.

PURITAN: a term first applied during the reign of Elizabeth I to members of the extreme Protestant party in the Anglican Church; under the Stuarts, one opposed to Episcopacy and the Monarchy.

QUARREL: a short, heavy, square-headed arrow or bolt, as used in conjunction with the cross-bow or arbalast.

REDE: counsel or advice.

REDELESS: devoid or destitute of counsel.

RELIEF: a payment made to an overlord by the heir of a feudal tenant on taking up possession of the vacant estate.

REEVE: a title applied to several classes of official who was the chief magistrate of a town or district—high-reeve, port-reeve, shire-reeve (sheriff).

RENAISSANCE: a rebirth, with particular reference to the revival of classical (ancient Greek) art, learning, and literature in Western Europe during the fifteenth and sixteenth centuries.

RESTORATION: the re-establishment of the monarchy with the return of Charles II in 1660; the period following this event.

ROUNDHEAD: the name given to members of the Parliamentary party in the great Civil War of 1642–49, who were so called because of their close-cropped hair.

SALIC LAW: the alleged fundamental law of the French monarchy, attributed to the Salian Franks, by which females were excluded from succession to the throne.

SALLY-PORT: an inconspicuous or concealed postern gate in the walls of a castle or fortress.

SAP: to destroy by digging underneath; a trench (usually covered or zigzag) by means of which an approach is made to an enemy position.

SCUTAGE: shield-money; a tax paid to the Crown by a holder of a knight's fee, in lieu of military service. Henry I demanded 30s. per knight's fee; in the time of Henry II, 2 marks (26s. 8d.) was the usual sum.

SEE: the official seat of a Bishop or Archbishop; the ecclesiastical unit over which he rules.

SENESCHAL: in the Middle Ages, the steward or bailiff of a royal palace or castle.

SHELL KEEP: a ring wall built on an earthen mound (motte), almost invariably the site of an earlier fortress.

SHERIFF: a shire-reeve, an official representative of the Crown in the various counties (shires) of England, Wales, Scotland, and Ireland; the deputy of an Ealdorman.

SHIP MONEY: an ancient tax, levied in time of war on the ports and maritime towns, cities, and counties of England to provide ships for the King's service.

SHIRE: an administrative district consisting of a number of smaller districts (hundreds), united for purposes of local government and ruled jointly by an Ealdorman and a Sheriff.

SLIGHT: (*obs.*) as applied to a fortification, to level to the ground; to raze.

SUZERAIN: in the feudal system, one who has supreme power; the dominant authority.

TALLAGE: an arbitrary tax levied by the Norman and early Angevin Kings upon the towns and demesne lands of the Crown.

TESTUDO: a protective cover, utilized by Roman soldiers when attacking a wall, and formed by overlapping their oblong shields above their heads; hence the name given to a mobile shelter capable of being wheeled up to the walls of an enemy-held castle or fortress.

THANE: same as thegn.

THEGN: a retainer; a member of the lesser nobility; a rank below that of Ealdorman (Eorl) and above the status of Ceorl (Churl), corresponding in its various grades to the post-Conquest Baron and Knight.

TORTOISE: the name given to a form of penthouse, under which those besieging a castle were protected as a tortoise by its shell. (See also testudo.)

TREBUCHET: a medieval siege engine, akin to the ballista.

TUNNAGE: a tax or duty levied upon wine imported in tuns (large casks) commonly associated with poundage.

TWELFHYNDE: the weregeld payable in respect of a thegn, usually reckoned at 1,200s.

TWYHYNDE: the weregeld payable in respect of a churl—200s.

VASSAL: in the feudal system, one holding lands from a superior on condition of homage and allegiance.

VILL: a village; under the feudal system, a territorial unit or division, consisting of a number of dwellings with their associated buildings and adjacent lands.

VILLEIN: a person of low birth; a churl; one of a class of serfs under the feudal system; a peasant entirely subject to a lord.

VIRGATE: an old English measure of area, varying in size but notationally about thirty acres, or a quarter of a hide.

WARD: a castle courtyard or bailey.

WARDSHIP: the guardianship and custody of the person and lands of a minor, together with all profits accruing during his minority.

WERE: an abbreviated form of weregeld.

WEREGELD: in old English law, the price set upon a man according to his rank; a composition whereby homicide and other serious crimes against the person were expiated. See twelfhynde and twyhynde.

WITAN: members of the Witenagemot; a gathering of notables and elders.

Selected Bibliography

Adams, G. B., *The History of England* (Longmans, Green & Co., London, 1905).

Allen, A. B., *Stuart England* (Rockcliff Publishing Corporation, London, 1954).

Armitage, E. S., *The Early Norman Castles of the British Isles* (John Murray, London, 1912).

Ashdown, C. H., *British Castles* (Adam & Charles Black, London, 1911).

Bagley, J. J., *Life in Medieval England* (B. T. Batsford Ltd., London, 1960).

Barrow, G. W. S., *Feudal Britain* (Edward Arnold (Publishers) Ltd., London, 1956).

Bentley, S., Ed., *Excerpta Historica* (Samuel Bentley, London, 1831).

Black, J. B., *The Reign of Elizabeth* (Oxford University Press, London, 1959).

Bowen, C. D., *The Lion and the Throne* (Hamish Hamilton, London, 1957).

Braun, H., *The English Castle* (B. T. Batsford Ltd., London, 1947).

Brett, S. R., *The Stuart Century* (George G. Harrap & Co. Ltd., London, 1961).

Brooke, Z. N., *A History of Europe* (Methuen & Co. Ltd., London, 1960).

Brown, R. A., *English Medieval Castles* (B. T. Batsford Ltd., London, 1954).

Bryant, A., *The Story of England* (Collins, London, 1961).

Burne, A. H. and Young, P., *The Great Civil War* (Eyre & Spottiswoode, London, 1959).

Chapman, H. W., *The Last Tudor King* (Jonathan Cape, London, 1958).

Cheyney, E. P., *A History of England* (Longmans, Green & Co., London, 1926).

Clark, G. N., *The Later Stuarts 1660–1714* (Oxford University Press, London, 1934).

Clemoes, P., Ed., *The Anglo-Saxons* (Bowes & Bowes Publishers Ltd., London, 1959).

Coate, M., *Social Life in Stuart England* (Methuen & Co. Ltd., London, 1924).

Cobbe, T., *History of the Norman Kings of England* (Longmans, Green & Co., London, 1869).

Curtiss, E., *A History of Ireland* (Methuen & Co. Ltd., London, 1950).

Darby, H. C., Ed., *An Historical Geography of England* (Cambridge University Press, Cambridge, 1948).

Darcie, A., *Annales* (Benjamin Fisher, London, 1625).

Davies, G., *The Early Stuarts* (Oxford University Press, London, 1937).

Davies, R. T., *Documents of Medieval England* (Methuen & Co. Ltd., London, 1926).

Davis, H. W. C., Ed., *Medieval England* (Oxford University Press, London, 1924).

— *England Under the Normans and Angevins* (Methuen & Co. Ltd., London, 1930).

Dickens, A. G., *Thomas Cromwell and the Reformation* (The English Universities Press Ltd., London, 1959).

Douglas, D. C. and Greenaway, G. W., *English Historical Documents 1042–1189* (Eyre & Spottiswoode Ltd., London, 1953).

Dutton, R., *The Châteaux of France* (B. T. Batsford Ltd., London, 1957).

Edwards, J. G., *Edward I's Castle-Building in Wales* (The British Academy, London, 1944).

Evans, H. T., *Wales and the Wars of the Roses* (Cambridge University Press, Cambridge, 1915).

Fedden, R., *Crusader Castles* (Art & Technics, London, 1960).

Feiling, K., *A History of England* (Macmillan & Co. Ltd., London, 1950).

Finn, R. W., *The Domesday Inquest* (Longmans, Green & Co. Ltd., London, 1961).

Freeman, E. A., *The Reign of William Rufus* (Oxford University Press, London, 1882).

– *William the Conqueror* (Macmillan & Co. Ltd., London, 1903).

Froude, J. A., *The Reign of Mary Tudor* (J. M. Dent & Sons Ltd., London, 1910).

Gairdner, J., *Richard the Third* (Longmans, Green & Co. Ltd., London, 1879).

Gardiner, S. R., *History of the Great Civil War* (Longmans, Green & Co., Ltd, London, 1893).

— *What Gunpowder Plot Was* (Longmans, Green & Co., Ltd., London, 1897).

Garmonsway, G. N., Trans., *The Anglo-Saxon Chronicle* (J. M. Dent & Sons Ltd., London, 1953).

Gerard, J., *What Was the Gunpowder Plot?* (Osgood McIlvaine & Co., London, 1897).

Harrison, D., *Tudor England* (Cassell & Co. Ltd., London, 1953).

Harvey, A., *The Castles and Walled Towns of England* (Methuen & Co. Ltd., London, 1925).

Hassall, W. O., *They Saw it Happen (55* B.C.–A.D. *1485)* (Basil Blackwell, Oxford, 1957).

Hennings, M. A., *England Under Henry III* (Longmans, Green & Co. Ltd., London, 1932).

Hopkins, R. T., *Moated Houses of England* (Country Life Ltd., London, 1935).

Jacob, E. F., *Henry V and the Invasion of France* (Hodder & Stoughton Ltd., London, 1947).

— *The Fifteenth Century* (Oxford University Press, London, 1961).

Jerrold, D., *An Introduction to the History of England* (Collins, London, 1949).

Kendall, P. M., *The Yorkist Age* (George Allen & Unwin Ltd., London, 1962).

— *Warwick the Kingmaker* (George Allen & Unwin Ltd., London, 1957).

Kenyon, J. P., *The Stuarts* (B. T. Batsford Ltd., London, 1958).

Langer, W. L., Ed., *An Encyclopedia of World History* (George G. Harrap & Co. Ltd., London, 1951).

Mackie, J. D., *The Earlier Tudors* (Oxford University Press, London, 1957).

Maclagan, E., *The Bayeux Tapestry* (Penguin Books Ltd., London, 1943).

Mahler, M., *Chirk Castle and Chirkland* (George Bell & Sons Ltd., London, 1912).

Maurois, A., *A History of England* (The Bodley Head, London, 1956),

McKisack, M., *The Fourteenth Century* (Oxford University Press. London, 1959).

Milward, J. S., Ed., *Sixteenth Century* (Hutchinson Educational Ltd., London, 1961).

Montague, F. C., *The History of England from the Accession of James I to the Restoration* (Longmans, Green & Co., London, 1907).

Morgan, O. M., *A History of Wales* (Edward Howell, Liverpool, 1911).

Morrah, P., *The Year of Restoration* (Chatto & Windus, London, 1960).

Morris, C., *The Tudors* (B. T. Batsford Ltd., London, 1955).

Morshead, O. *Windsor Castle* (Phaidon Press, London, 1957).

Mowatt, R. B., *The Wars of the Roses* (Crosby Lockwood & Son, London, 1914).

Neaverson, E., *Medieval Castles in North Wales* (Hodder & Stoughton Ltd., London, 1947).

Oman, C., *Castles* (The Great Western Railway, London, 1926).

— *England Before the Norman Conquest* (Methuen & Co. Ltd., London, 1930).

— *The Art of War in the Middle Ages* (Cornell University Press, Ithaca, New York, 1953).

O'Neil, B. H. St. J., *Castles* (H.M. Stationery Office, London, 1953).

Pearson, H., *Charles II* (William Heinemann Ltd., London, 1960).

Perroy, E., *The Hundred Years War* (Eyre & Spottiswoode Ltd., London, 1951).

Perry, E. W., *Under Four Tudors* (George Allen & Unwin Ltd., London, 1940).

Petrie, C., *The Stuarts* (Eyre & Spottiswoode Ltd., London, 1958).

Pirenne, H., *A History of Europe* (George Allen & Unwin Ltd., London, 1948).

Pollard, A. F., *Henry VII* (Longmans, Green & Co. Ltd., London, 1951).

Poole, A. L., Ed., *Medieval England* (Oxford University Press, London, 1958).

Potter, K. R., Ed., *Gesta Stephani* (Thomas Nelson & Sons Ltd., London, 1955).

— *Historia Novella* (Thomas Nelson & Sons Ltd., London, 1957).

Powicke, F. M., *The Thirteenth Century* (Oxford University Press, London, 1953).

Round, J. H., *Geoffrey de Mandeville* (Longmans, Green & Co. Ltd., London, 1892).

Simpson, W. D., *Castles from the Air* (London Country Life Ltd., London, 1949).

— *Dunstaffnage Castle* (Oliver & Boyd, Edinburgh, 1958).

— *Scottish Castles* (H.M. Stationery Office, Edinburgh, 1959).

Slocombe, G., *William the Conqueror* (Hutchinson & Co. (Publishers) Ltd., London, 1959).

Smith, A. G., *The Babington Plot* (Macmillan & Co. Ltd., London, 1936).

Smith, F. R., *The Historical Architecture of Britain* (Sir Isaac Pitman & Son Ltd., London, 1948).

Steel, A., *Richard II* (Cambridge University Press, Cambridge, 1941).

Stenton, F. M., *Anglo-Saxon England* (Oxford University Press, London, 1943).

— *The First Century of English Feudalism* (Oxford University Press, London, 1932).

Stephenson, C., *Medieval History* (Harper and Brothers, New York, 1951).

Stubbs, W., *Lectures on Early English History* (Longmans, Green & Co. Ltd., London, 1906).

— *Lectures on European History* (Longmans, Green & Co. Ltd., London, 1904).

Thornton, P. M., *The Stuart Dynasty* (William Ridgway, London, 1890).

Toy, S., *A History of Fortification* (William Heinemann Ltd., London, 1955).

Trevelyan, G. M., *England Under the Stuarts* (Methuen & Co. Ltd., London, 1961).

— *Illustrated History of England* (Longmans, Green & Co. Ltd., London, 1956).

Tuulse, A., *Castles of the Western World* (Thames & Hudson, London, 1958).

Vickers, K. H., *England in the Later Middle Ages* (Methuen & Co. Ltd., London, 1950).

Waters, W. H., *The Edwardian Settlement of North Wales* (University of Wales Press Board, Cardiff, 1935).

Williamson, J. A., *The Evolution of England* (Oxford University Press, London, 1944).

— *The Tudor Age* (Longmans, Green & Co. Ltd., London, 1957).

Willson, D. H., *King James VI and I* (Jonathan Cape, London, 1956).

Woolrych, A., *Battles of the English Civil War* (B. T. Batsford Ltd., London, 1961).

Young, N. D., *Vita Edwardi Secundi* (Thomas Nelson & Sons Ltd., London, 1957).

Index